THE TRIAL

OF

THEODORE PARKER,

FOR THE

"MISDEMEANOR"

OF

A Speech in Faneuil Hall against Kidnapping,

BEFORE THE CIRCUIT COURT OF THE UNITED STATES,

AT BOSTON, APRIL 3, 1855

WITH

THE DEFENCE,

BY

THEODORE PARKER,

MINISTER OF THE TWENTY-EIGHTH CONGREGATIONAL SOCIETY IN BOSTON.

BOSTON:

PUBLISHED FOR THE AUTHOR.

1855.

CAMBRIDGE:
ALLEN AND FARNHAM, PRINTERS.

TO

JOHN PARKER HALE

AND

CHARLES MAYO ELLIS,

MAGNANIMOUS LAWYERS,

FOR THEIR LABORS IN A NOBLE PROFESSION,

WHICH HAVING ONCE IN ENGLAND ITS KELYNG, ITS SAUNDERS, ITS JEFFREYS, AND ITS SCROGGS, AS NOW IN AMERICA ITS SHARKEY, ITS GRIER, ITS CURTIS, AND ITS KANE, HAS YET ALSO SUCH GENEROUS ADVOCATES OF HUMANITY AS EQUAL THE GLORIES OF HOLT AND ERSKINE, OF MACKINTOSH AND ROMILLY,

FOR THEIR ELOQUENT AND FEARLESS DEFENCE OF TRUTH, RIGHT, AND LOVE,

THIS VOLUME IS DEDICATED,

BY THEIR CLIENT AND FRIEND,

THEODORE PARKER.

PREFACE.

TO THE PEOPLE OF THE FREE STATES OF AMERICA.

FELLOW-CITIZENS AND FRIENDS,—

IF it were a merely personal matter for which I was arraigned before the United States Court, after the trial was over I should trouble the public no further with that matter; and hitherto indeed, though often attacked, nay, almost continually for the last fourteen years, I have never returned a word in defence. But now, as this case is one of such vast and far-reaching importance, involving the great Human Right to Freedom of Speech, and as the actual question before the court was never brought to trial, I cannot let the occasion pass by without making further use of it.

When Judge Curtis delivered his charge to the Grand-Jury, June 7th, 1854, I made ready for trial, and in three or four days my line of defence was marked out — the fortifications sketched, the place of the batteries determined; I began to collect arms, and was soon ready for his attack. When that Grand-Jury, summoned with no special reference to me, refused to find a bill and were discharged, I took public notice of the conduct of Judge Curtis, in a Sermon for the Fourth of July.[1] But I knew the friends of the fugitive slave bill at Boston and Washington too well to think they would let the matter sleep; I knew what arts could be used to pack a jury and

[1] 2 Parker's Additional Speeches, 178 – 283.

procure a bill. So I was not at all surprised when I heard of the efforts making by the Slave Power in Boston to obtain an indictment by another grand-jury summoned for that purpose. It need not be supposed that I was wholly ignorant of their doings from day to day. The arrest was no astonishment to me. I knew how much the reputation of this Court and of its Attorney depended on the success of this prosecution. I knew what private malignity was at work.

After my arraignment I made elaborate preparation for my defence. I procured able counsel, men needing no commendation, to manage the technical details which I knew nothing about and so could not meddle with, while I took charge of other matters lying more level to my own capacity. I thought it best to take an active part in my own defence,—for the matter at issue belonged to my previous studies and general business; my personal friends and the People in general, seemed to expect me to defend myself as well as I could.

A great political revolution took place between the Judge's charge and my arraignment, June 7th, and November 29th, 1854, and I thought the Court would not allow the case to come to open argument. For certainly, it would not be a very pleasant thing for Judge Sprague and Judge Curtis, who have taken such pains to establish slavery in Massachusetts, to sit there—each like a travestied Prometheus, chained up in a silk gown because they had brought to earth fire from the quarter opposite to Heaven—and listen to Mr. Hale, and Mr. Phillips and other anti-slavery lawyers, day after day: there were facts, sure to come to light, not honorable to the Court and not pleasant to look at in the presence of a New England community then getting indignant at the outrages of the Slave Power. I never thought the case would come to the jury. I looked over the indictment, and to my unlearned eye it seemed so looped and windowed with breaches that a skilful lawyer might drive a cart and six oxen through it in various directions; and so the Court might easily quash the indictment and leave all the blame of the failure on the poor Attorney—whom they seemed to despise, though using him for their purposes—while they themselves should escape with a whole reputation, and ears which had not tingled under manly speech.

Still, it was possible that the trial would come on. Of course, I knew the trial would not proceed on the day I was ordered to appear—the eighty-fifth anniversary of the Boston Massacre. It would be "unavoidably postponed," which came to pass accordingly. The Attorney, very politely, gave me all needed information from time to time.

At the "trial," April 3d, it was optional with the defendant's counsel to beat the Government on the indictment before the Court; or on the merits of the case before the Jury. The latter would furnish the most piquant events, for some curious scenes were likely to take place in the examination of witnesses, as well as instruction to be offered in the Speeches delivered. But on the whole, it was thought best to blow up the enemy in his own fortress and with his own magazine, rather than to cut him to pieces with our shot in the open field. So the counsel rent the indictment into many pieces—apparently to the great comfort of the Judges, who thus escaped the battle, which then fell only on the head of the Attorney.

At the time appointed I was ready with my defence—which I now print for the Country. It is a Minister's performance, not a lawyer's. Of course, I knew that the Court would not have allowed me to proceed with such a defence—and that I should be obliged to deliver it through the press. Had there been an actual jury trial, I should have had many other things to offer in reference to the Government's evidence, to the testimony given before the grand-jury, and to the conduct of some of the grand-jurors themselves. So the latter part of the defence is only the skeleton of what it otherwise might have been,—the geological material of the country, the Flora and Fauna left out.

It would have been better to publish it immediately after the decision of the case: but my *brief* was not for the printer, and as many duties occurred at that time, it was not till now, in a little vacation from severer toils, that I have found leisure to write out my defence in full. Fellow-Citizens and Friends, I present it to you in hopes that it may serve the great cause of Human Freedom in America and the world; surely, it has seldom been in more danger.

THEODORE PARKER.

BOSTON, 24*th* *August*, 1855.

INTRODUCTION.

On Tuesday, the 23d of May, 1854, Charles F. Suttle of Virginia, presented to Edward Greeley Loring, Esquire, of Boston, Commissioner, a complaint under the fugitive slave bill — Act of September 18th, 1850 — praying for the seizure and enslavement of Anthony Burns.

The next day, Wednesday, May 24th, Commissioner Loring issued the warrant: Mr. Burns was seized in the course of the evening of that day, on the false pretext of burglary, and carried to the Suffolk County Court House in which he was confined by the Marshal, under the above-named warrant, and there kept imprisoned under a strong and armed guard.

On the 25th, at about nine o'clock in the morning, the Commissioner proceeded to hear and decide the case in the Circuit Court room, in which were stationed about sixty men serving as the Marshal's guard. Seth J. Thomas, Esquire, and Edward Griffin Parker, Esquire, members of the Suffolk Bar, appeared as counsel for Mr. Suttle to help him and Commissioner Loring make a man a Slave. Mr. Burns was kept in irons and surrounded by "the guard." The Slave-hunter's documents were immediately presented, and his witness was sworn and proceeded to testify.

Wendell Phillips, Theodore Parker, Charles M. Ellis, and Richard H. Dana, with a few others, came into the Court room. Mr. Parker and some others, spoke with Mr. Burns, who sat in the dock ironed, between two of the Marshal's guard. After a little delay and conference among these four and others, Mr. Dana interrupted the proceedings and asked that counsel might be assigned to Mr. Burns, and so a defence allowed. To this Mr. Thomas, the senior counsel for the Slave-hunters, objected. But after repeated protests on the part of Mr. Dana and Mr. Ellis, the Commissioner adjourned the hearing until ten o'clock, Saturday, May 27th.

On the evening of Friday, May 26th, there was a large and earnest meeting of men and women at Faneuil Hall. Mr. George R. Russell, of West Roxbury, presided; his name is a fair exponent of the character and purposes of the meeting, which Dr. Samuel G. Howe called to order.

Speeches were made and Resolutions passed. Mr. Phillips and Mr. Parker, amongst others, addressed the meeting; Mr. Parker's speech, as reported and published in the newspapers, is reprinted in this volume, page 199. While this meeting was in session there was a gathering of a few persons about the Court House, the outer doors of which had been unlawfully closed by order of the Marshal; an attempt was made to break through them and enter the building, where the Supreme Court of Massachusetts was sitting engaged in a capital case; and the Courts of this State must always sit with open doors. In the strife one of the Marshal's guard, a man hired to aid in the Slave-hunt, was killed — but whether by one of the assailing party, or by the Marshal's guard, it is not yet quite clear. It does not appear from the evidence laid before the public or the three Grand-Juries, that there was any connection between the meeting at Faneuil Hall and the gathering at the Court House.

Saturday, 27th, at ten o'clock, the Commissioner opened his Court again, his prisoner in irons before him. The other events are well known. Mr. Burns was taken away to Slavery on Friday, June 2d, by an armed body of soldiers with a cannon.

The May Term of the Circuit Court at Boston began on the 15th of that month, and the Grand-Jury for that term had already been summoned. Here is the list: —

UNITED STATES CIRCUIT COURT,
MASSACHUSETTS DISTRICT. }

May Term, 1854. ss. May 15, 1854.

GRAND-JURY.

1	Sworn.	Isaac Tower,	Randolph,	Foreman.
2	"	Elbridge G. Manning,	Andover.	
3	"	Asa Angier,	"	
4	"	Ballard Lovejoy,	"	
5	"	Levi Eldridge,	Chatham.	
6	"	Isaac B. Young,	"	
7	"	Josiah Peterson,	Duxbury.	
8	"	James Curtis,	"	
9	Not Sworn.	William Amory,	Boston,	Excused first day. Member of the bar.
10	Sworn.	James P. Bush,	"	Absent June 28th.
11	"	John Clark,	"	
12	"	Charles H. Mills,	"	
13	"	William N. Tyler,	"	
14	"	Samuel Weltch,	"	
15	"	Reuben Nichols,	Reading.	
16	"	Benjamin M. Boyce,	"	
17	"	Ephraim F. Belcher,	Randolph.	
18	"	Thomas S. Brimblecome,	Fairhaven.	
19	"	Obed F. Hitch,	"	
20	"	Lowell Claflin,	Hopkinton.	
21	"	William Durant,	Leominster.	
22	"	Charles Grant,	"	
23	"	Jeremiah B. Luther,	Douglas.	

On the 7th of June, Judge Curtis gave to this Grand-Jury his charge.[1] In that he spoke of the enforcement of the fugitive slave bill; and he charged the Jury especially and minutely upon the Statute of the United States of 1790, in relation to resisting officers in service of process as follows,

That not only those who are present and actually obstruct, resist, and oppose, and all who are present leagued in the common design, and so situated as to be able in case of need, to afford assistance to those actually engaged; but all who, though absent, did procure,

[1] The charge is printed below, at page 170.

counsel, command, or abet others to commit the offence; and all who, by indirect means, by *evincing an express liking, approbation, or assent to the design, were liable as principals.* And he added, "My instruction to you is, that language addressed to persons who immediately afterwards commit an offence, actually intended by the speaker to incite those addressed to commit it, and adapted thus to incite them, is such a counselling, or advising to the crime as the law contemplates, and the person so inciting others is liable to be indicted as a principal," and *it is of no importance that his advice or directions were departed from in respect to the time, or place, or precise mode, or means of committing it.*

That Jury remained in session a few weeks: pains were taken to induce them to find bills against the speakers at Faneuil Hall; but they found no indictment under the law of 1790, or that of 1850; they were discharged.

On the 22d of September, *venires* were issued by order of the Court for a new Grand-Jury; and, on the 16th of October, twenty-three were returned by Marshal Freeman, and impanelled. Here is the list of new Grand-Jurors: —

UNITED STATES CIRCUIT COURT,
MASSACHUSETTS DISTRICT. } ss. October 16, 1854.

October Term, 1854.

GRAND-JURY.

1	Sworn.	Enoch Patterson, Jr.,	Boston,	Foreman.
2	"	David Alden,	"	
3	"	Stephen D. Abbott,	Andover.	
4	"	Isaac Beal,	Chatham.	
5	"	John Burrill,	Reading.	
6	"	Mathew Cox,	Boston.	
7	"	Richard B. Chandler,	Duxbury.	
8	"	Charles L. Cummings,	Douglas.	
9	"	Charles Carter,	Leominster.	
10	"	Warren Davis,	Reading.	
11	"	William W. Greenough,	Boston.	
12	"	George O. Hovey,	"	
13	"	John M. Howland,	Fairhaven.	

14 Sworn.	Manson D. Haws,	Leominster.	
15 "	John Holbrook,	Randolph.	
Excused.	Nathaniel Johnson,	Hopkinton,	Excused first day, October 16th, for the term.
16 Sworn.	George Londen,	Duxbury.	
17 "	Nathan Moore,	Andover.	
18 "	Samuel P. Ridler,	Boston.	
19 "	Christopher Ryder,	Chatham.	
20 "	John Smith,	Andover.	
21 "	Appollos Wales,	Randolph.	
22 "	Samuel L. Ward,	Fairhaven.	

This Grand-Jury was not charged by the Judge upon the statute of 1790, or 1850, but was referred to Mr. Hallett, the Attorney, for the instructions previously given to the Jury that had been discharged, namely, for his charge of June 7th, already referred to. Mr. William W. Greenough, brother-in-law of Judge Curtis, was one of the Jury. They found the following indictment against Mr. Parker: —

UNITED STATES OF AMERICA.

Circuit Court of the United States of America, for the District of Massachusetts.

At a Circuit Court of the United States of America, for the District of Massachusetts, begun and holden at Boston, the aforesaid District, on the sixteenth day of October, in the year of our Lord one thousand eight hundred and fifty-four (the fifteenth day of said October being Sunday).

The Jurors of the United States within the aforesaid District, on their oath, present.

1st. That heretofore to wit, — on the twenty-fourth day of May, in the year of our Lord one thousand eight hundred and fifty-four, a certain warrant and legal process directed to the Marshal of the said District of Massachusetts, or either of his Deputies, was duly issued under the hand and seal of Edward G. Loring, Esquire, who was then and there a Commissioner of the Circuit Court of the United States, for said District, which said warrant and legal process was duly delivered to Watson Freeman, Esquire, who was then and there an officer of the United States, to wit, Marshal of the United States, for the said District of Massachusetts, at Boston, in the District aforesaid, on the said twenty-fourth day of May in the year aforesaid, and was of the purport and effect following, that is to say: —

UNITED STATES OF AMERICA.

MASSACHUSETTS DISTRICT, ss.

To the Marshal of our District of Massachusetts, or either of his Deputies, *Greeting:*

In the name of the President of the United States of America, you are hereby commanded forthwith to apprehend Anthony Burns, a negro man, alleged now to be in your District, charged with being a fugitive from labor, and with having escaped from service in the State of Virginia, if he may be found in your precincts, and have him forthwith before me, Edward G. Loring, one of the Commissioners of the Circuit Court of the United States for the said District, then and there to answer to the complaint of Charles F. Suttle, of Alexandria, in the said State of Virginia, Merchant, alleging under oath that the said Anthony Burns on the twenty-fourth day of March last, did and for a long time prior thereto had, owed service and labor to him the said Suttle, in the said State of Virginia, under the laws thereof, and that, while held to service there by said Suttle, the said Burns escaped from the said State of Virginia, into the State of Massachusetts; and that the said Burns still owes service and labor to said Suttle in the said State of Virginia, and praying that said Burns may be restored to him said Suttle in said State of Virginia, and that such further proceedings may then and there be had in the premises as are by law in such cases provided.

Hereof fail not, and make due return of this writ, with your doings therein before me.

Witness my hand and seal at Boston, aforesaid, this twenty-fourth day of May, in the year one thousand eight hundred and fifty-four.

EDWARD G. LORING, *Commissioner.* [L. S.]

And the Jurors aforesaid do further present, that the said warrant and legal process, being duly issued and delivered as aforesaid, afterwards to wit, on the twenty-fifth day of May, in the year aforesaid, at Boston in said District, the said Watson Freeman then and there being an officer of the said United States, to wit Marshal of the District aforesaid, and in pursuance of said warrant and legal process, did then and there arrest the said Anthony Burns named therein, and had him before the said Edward G. Loring, Commissioner, for examination — and thereupon the hearing of the said case was adjourned by the said Commissioner until Saturday the twenty-seventh day of May, in the year aforesaid, at ten o'clock in the forenoon; and the said Marshal, who had so made return of the said Warrant, was duly ordered by the said Commissioner to retain the said Anthony Burns in his custody, and have him before the said Commissioner on the said twenty-seventh day of May in the year aforesaid, at the Court House in said Boston, which said last-mentioned legal process and order was duly issued under the hand of the said Edward G. Loring, Commissioner, and was of the purport and effect following, that is to say:

U. S. of AMERICA, District of Massachusetts.

Boston, May 25, 1854.

And now the hearing of this case being adjourned to Saturday, May 27, 1854, 10 A. M., the said Marshal, who has made return of this warrant, is hereby ordered to retain the said Anthony Burns in his custody, and have him before me at the time last mentioned, at the Court House in Boston, for the further hearing of the Complaint on which the warrant was issued.

EDWARD G. LORING, *Commissioner.*

And the Jurors aforesaid do further present, that on the twenty-sixth day of May, in the year aforesaid, in pursuance of the warrant and legal process aforesaid, and of said further legal process and order last mentioned, the said Watson Freeman, Marshal as aforesaid, then and there, at the said Court House in said Boston, had in his custody the person of the said Anthony Burns, in the due and lawful execution of the said warrant and legal process, and of the said further legal process and order, in manner and form as he was therein commanded — and one Theodore Parker, of Boston, in said District, Clerk, then and there well knowing the premises, with force and arms did knowingly and wilfully obstruct, resist, and oppose the said Watson Freeman, then and there being an officer of the said United States, to wit, Marshal of the said District, in serving and attempting to serve and execute the said warrant and legal process, and the said further legal process and order in manner and form as he was therein commanded, to the great damage of the said Watson Freeman, to the great hinderance and obstruction of Justice, to the evil example of all others, in like case offending, against the peace and dignity of the said United States, and contrary to the form of the Statute in such case made and provided.

2d. And the Jurors aforesaid, on their oath aforesaid, do further present, that on the twenty-sixth day of May, in the year of our Lord one thousand eight hundred and fifty-four, at Boston, in said District, one Theodore Parker, of Boston, in said District, Clerk, with force and arms, did knowingly and wilfully obstruct, resist, and oppose one Watson Freeman, who was then and there the Marshal of the United States of America, for the District of Massachusetts, and an officer of the said United States, in serving and attempting to serve and execute a certain warrant and legal process, which before that time, to wit, on the twenty-fourth day of May, in the year of our Lord one thousand eight hundred and fifty-four, had been duly issued under the hand and seal of Edward G. Loring, Esquire, a Commissioner of the Circuit Court of the United States, for said District of Massachusetts, and directed to the Marshal of the District of Massachusetts, or either of his deputies, which said warrant and legal process the said Freeman, in the due and lawful execution of his said office, had then and there in his hands and possession for service of the same, and which he was then and there serving and attempting to serve and execute; which said warrant commanded the said Freeman to apprehend one Anthony Burns and to have him forthwith before the said Commissioner, then and there to be dealt with according to law. Against the peace and dignity of the said United States, and contrary to the form of the Statute in such case made and provided.

3d. And the Jurors aforesaid, on their oath aforesaid, do further present, that on the twenty-sixth day of May, in the year of our Lord one thousand eight hundred and fifty-four, at Boston, in said District, the said Theodore Parker, with force and arms, did knowingly and wilfully obstruct, resist, and oppose one Watson Freeman, who was then and there an officer of the said United States, to wit, the Marshal of the United States for the said District of Massachusetts, in serving and attempting to serve and execute a certain legal process which before that time, to wit, on the 25th day of May, in the year of our Lord one thousand eight hundred and fifty-four, had been duly issued under the hand of Edward G. Loring, who was then and there a Commissioner of the Circuit Court of the United States, for the said District of Massachusetts, and was then and there duly empowered to issue said legal process, and which said legal process was duly committed for obedience and execution to the said Freeman, Marshal as aforesaid, wherein and whereby and in pursuance of the command whereof the said Freeman was then and there lawfully retaining, detaining, and holding one Anthony Burns for the further hearing and determination of a certain complaint, upon which a warrant before that time, to wit, on the twenty-fourth day of said May, had been duly issued under the hand and seal of the said Commissioner, by force of which warrant the said Anthony Burns had been duly arrested and apprehended by the said Freeman, and in execution of the same, on the twenty-fifth day of said May had been brought by the said Freeman before the said Commissioner.

4th. And the jurors aforesaid, on their oath aforesaid, do further present, that on the twenty-sixth day of May, in the year of our Lord one thousand eight hundred and fifty-four, at Boston, in said district, the said Theodore Parker, with force and arms, did knowingly and wilfully obstruct, resist, and oppose one Watson Freeman, who was then and there an officer of the said Uuited States, to wit, Marshal of the United States, for the District of Massachusetts, in serving and attempting to serve and execute a certain warrant and legal process, which before that time, to wit, on the twenty-fourth day of May, in the year of our Lord one thousand eight hundred and fifty-four, had been duly issued under the hand and seal of Edward G. Loring, Esquire, a Commissioner of the Circuit Court of the United States, for the District of Massachusetts, and directed to the Marshal of the said District of Massachusetts or either of his Deputies, which the said Freeman, in the due and lawful execution of his said office, had then and there in his hands and possession for service of the same, and which he was then and there serving and attempting to serve and execute; which warrant commanded the said Freeman to apprehend one Anthony Burns, and to have him forthwith before the said commissioner and that such further proceedings might then and there be had in the premises, as are by law in such cases provided, — and also in serving and attempting to serve and execute a certain further legal process which before that time, to wit, on the twenty-fifth day of May, in the year aforesaid, had been duly issued under the hand of the said Commissioner, and duly committed for obedience and execution to the said Freeman, wherein and whereby, and in pursuance of the command whereof, the said Freeman was then and there lawfully retaining, detaining, and holding the said Anthony Burns for the further hearing and determination of a certain complaint upon which the warrant aforesaid had been issued by the said Commissioner.

5th. And the Jurors aforesaid on their oath aforesaid, do further present that one Theodore Parker, of Boston, in said District, Clerk, on the 26th day of May, in the year of our Lord one thousand eight hundred and fifty-four, at Boston, in the said District of Massachusetts, with force and arms, in and upon one Watson Freeman, then and there in the peace of the said United States being, an assault did make, he the said Freeman also then and there being an officer of the said United States, to wit, Marshal of the United States, for the said District of Massachusetts, and then and there also being in the due and lawful discharge of his duties as such officer. And so the jurors aforesaid, on their oath aforesaid, do say and present that the said Theodore Parker, at Boston aforesaid, on the said twenty-sixth day of said May, with force and arms assaulted the said Freeman as such officer, and knowingly and wilfully obstructed, resisted, and opposed him in the discharge of his lawful duties in manner and form aforesaid, against the peace and dignity of the said United States, and contrary to the form of the Statute in such cases made and provided. And the Jurors aforesaid, on their oath aforesaid, do further present that the said Theodore Parker was first apprehended in said District of Massachusetts, after committing the aforesaid offence, against the peace and dignity of the said United States, and contrary to the form of the statute in such case made and provided. A true bill.

ENOCH PATTERSON, Jr., *Foreman.*
B. F. HALLETT, *United States Attorney for the District of Massachusetts.*

Similar indictments were found against Mr. Phillips, Mr. Stowell, Rev. T. W. Higginson, John Morrison, Samuel T. Proudman, and John C. Cluer.

Mr. Parker was arraigned on Wednesday, November 29th, and ordered to recognize in bonds of $1,500 for his appearance at that Court, on the 5th of March, 1855. His bondsmen were Messrs. Samuel May, Francis Jackson, and John R. Manley; his counsel were Hon. John P. Hale, and Charles M. Ellis, Esq. The other gentlemen were arraigned afterwards at different times.

After considerable uncertainty about the engagements of Hon. Justice Curtis, Tuesday, April 3d, was fixed for the commencement of the trials. At that time there appeared as counsel for the government, Hon. Benjamin F. Hallett, District Attorney, and Elias Merwin, Esq., formerly a law partner of Judge Curtis; on the other side were Hon. John P. Hale, and Charles M. Ellis, Esq., for Mr. Parker; Wm. L. Burt, Esq., John A. Andrew, Esq., and H. F. Durant, Esq., counsel for Messrs. Phillips, Higginson, Stowell, Bishop, Morrison, Proudman, and Cluer.

Mr. Hale, as senior counsel, stated to the court that the counsel for the defendants in several of the cases had conferred, and concluded — on the supposition that the Court and Government would assent to the plan as most for their own convenience, as well as that of the defendants' counsel — to file the like motion on the different cases; and, instead of each counsel going over the whole ground for each case, to divide the matter presented for debate, and for each to discuss some particular positions on behalf of them all. This was assented to; and motions, of which the following is a copy, were filed in the several cases: —

CIRCUIT COURT OF THE UNITED STATES, MASSACHUSETTS DISTRICT, SS.

United States by Indictment v. *Theodore Parker.*

And now said Theodore Parker comes and moves that the indictment against him be quashed, because,

"1. The writ of venire for the jury that found said indictment was directed to and returned by Watson Freeman, the Marshal, who was not an indifferent person, and it was not served and returned as the law directs.

"2. Because said Jury was not an impartial Jury of the District, designated as the laws require, but the jury Districts for this court embrace but a portion of the District and of the population, and said jury was in fact chosen and designated from but a fraction of the District and contrary to law.

"3. Because the matters and things alleged in said indictment do not constitute any crime under the statute on which said indictment is framed, the said statute not embracing them, or being, so far as it might embrace them, repealed by the statute of eighteen hundred and fifty.

"4. Because said indictment does not allege and set forth fully and sufficiently the authority and the proceedings whereon the alleged warrant and order were based, or facts sufficient to show that the alleged process and order were lawfully issued by any person duly authorized, and his authority and jurisdiction, and that the same were within such jurisdiction, and issued by the authority of the law, and originated, issued, and directed as the law prescribes; said warrant and order not being alleged to have issued from any court or tribunal of general or special jurisdiction, but by a person vested with certain specific statute authority.

"5. Because said indictment and the several counts thereof are bad on the face of them, as follows, viz.: —

"First, it nowhere appearing that the same were found by a grand-jury, because the second and third counts do not conclude, against the form of the statute, and have no conclusion, because the third and fourth counts do not set forth the estate, degree, or mystery of the person therein charged.

"Because said indictment and the counts thereof are repugnant and inconsistent, the same being based on an alleged obstruction, resistance, and opposition to the service of an action, order, or warrant, which is therein averred to have been already served, executed, and returned.

"Because the first and fifth counts are double.

"Because the alleged order of May 25th, referred to therein, was a void and illegal, order.

"Because, if the alleged warrant was served as therein alleged, said Watson Freeman did not, and by law could not thereafter, hold the person described therein, under any process or order.

"And because the same do not set forth and allege fully and specifically the acts charged to be offences against the statute, so as to inform said party charged, of the nature and cause of the accusation.

"6. Because the warrant set forth and referred to therein was void on its face, and issued from and ran into a jurisdiction not authorized by law, and directed the arrest of a person without legal cause, and because said indictment is otherwise bad, uncertain, and insufficient."

Mr. Wm. L. Burt commenced the argument of the motions, and presented several of the points. He was followed by Mr. C. M. Ellis, J. A. Andrew, and H. F. Durant, who severally discussed some of the grounds of the motions.

Elias Merwin, Esquire, and Mr. Attorney Hallett, replied.

The Court stated that they did not wish to hear Hon. John P. Hale, who was about to rejoin and close in support of the motion, and decided that the allegation, on the indictment, that Edward G. Loring was a Commissioner of the Circuit Court of the United States for said District, was not a legal averment that he was such a Commissioner as is described in the bill of 1850, and therefore the indictments were bad.

The Court said they supposed it to be true that Mr. Loring was such a Commissioner, and that his authority could be proved by producing the record of his appointment; that they did not suppose the absence of this averment could be of any practical consequence to the defendants, so far as respected the substantial merits of the cases; and it was true the objection to the indictment was "technical;" but they held it sufficient, notwithstanding the averment that the warrant was "*duly issued*," and ordered the indictment against Stowell to be quashed. On every other point, save that that the Court could properly construct the Jury *roster* and return the Jury from a portion of the District, the Judge said they would express no opinion.

Mr. Hallett insisted on his right to enter a *nolle prosequi* in the other cases; and the Judges decided that, though all the cases had been heard upon the motion, yet as it could make no difference whether an entry were made that this indictment be quashed, or an entry of *nolle prosequi*, the Attorney might enter a *nolle prosequi* if he chose to do so *then*, before the Court passed any order on the motions.

Mr. Hallett accordingly entered a *nolle prosequi* in all the other cases, and the whole affair was quashed.[1]

[1] See Law Reporter for June, 1855.

DEFENCE.

May it please the Court:

Gentlemen of the Jury.—It is no trifling matter which comes before you this day. You may hereafter decide on millions of money, and on the lives of your fellow men; but it is not likely that a question of this magnitude will ever twice be brought before the same jurymen. Opportunities to extend a far-reaching and ghastly wickedness, or to do great service for mankind, come but seldom in any man's life. Your verdict concerns all the people of the United States; its influence will reach to ages far remote, blessing or cursing whole generations not yet born. The affair is national in its width of reach,—its consequences of immense duration.

In addressing you, Gentlemen, my language will be more didactic than rhetorical, more like a lecture, less like a speech; for I am not a lawyer but a minister, and do not aim to carry a Measure, which with you will go of its own accord, so much as to set forth a Principle that will make such prosecutions as impossible hereafter, as a conviction now is to-day.

Gentlemen, I address you provisionally, as Representatives of the People. To them, my words are ultimately addressed,—to the People of the Free States of America. I must examine many things minutely, not often touched upon in courts like this. For mine is a Political Trial; I shall treat it accordingly. I am charged with no immoral act—with none even of selfish ambition. It is not pretended that I have done a deed, or spoken a word, in the heat of passion, or vengeance, or with calculated covetousness, to bring money, office, or honor, to myself or any friend. I am not suspected of wishing to do harm to man or woman; or with disturbing any man's natural rights. Nay, I am not even charged with such an offence. The Attorney and the two Judges are of one heart and mind in this prosecution; Mr. Hallett's "Indictment" is only the beast of burthen to carry to its own place Mr. Curtis's "Charge to the

Grand-Jury," fit passenger for fitting carriage! The same tree bore the Judge's blossom in June, and the Attorney's fruit in October,—both reeking out the effluvia of the same substance. But neither Attorney nor Judge dares accuse me of ill-will which would harm another man, or of selfishness that seeks my own private advantage. No, Gentlemen of the Jury, I am on trial for my love of Justice; for my respect to the natural Rights of Man; for speaking a word in behalf of what the Declaration of Independence calls the "self-evident" Truth,—that all men have a natural, equal, and unalienable Right to Life, Liberty, and the pursuit of Happiness. I am charged with words against what John Wesley named, the "Sum of all Villanies," against a national crime so great, that it made freethinking Mr. Jefferson, with all his "French Infidelity," "tremble" when he remembered "that God is just." I am on trial for my manly virtue,—a Minister of the Christian Religion on trial for keeping the Golden Rule! It is alleged that I have spoken in Boston against kidnapping in Boston; that in my own pulpit, as a minister, I have denounced Boston men for stealing my own parishioners; that as a man, in Faneuil Hall, the spirit of James Otis, of John Hancock, and three Adams's about me, with a word I "obstructed" the Marshal of Boston and a Boston Judge of Probate, in their confederated attempts to enslave a Boston man. When the Government of the United States has turned kidnapper, I am charged with the "misdemeanor" of appealing from the Atheism of purchased officials to the Conscience of the People; and with rousing up Christians to keep the golden rule, when the Rulers declared Religion had nothing to do with politics and there was no Law of God above the fugitive slave bill!

Such are the acts charged. Gentlemen of the Jury, you are summoned here to declare them a Crime, and then to punish me for this "offence!" You are the Axe which the Government grasps with red hand to cleave my head asunder. It is a trial where Franklin Pierce, transiently President of the United States, and his official coadjutors,—Mr. Caleb Cushing, Mr. Benj. R. Curtis, and Mr. Benj. F. Hallett,—are on one side, and the People of the United States on the other. As a Measure, your decision may send me to jail for twelve months; may also fine me three hundred dollars. To me personally it is of very small consequence what your verdict shall be. The fine is nothing; the imprisonment for twelve months—Gentlemen, I laugh at it! Nay, were it death, I should smile at the official gibbet. A verdict of guilty would affix no stain to my reputation. I am sure to come out of this trial with honor—it is the Court that is sure to suffer loss—at least shame. I do not mean the Court will ever feel remorse, or even shame, for this conduct; I am no young man now, I know these men,—but the People are sure to burn the brand of shame deep into this tribunal. The blow of that axe, if not parried, will do me no harm.

But it is not I, merely, now put to trial. Nay, it is the unalienable Rights of Humanity, it is truths self-evident. For on the back of that compliant Measure, unseen, there rides a Principle. The verdict expected of you condemns liberal institutions: all Religion but priestcraft — the abnegation of religion itself; all Rights but that to bondage — the denial of all rights. The word which fines me, puts your own purse in the hands of your worst enemies; the many-warded key which shuts me in jail, locks your lips forever — your children's lips forever. No complaint against oppression hereafter! Kidnapping will go on in silence, but at noonday, not a minister stirring. Meeting-houses will be shut; all court houses have a loaded cannon at their door, chains all round them, be stuffed with foreign soldiers inside, while commissioners swear away the life, the liberty, and even the Estate of the subjected "citizens." All Probate Judges will belong to the family of man-stealers. Faneuil Hall will be shut, or open only for a "Union Meeting," where the ruler calls together his menials to indorse some new act of injustice, — only creatures of the Government, men like the marshal's guard last June, allowed to speak words paid for by the People's coward sweat and miserable blood. The blow which smites my head will also cleave you asunder from crown to groin.

Your verdict is to vindicate Religion with Freedom of Speech, and condemn the stealing of men; or else to confirm Kidnapping and condemn Religion with Freedom of Speech. You are to choose whether you will have such men as Wendell Phillips for your advisers, or such as Benjamin F. Hallett and Benjamin R. Curtis for your masters, with the marshal's guard, for their appropriate servants. Do you think I doubt how you will choose?

Already a power of iniquity clutches at your children's throat; stabs at their life — at their soul's life. I stand between the living tyrant and his living victim; aye, betwixt him and expected victims not yet born, — your children, not mine. I have none to writhe under the successful lash which tyrants now so subtly braid therewith, one day, to scourge the flesh of well-descended men. I am to stand the champion of human Rights for generations yet unborn. It is a sad distinction! Hard duties have before been laid on me, — none so obviously demanding great powers as this. Whereto shall I look up for inspiring aid? Only to Him who gave words to the slow tongue of Moses and touched with fire Esaias' hesitating lips, and dawned into the soul of tent-makers and fishermen with such great wakening light, as shining through them, brought day to nations sitting in darkness, yet waiting for the consolation. May such

Truth and Justice enable me also, to speak a testimony unto the Gentiles; He who chose the weak things, to bring to nought the mighty, may not despise such humble services as mine.

Gentlemen of the Jury, my ministry deals chiefly with the Laws of God, little with the statutes of men. My manhood has been mainly passed in studying absolute, universal truth, teaching it to men, and applying it to the various departments of life. I have little to do with courts of law. Yet I am not now altogether a stranger to the circuit court room of the United States, having been in it on five several occasions before.

1. A Polish exile, — a man of famous family, ancient and patrician before Christendom had laid eyes on America, once also of great individual wealth, a man of high rank alike acquired and inherited, once holding a high place at the court of the Czar, — became a fugitive from Russian despotism, seeking an asylum here; he came to the circuit court room to lecture on the Roman Law. I came to contribute my two mites of money, and receive his wealth of learning.

2. The next time, I came at the summons of Thomas Sims. For a creature of the slave-power had spontaneously seized that poor and friendless boy and thrust him into a dungeon, hastening to make him a slave, — a beast of burthen. He had been on his mock trial seven days, and had never seen a Judge, only a commissioner, nor a Jury; no Court but a solitary kidnapper. Some of his attendants had spoken of me as a minister not heedless of the welfare and unalienable rights of a black man fallen among a family of thieves. I went to the court house. Outside it was belted with chains. In despotic Europe I had seen no such spectacle, save once when the dull tyrant who oppressed Bavaria with his licentious flesh, in 1844 put his capital in a brief state of siege and chained the streets. The official servant of the kidnapper, club in hand, a policeman of this city, goaded to his task by Mayor Bigelow and Marshal Tukey, — men congenitally mingled in such appropriate work, — bade me "Get under the chain." I pressed it down and went over. The Judges of our own Supreme Court, *they went under*, — had gone out and in, beneath the chain! How poetry mingles with fact! The chain was a symbol, and until this day remaineth the same chain, untaken away in the reading of the fugitive slave bill; and when the law of Massachusetts is read, the chain is also upon the neck of that court! Within the court house was full of armed men. I found Mr. Sims in a private room, illegally, in defiance of Massachusetts law, converted into a jail to hold men charged with no crime. Ruffians mounted guard at the entrance, armed with swords, fire-arms,

and bludgeons. The door was locked and doubly barred besides. Inside the watch was kept by a horrid looking fellow, without a coat, a naked cutlass in his hand, and some twenty others, their mouths nauseous with tobacco and reeking also with half-digested rum paid for by the city. In such company, I gave what consolation Religion could offer to the first man Boston ever kidnapped,—consolations which took hold only of eternity, where the servant is free from his master, for there the wicked cease from troubling. I could offer him no comfort this side the grave.

3. I visited the United States court a third time. A poor young man had been seized by the same talons which subsequently griped Sims in their poison, deadly clutch. But that time, wickedness went off hungry, defeated of its prey; "for the Lord delivered him out of their hands," and Shadrach escaped from that Babylonish furnace, heated seven times hotter than its wont: no smell of fire had passed on him. But the rescue of Shadrach was telegraphed as "treason." The innocent lightning flashed out the premeditated and legal lie,—"it is levying war!" What offence it was in that Fourth One who walked with the Hebrew children, "making their good confession," and sustained the old Shadrach, Meshech, and Abednego, I know not. But the modern countrymen of the African Shadrach, charged with some great crime, were haled into this court to be punished for their humanity! I came to look on these modern Angels of the Deliverance, to hear counsel of Mr. Dana, then so wise and humane, and to listen to the masterly eloquence which broke out from the great human heart of my friend, Mr. Hale, and rolled like the Mississippi, in its width, its depth, its beauty, and its continuous and unconquerable strength.

4. The fourth time, a poor man had been kidnapped, also at night, and forced into the same illegal jail. He sat in the dock—an innocent man, to be made into a beast. The metamorphosis had begun;—he was already in chains and his human heart seemed dead in him; sixty ruffians were about him, aiding in this drama, hired out of the brothels and rum-shops for a few days, the lust of kidnapping serving to vary the continual glut of those other and less brutal appetites of unbridled flesh. While that "trial" lasted, whoredom had a Sabbath day, and brawlers rested from their toil. Opposite sat the Boston Judge of Probate, and the Boston District Attorney,—the Moses and Elias of this inverted transfiguration; there sat the marshal, two "gentlemen" from Virginia, claiming that a Boston man was their beast of burthen, owing service and labor in Richmond; two "lawyers," "members of the Suffolk bar," pistols in their coats, came to support the allegation and enforce the claim. Honorable men stood up to defend him. There is one of them,—to defend

me [Charles M. Ellis.] You know very well the rest of that sad story, — the mock trial of Anthony Burns lasted from May 25th till June 2d. I was here in all the acts of that Tragedy. My own life was threatened; friend and foe gave me public or anonymous warning. I sat between men who had newly sworn to kill me, my garments touching theirs. The malaria of their rum and tobacco was an offence in my face. I saw their weapons, and laughed as I looked those drunken rowdies in their coward eye. They touch me!

5. The fifth time I came here at the summons of an officer of this court, — very politely delivered, let me say it to his credit, — indicted and arrested for a "misdemeanor." I gave bail and withdrew.

6. The sixth time, — Gentlemen, — it is the present, whereof I shall erelong have much to say.

At the first visit I found only scholarly and philanthropic gentlemen, coming out of sympathy with a Polish exile, a defeated soldier of freedom, from his broken English to learn sound Roman Law. On each of the other visits I have been in quite different company. I have invariably met this Honorable Court, its kinsfolk and its most intimate friends, — some member of the family of the distinguished Judge, now fitly presiding over this trial.

1. It was Mr. George T. Curtis, the only brother of the honorable Justice now on the bench, — born of the same mother and father, — who had the glory of kidnapping Mr. Sims; it was he who seized Shadrach, and gave such witness against one of the Angels of the Deliverance, and then came back and enlarged his testimony; it was he who declared the rescue an act of "treason;" he who hung the court house in chains, and brought down the pliant neck of the Massachusetts Judges beneath that symbolic line of linked fetters long drawn out. To what weak forces will such necks bow when slavery commands!

2. It was the honorable Judge now on the distinguished bench who tried men for the rescue of Shadrach. How he tried them is well known.

3. It was Edward G. Loring, another of this family so distinguished, who kidnapped Mr. Burns and held him in irons; he whose broom swept up together the marshal's guard; he who advised Mr. Burns's counsel to make no defence, — "put no obstructions in the way of his going back, as he probably will;" he who, in the darkness of midnight, sought to sell his victim, before he had examined the evidence which might prove him a free man; he who delivered him up as a slave, against evidence as against law.

4. Another of the same family, William W. Greenough, brother-in-law of Hon. Judge Curtis, was one of the grand-jury which

found the indictment against me, and "the most active of all in that work."

5. When I came here on the 29th of last November, the Hon. Judge Curtis sat on the bench and determined the amount of my bail, and the same eye which had frowned with such baleful aspect on the rescuers of Shadrach, quailed down underneath my look and sought the ground.

In thus mentioning my former visits to the court, I but relate the exploits of the Hon. Justice Curtis, of his kinsfolk and friends, adding to their glory and their renown. Their chief title to distinction rests on their devotion to the fugitive slave bill. It and their honor are "one and inseparable." Once only humanity and good letters brought me here, I met only scholars and philanthropists; on five other occasions, when assaults on freedom compelled my attendance, I have been confronted and surrounded with the loyalty of the distinguished Judge and his kinsfolk and friends, valiantly and disinterestedly obeying the fugitive slave bill "with alacrity;" patriotically conquering their prejudices against man-stealing — if such they ever had; — and earning for themselves an undying reputation by "saving the Union" from Justice, Domestic Tranquillity, general Welfare, and the Blessings of Liberty.

If I am to be arraigned for any act, I regard it as a special good fortune that I am charged with such deeds, with seeking to arouse the noblest emotions of Human Nature; and by means of the grandest Ideas which Human History has brought to light. I could not have chosen nobler deeds in a life now stretching over nearly half a hundred years. I count it an honor to be tried for them. Nay, it adds to my happiness to look at the Court which is to try me — for if I were to search all Christendom through, nay, throughout all Heathendom, I know of no tribunal fitter to try a man for such deeds as I have done. I am fortunate in the charges brought; thrice fortunate in the judges and the attorney, — the Court which is to decide; — its history and character are already a judgment.

6. For my sixth visit, I was recognized to appear on the fifth of March, 1855 — the eighty-fifth anniversary of the Boston Massacre. I might have been bound over to any other of the great days of American history — 22d of December, 19th of April, 17th of June, or the 4th of July. But as I am the first American ever brought to trial for a speech in Faneuil Hall against kidnapping; as I am the first to be tried under the act of 1790 for "obstructing an officer" with an argument, committing a "misdemeanor" by a word which appeals to the natural justice of mankind, so there could not perhaps be a fitter time chosen. For on the fifth of March, 1770, British

despotism also delivered its first shot into the American bosom. Not far from this place the hand of George III. wounded to death five innocent citizens of Boston, — one of them a negro. It was the first shot Britain ever fired into the body of the American people, then colonial subjects of the king-power. That day the fire was not returned, — only with ringing of bells and tumult of the public, with words and resolutions. The next day that American blood lay frozen in the street. Soon after the British government passed a law exempting all who should aid an officer in his tyranny from trial for murder in the place where they should commit their crime. Mr. Toucey has humbly copied that precedent of despotism. It was very proper that the new tyranny growing up here, should select that anniversary to shoot down freedom of thought and speech among the subjects of the slave-power. I welcomed the omen. The Fifth of March is a red-letter day in the calendar of Boston. The Court could hardly have chosen a better to punish a man for a thought and a word, especially a Boston man, for such a word in Faneuil Hall — a word against man-stealing. But I knew the case would never come to trial on that day — of course it was put off.

Mr. Sims and Mr. Burns were accused of no crime but birth from a mother whom some one had stolen. They had only a mock trial, without due process of law, with no judge, no jury, no judicial officer. But I, accused of a grave offence, am to enjoy a trial with due process of law. It is an actual judge before me and another judge at his side, both judicial officers known to the constitution. I know beforehand the decision of the court — its history is my judgment. Justice Curtis's Charge of last June, would make my daily talk a "misdemeanor," my public preaching and my private prayers a "crime," nay, my very existence is constructively an "obstruction" to the marshal. On that side my condemnation is already sure.

But there is another element. Gentlemen of the Jury, the judges and attorney cannot lay their hand on me until you twelve men with one voice say, "Yes! put him in jail." In the mock trial of Sims and Burns it was necessary to convince only a single official of the United States Court, a "ministerial" officer selected and appointed to do its inferior business, a man who needed no conviction, no evidence but the oath of a slave-hunter and the extorted "admission" of his victim, an official who was to have ten dollars for making a slave, five only for setting free a man! But you are a Massachusetts Jury, not of purchased officials, but of honest men. I think you have some "prejudices" to conquer in favor of justice. It has not appeared that you are to be paid twice as much for sending me to jail, as for acquitting me of the charge. I doubt that you have yet advised my counsel to make no defence, "put no obstructions in the way" of my being sent to jail as "he probably will."

Gentlemen, a United States Commissioner has his place on condition that he performs such services as his masters "require." These United States Judges have their seat in consequence of services rendered to the ruling power of America, and for others of like sort yet to be paid to the stealers of men. Other rewards shine before them alluring to new service, — additional salary can pay additional alacrity. But you, Gentlemen, are not office-holders nor seekers of office, not hoping to gain money, or power, or honor, by any wickedness. You are to represent the unsophisticated Conscience of the People,— not the slave-power, but the power of Freedom.

It is to you I shall address my defence! MY defence? No, Gentlemen, YOUR defence, the defence of your own Rights, inherent in your national Institutions as Americans, ay, in your Nature as Men. It is a singular good fortune that to you, as judges, I am pleading your own cause. You have more interest at stake than I. For at death my name will perish, while children and children's children, I trust, will gently mingle your memories in that fair tide of human life which never ends.

So much have I said by way of introduction, treating only of the accidents pertaining to this case. I will now come to the Primary Qualities and Substance thereof.

This is a Political Trial. In *form*, I am charged with violating a certain statute never before applied to actions like mine; never meant to apply to such actions; not legally capable of such application. But in *fact*, my offence is very different from what the indictment attempts to set forth. The judges know this; the attorney knows it, and "never expected to procure a conviction." It is your cause, even more than mine, that I plead. So it concerns you to understand the whole matter thoroughly, that you may justly judge our common cause. To make the whole case clear, I will *land* it out into four great parcels of matter, which your mind can command at once, and then come to the details of each, ploughing it all over before your face, furrow by furrow. I shall speak,

I. Of the State of Affairs in America which has led to this prosecution, — the Encroachments of a Power hostile to Democratic Institutions.

II. Of the Mode of Operation pursued by this Encroaching Power, in other times and in our own, — of Systematic Corruption of the Judiciary.

III. Of the great Safeguard which has been found serviceable in protecting Democratic Institutions and the Rights of Man they are designed to defend, — of the Trial by Jury.

IV. Of the Circumstances of this special case, UNITED STATES *versus* THEODORE PARKER.

I shall speak of each in its order, and begin at the head.

I. OF THE STATE OF AFFAIRS IN AMERICA, WHICH HAS LED TO THIS PROSECUTION — THE ENCROACHMENTS OF A POWER HOSTILE TO DEMOCRATIC INSTITUTIONS.

In a republic where all emanates from the People, political institutions must have a Basis of Idea in the Nation's Thought, before they can acquire a Basis of Fact in the Force of the Nation. Now in America there are two diverse Ideas recognized as principles of Action — the Idea of Freedom and the Idea of Slavery. Allow me to read my analysis and description of each.

The Idea of Freedom first got a national expression on the Fourth of July, 1776. Here it is. I put it in a philosophic form. There are five points to it.

First, All men are endowed by their Creator with certain natural rights, amongst which is the right to life, liberty, and the pursuit of happiness.

Second, These rights are unalienable; they can be alienated only by the possessor thereof; the father cannot alienate them for the son, nor the son for the father; nor the husband for the wife, nor the wife for the husband; nor the strong for the weak, nor the weak for the strong; nor the few for the many, nor the many for the few; and so on.

Third, In respect to these, all men are equal; the rich man has not more, and the poor less; the strong man has not more, and the weak man less: — all are exactly equal in these rights, however unequal in their powers.

Fourth, It is the function of government to secure these natural, unalienable, and equal rights to every man.

Fifth, Government derives all its divine right from its conformity with these ideas, all its human sanction from the consent of the governed.

That is the Idea of Freedom. I used to call it "the American Idea;" that was when I was younger than I am to-day. It is derived from human nature; it rests on the immutable Laws of God; it is part of the natural religion of mankind. It demands a government after natural Justice, which is the point common between the conscience of God and the conscience of mankind; it is the point common also between the interests of one man and of all men.

Now this government, just in its substance, in its form must be democratic: that is to say, the government of all, by all, and for all. You see what consequences must follow from such an idea, and the attempt to reënact the Law of God into political institutions. There will follow the freedom of the people, respect for every natural right of all men, the rights of their body and of their spirit — the rights of mind and conscience, heart and soul. There must be some restraint — as of children by their parents, as of bad men by good men; but it will be restraint for the joint good of all parties concerned; not restraint for the exclusive benefit of the restrainer. The ultimate consequence of this will be the material and spiritual welfare of all — riches, comfort, noble manhood, all desirable things.

That is the Idea of Freedom. It appears in the Declaration of Independence; it reappears in the Preamble to the American Constitution, which aims "to establish Justice, insure domestic tranquillity, provide for the common defence, promote the general welfare, and secure the blessings of Liberty." That is a religious idea; and when men pray for the "Reign of Justice" and the "Kingdom of Heaven" to come on earth politically, I suppose they mean that there may be a Commonwealth where every man has his natural rights of mind, body, and estate.

Next is the Idea of Slavery. Here it is. I put it also in a philosophic form. There are three points which I make.

First, There are no natural, unalienable, and equal rights, wherewith men are endowed by their Creator; no natural, unalienable, and equal right to life, liberty, and the pursuit of happiness.

Second, There is a great diversity of powers, and in virtue thereof the strong man may rule and oppress, enslave and ruin the weak, for his interest and against theirs.

Third, There is no natural law of God to forbid the strong to oppress the weak, and enslave and ruin the weak.

That is the Idea of Slavery. It has never got a national expression in America; it has never been laid down as a Principle in any act of the American people, nor in any single State, so far as I know. All profess the opposite; but it is involved in the Measures of both State and Nation. This Idea is founded in the selfishness of man; it is atheistic.

The idea must lead to a corresponding government; that will be unjust in its substance, — for it will depend not on natural right, but on personal force; not on the Constitution of the Universe, but on the compact of men. It is the abnegation of God in the universe and of conscience in man. Its form will be despotism, — the government of all, by a part, for the sake of a part. It may be a single-headed despotism, or a despotism of many heads; but whether a Cyclops or a Hydra, it is alike "the abomination which maketh desolate." Its ultimate consequence is plain to foresee — poverty to a nation, misery, ruin.

These two Ideas are now fairly on foot. They are hostile; they are both mutually invasive and destructive. They are in exact opposition to each other, and the nation which embodies these two is not a figure of equilibrium. As both are active forces in the minds of men, and as each idea tends to become a fact — a universal and exclusive fact, — as men with these ideas organize into parties as a means to make their idea into a fact, — it follows that there must not only be strife amongst philosophical men about these antagonistic Principles and Ideas, but a strife of practical men about corresponding Facts and Measures. So the quarrel, if not otherwise ended, will pass from words to what seems more serious; and one will overcome the other.

So long as these two Ideas exist in the nation as two political forces, there is no national unity of Idea, of course no unity of action. For there is no centre of gravity common to Freedom and Slavery. They will not compose an equilibrious figure. You may cry "Peace! Peace!" but so long as these two antagonistic Ideas remain, each seeking to organize itself and get exclusive power, there is no peace; there can be none.

The question before the nation to-day is, Which shall prevail — the Idea and Fact of Freedom, or the Idea and the Fact of Slavery; Freedom, exclusive and universal, or Slavery, exclusive and universal? The question is not merely, Shall the African be bond or free? but, Shall America be a Democracy or a Despotism? For nothing is so remorseless as an idea, and no logic is so strong as the historical development of a national idea by millions of men. A measure is nothing without its Principle. The Idea which allows Slavery in South Carolina will establish it also in New England.

The bondage of a black man in Alexandria imperils every white woman's daughter in Boston. You cannot escape the consequences of a first Principle more than you can "take the leap of Niagara and stop when half-way down." The Principle which recognizes Slavery in the Constitution of the United States would make all America a Despotism, while the Principle which made John Quincy Adams a free man would extirpate Slavery from Louisiana and Texas. It is plain America cannot long hold these two contradictions in the national consciousness. Equilibrium must come.[1]

These two ideas are represented by two parties which aim at the ultimate organization of their respective doctrines, the party indicating the special tendency towards Democracy or Despotism. The Party of Freedom is not yet well organized; that of Slavery is in admirable order and discipline. These two parties are continually at war attended with various success.

1. In the individual States of the North, since the Revolution, the Party of Freedom has gained some great victories; it has abolished Personal Slavery in every northern State, and on a deep-laid foundation has built up Democratic Institutions with well proportioned beauty. The Idea of Freedom, so genial to the Anglo-Saxon, so welcome to all of Puritanic birth and breeding, has taken deep root in the consciousness of the great mass of the People at the North. In the severe simplicity of national deduction they will carry it to logical conclusions not yet foreseen by human providence. The free States are progressively democratic.

But in all the Northern States, and more especially in its cities,—and here chiefly among the men of exclusive intellectual culture and the votaries of commerce and its riches,—there are exceptional men who embrace the Idea of Slavery and belong to its Party. They know no law higher than the transient interest of their politics or their commerce, their ease or ambition. They may not theoretically hate the People, but they so love their own money, their own ease or pleasure, that practically they oppose what promotes the welfare of mankind, and seek their own personal advancement to the injury of the human race. These are Northern men with Southern "Principles." They have their Journals too well known in Boston to need mention here.

2. In the individual States of the South, the Idea and Party of Slavery has also gained great victories and been uniformly successful; it has extended and strengthened personal slavery, which has now a firmer hold in the minds of the controlling classes of Southern men,—the rich and "educated,"—than in 1776, or ever before. The Southern States are progressively despotic.

Still, in all the Southern States there are exceptional men, hostile

[1] See this statement in Mr. Parker's Additional Speeches, Addresses, and Occasional Sermons. Boston, 1855, vol. ii. p. 250, *et seq.*

to slavery, — the intelligent and religious from conviction, others from mere personal interest. These are Southern men with Northern Principles. They are much oppressed at home — kept from political advancement or social respectability, as much as democrats would be at Rome or Naples, — have no journals and little influence.

3. In the Federal Government, the warfare goes on, each party seeking for mastery over the whole United States — the contest is carried on in Congress, in all the local legislatures; newspapers, speeches, even sermons, resound with the din of battle. See what forces contend and with what results.

The nation lives by its productive industry, whereof there are these five chief departments: — Hunting and Fishing, the appropriation of the spontaneous live products of the land and sea; Agriculture, the use of the productive forces of the earth's surface; Mining, the appropriation of the metallic products of her bosom; Manufactures, the application of toil and thought to the products of Hunting and Fishing, Mining and Agriculture; Commerce, the exchange of value, distribution of the products of these four departments of industry, directly productive.

Hunting and Fishing, Mining, Manufactures, Commerce, are mainly in the hands of Northern men — the South is almost wholly Agricultural. Her wealth consists of land and slaves. In 1850 the fifteen slave States had not fourteen hundred millions of other property. In the South property, with its consequent influence, is in few hands — in the North it is wide spread.

Now the few controlling men of the South, the holders of land and slaves, have Unity of pecuniary Interest — the support of Slavery as a local measure, — for it is the source of their material wealth, and also a consequent Unity of political Idea, the support of Slavery as a universal Principle, for it is the source likewise of their political power. Accordingly the South presents against the North an even and well-disciplined front of veteran soldiers, is always hostile to Freedom, and as her "best educated" men devote much time to politics, making it the profession of their whole lives, it is plain they become formidable antagonists.

But the North has a great variety of conflicting interests, a great amount of intellectual activity, where education and its consequent habits of reading and thinking are so wide spread, and therefore a great variety of opinion. Accordingly there is not the same Unity of pecuniary Interest and of political Idea, which distinguishes the South. Besides, in the North the ablest and best educated men do not devote their time to the thankless and stormy calling of politics; Virginia cares for nothing but Negroes and Politics, her loins and her brains gender but this twofold product: Massachusetts and New

York care for much beside. So the North does not present against the South an even and well-disciplined front of veteran soldiers, but a ragged, discordant line of raw recruits, enlisting for a short time with some special or even personal local interest to serve.

What makes the matter yet worse for us, Gentlemen of the Jury, is this: While the great mass of the people at the North, engrossed in direct productive industry, are really hostile to slavery, those absorbed in the large operations of commerce, taken as a whole class, feel little interest in the Idea of Freedom; nay, they are positively opposed to it. Before the African Slave-trade was treated like other kindred forms of piracy, as a capital crime, they had their ships in that felonious traffic; and now their vessels engage in the American Slave-trade and their hand still deals in the bodies of their fellow men. In all the great commercial cities, like Philadelphia, New York and Boston these men prevail, and are the "eminent citizens," overslaughing the press, the pulpit, the bar, and the court, with the Ideas of their lower law, and sweeping along all metropolitan and suburban fashion and respectability in their slimy flood. Hence the great cities of the North, governed by the low maxims of this class, have become the asylum of Northern men with Southern "Principles," and so the strong-hold of Slavery. And hitherto these great cities have controlled the politics of the Northern States, crowding the Apostles of Freedom out from the national board, and helping the party of slavery to triumph in all great battles.

Thus aided, for many years the South has always elected her candidate for the Presidency by the vote of the people. But the American Executive is twofold,—part Presidential, part Senatorial. Sometimes these two Executives are concordant, sometimes discordant. The Senatorial Executive has always carried the day against the less permanent Presidential power, except in the solitary case where General Jackson's unconquerable will and matchless popularity enabled him to master the senate itself, who "registered" his decrees, or "expunged" their own censure, just as the iron ruler gave orders.

Now by means of the control which the Northern Cities have over the Northern States, and such Commercial Men over those cities, it has come to pass that not only the Presidential, but also the Senatorial Executive, has long been hostile to the Idea of Freedom.

Gentlemen of the Jury, the direct consequence is obvious,—the Party of Slavery has long been the conqueror in the field of Federal politics. In the numerous and great conflicts between the two, Freedom has prevailed against Slavery only twice since the close of the Revolutionary War,—in prohibiting involuntary servitude in the North-west Territory in 1787, and in the abolition of the African

Slave-trade in 1808. Her last triumph was forty-seven years ago,— nay, even that victory was really achieved twenty years before at the adoption of the constitution. In this warfare we have not gained a battle for freedom since 1788!

For a time it seemed doubtful which would triumph, though Slavery gained Kentucky and Tennessee, and Louisiana was purchased as slave soil in 1803. But in 1820 slavery became the obvious and acknowledged master in the Federal Territory, marched victorious over the Mississippi, planted itself in Missouri, and has subsequently taken possession of Mississippi, Alabama and Arkansas, all slave States; has purchased Florida; "reannexed" Texas; conquered Utah, New Mexico and California, all slave soil; and from Freedom and the North has just now reconquered Kanzas and Nebraska. Ever since the Missouri Compromise in 1820 Slavery has been really the master, obviously so since the annexation of Texas in 1845. The slave-power appoints all the great national officers, executive, diplomatic, judicial, naval and military,—it controls the legislative departments. Look at this Honorable Court, Gentlemen, and recognize its power!

The idea of Slavery must be carried out to its logical consequence, so our masters now meditate two series of Measures, both necessary to the development of Slavery as a Principle.

(I.) African Slavery is to be declared a Federal Institution, national and sectional, and so extended into all the Territories of the United States. New soil is to be bought or plundered from Hayti, Spain, Mexico, South America "and the rest of mankind," that slavery may be planted there; that is the purpose of all the Official Fillibustering of the Government, and the Extra-official Fillibustering which it starts, or allows; Quitman "Enterprises," Kinney "Expeditions," Black Warrior and El Dorado "difficulties," all point to this; the "Ostend Conference" is a step in that direction; Slavery is to be restored to the so called "Free States," reëstablished in all the North. That is the design of the fugitive slave bill in 1850, and the kidnapping of northern men consequent thereon for the last five years; of President Pierce's inaugural declarations in behalf of slavery in 1853; of Mr. Toombs's threat in 1854, that "soon the master with his slaves will sit down at the foot of Bunker Hill Monument;" of Mr. Toucey's Bill in 1855, providing that when a kidnapper violates the local laws of any State, he shall be tried by the fugitive slave bill court. Then the African Slave-trade is to be restored by federal enactments, or judicial decisions of the "Supreme Court of the United States." All these steps belong to Measure number One. The Supreme Court is ready to execute the commands of its lord. Soon you will see more "decisions" adverse to humanity.

(II.) The next movement is progressively to weaken and ultimately to destroy the Democratic Institutions of the North, — yes, also of the South. This design is indicated and sustained by some of the measures already mentioned as connected with the first purpose.

To this point tend the words of President Pierce addressed to the soldiers of 1812 on the 8th of January 1855, in which he speaks of such as "disseminate political heresies," that is, the Idea of Freedom; "revile the government," — expose its hostility against the unalienable Rights of man; "deride our institutions," — to wit, the patriarchal institution of Slavery; "sow political dissensions," — advise men not to vote for corrupt tools of the government; "set at defiance the laws of the land," — meaning the fugitive slave bill which commands kidnapping.

There belong the attempts of the Federal courts to enlarge their jurisdiction at the expense of State Rights; the cry, "Union first and Liberty afterwards;" the shout "No higher law," "Religion nothing to do with Politics."

Thence come the attacks made on the freedom of the pulpit, of the press, and all freedom of speech. The Individual State which preserves freedom must be put down, — the individual person who protests against it must be silenced. No man must hold a federal office, — executive, diplomatic, judicial, or "ministerial," — unless he has so far conquered his "prejudices" in favor of the natural Rights of man that he is ready to enslave a brother with alacrity. All these steps belong to Measure number Two.

This latter Measure advances to its execution, realizing the Idea of Slavery, with subtle steps, yet creeps on rapid-moving feet. See how it has gained ground latterly. Obviously the fugitive slave bill struck only at the natural Rights of Colored men — as valuable as those of white men, but the colored are few and the white many, — the experiment must be made on the feebler body. But this despotism cannot enslave a black girl without thereby putting in peril the liberty of every white man. At first our masters only asked of Boston a little piece of chain, but just long enough to shackle the virtuous hands of Ellen Craft, a wife and mother, whom her Georgian "owner" wished to sell as a harlot at New Orleans! A meeting was summoned at Faneuil Hall, and Boston answered, "Yes, here is the chain. Let the woman-hunter capture Ellen Craft, make her a Prostitute at New Orleans. She is a virtuous wife and mother, — but no matter. Slavery is king and commands it. Let the 'owner' have his chain."

There is no escaping the consequence of a first Principle. Soon that little chain lengthened itself out, and coiled itself all round the court house, and how greedily your judges stooped to go under! This Anaconda of the Dismal Swamp wound its constricting twists about the neck of all your courts, and the Judges turned black in the face, and when questioned of law, they could not pronounce "Habeas Corpus," "Trial by Jury," nor utter a syllable for the Bible or the Massachusetts Constitution, but only wheeze and gurgle and squeak and gibber out their defences of Slavery! No, Boston could not bewray a woman wandering towards freedom, without chaining the court house and its judges, putting the town in a state of siege,—insolent soldiers striking at the people's neck. Now the attempt is making by this Honorable Court to put the same chain round Faneuil Hall, so that the old Cradle of Liberty shall no more rock to manhood the noble sons of freedom, but only serve as a nest that the spawn of Bondage may hibernate therein.

I am on trial because I hate Slavery, because I love freedom for the black man, for the white man, and for all the human Race. I am not arraigned because I have violated the statute on which the indictment is framed—no child could think it—but because I am an advocate of Freedom, because my Word, my Thoughts, my Feelings, my Actions, nay, all my Life, my very Existence itself, are a protest against Slavery. Despotism cannot happily advance unless I am silenced. It is very clear logic which indicts me. Private personal malice, deep, long cherished, rancorous, has doubtless jagged and notched and poisoned too the public sword which smites at my neck. Still it is the public sword of Slavery which is wielded against me. Against ME? Against YOU quite as much—against your children. For as Boston could not venture to kidnap a negro woman, without bringing down that avalanche of consequences connected with the Principle of Slavery,—without chains on her Judges, falsehood in her officers, blood in her courts, and drunken soldiers in her streets, and hypocrisy in her man-hunting ministers,—no more can she put me to silence alone. The thread which is to sew my lips together, will make your mouths but a silent and ugly seam in your faces. Slavery is Plaintiff in this case; Freedom Defendant. Before you as Judges, I plead your own cause—for you as defendant. I will not insult you by the belief or the fear that you can do other than right, in a matter where the law is so plain, and the Justice clear as noonday light. But should you decide as the wicked wish, as the court longs to instruct you, you doom your mouths to silence; you bow your manly faces to the ground, destine your memories to shame, and your children to bondage worse than negro slavery.

Such, Gentlemen of the Jury, is the state of affairs leading to this Prosecution—such the past, present, and prospective Encroachments

2*

of a Power hostile to Democratic Institutions and the unalienable Rights they were designed to protect. Such also are the two Measures now in contemplation, — the Extension of African Bondage, and the Destruction of American Freedom.

II. Look next at the Mode of Operation hitherto pursued by this Encroaching Power, in other times and nations, and in our own, systematic corruption of the Judiciary.

Here I shall show the process by which that Principle of Slavery becomes a Measure of political ruin to the People.

In substance Despotism is always the same, Spanish or Carolinian, but the form varies to suit the ethnologic nature and historical customs of different people. I shall mention two forms — one to illustrate, the other to warn.

(I.) The open Assumption of Power by military violence. This method is followed in countries where love of Individual Liberty is not much developed in the consciousness of the people, and where democratic institutions are not fixed facts in their history; where the nation is not accustomed to local self-government, but wonted to a strong central power directed by a single will. This form prevails in Russia, Turkey, and among all the Romanic tribes in Europe, and their descendants in America. Military usurpation, military rule is indigenous in France, — where two Napoleons succeed thereby, — in Italy, in Spain, and most eminently in Spanish America. But no people of the Teutonic family for any length of time ever tolerated a usurping soldier at the head of affairs, or submitted to martial arbirary rule, or military violence in the chief magistrate. It is against our habit and disposition.

Neither Cromwell nor William of Orange could do with the Anglo-Saxon what it would have been impossible not to do with Spaniards or Italians. Even warlike Swiss — Teutonic tribes — will have a government with due process of law, not by the abrupt violence of the soldier. Washington could not have established a military monarchy in America had he been so wickedly disposed. Even William the Conqueror must rule the Saxons by Saxon law.

(II.) The corruption of the acknowledged safeguards of public security. This is attempted in nations who have a well-known love of individual liberty, and institutional defences thereof, the habit of Local Self-government by Democratic Law-making and Law-administering. For example, this experiment has been repeatedly made in England. The monarch seeking to destroy the liberty of the people, accomplishes his violent measure by the forms of peaceful law, by getting the judicial class of men on the side of despotism. Then all the wickedness can be done in the name, with the forms, and by "due process" of law, by regular officers thereof—done solemnly with the assistance of slow and public deliberation.

Gentlemen of the Jury, this is a matter of such importance to the People of America just now, that I must beg you to bear with me while I explain this subtle operation. I will select examples from the history of England which are easy to understand, because her blood is kindred to our own, and the institutions of the two countries are related as parent and child. And besides, her past history affords alike warning and guidance in our present peril.

(1.) The first step in this process of political iniquity is, to appoint men for judges and other officers of the court, who know no law higher than the selfish will of the hand that feeds them, mere creatures of the rest.

I will select instances of this from the reign of the Stuart kings and one of their successors, from a period full of melancholy warning to America.

I will begin with James I. (1603–1625), the first King of New England. At his very accession he had high notions of his royal Prerogative, and maintained that all the privileges of the House of Commons were derived from his royal grant. "I am your King," said he, "I am placed to govern you, and I shall [must] answer for your errors." It was quite enough to answer for his own,—poor man. "Let me make the Judges," said he, "and I care not who makes the laws."

Accordingly for judicial officers he appointed such men as would execute his unlawful schemes for the destruction of public liberty. To such considerations was Francis Bacon mainly indebted for his elevation from one legal rank to another, until he reached the seat of the Lord Chancellor. A man whom Villers declared, "of excellent parts, but withal of a base and ungrateful temper, and an arrant knave, yet a fit instrument for the purposes of the government." He did not receive his appointment for that vast, hard-working genius which makes his name the ornament of many an age, but only for his sycophantic devotion to the royal will. Sir Edward Coke was promoted rapidly enough, whilst wholly subservient to the despotic court, but afterwards, though a miracle of legal knowledge, not equalled yet perhaps, he must not be appointed Lord Chancellor on account of "his occasional fits of independence." Chief Justice Ley was one of the right stamp, but it was thought "his subserviency might prove more valuable by retaining him to preside over the Court of King's Bench." "For in making the highest judicial appointments the only question was, what would suit the arbitrary schemes of governing the country."[1] Hobart had resisted some illegal monopolies of the all-powerful Buckingham, and he was "unfit for promotion."

James thought the Prerogative would be strengthened by the appointment of clergymen of the national church, perhaps the only class of men not then getting fired with love of liberty, — and made Williams, Bishop of Lincoln, Lord Keeper, a "man of rash and insolent, though servile temper, and of selfish, temporizing, and trimming political conduct," who at that time had never acted as "a judge except at the Waldegrave Petty Sessions in making an order of bastardy or allowing a rate for the Parish poor," and was "as ignorant of the questions coming before him as the door-keepers of his court." But he was subservient, and had pleased the King by preaching the courtly doctrine that "subjects hold their liberties and their property at the will of the Sovereign whom they are bound in every extremity passively to obey."[2] Men like Fleming and other creatures of the throne, sanctioning the King's abundant claim to absolute power, were sure of judicial distinction; while it was only the force of public opinion which gave the humblest place of honor to such able and well-studied lawyers as would respect the constitutional Rights of the People and the just construction of the laws, and at all hazards maintain their judicial independence. Ecclesiastics who taught that the King "is above the laws by his absolute power," and "may quash any law passed by Parliament," were sure of rapid preferment. Thus Bancroft was promoted; thus Abbot was pushed aside; and for his mean, tyrannical and subservient disposition Rev. William Laud was continually promoted in expectation of the services which, as Archbishop, he subsequently performed in the overthrow of the Liberty of the People. But time would fail me to read over the long dark list of men whose personal shame secured them "official glory."

In his address to the Judges in the Star-Chamber in 1616 James gave them this charge, "If there falls out a question which concerns any Prerogative or mysterie of State, *deale not with it till you consult with the King* or his Council, or both; for they are Transcendent Matters, and must not be slibberly carried with over rash wilfullnesse." "And this I commend unto your special care, as some of you of late have done very much, to *blunt the edge and vaine popular humor of some lawyers at the Barre*, that think they are not eloquent and bold-spirited enough, except they *meddle with the King's Prerogative.*" "*That which concerns the mysterie of the King's Power is not lawful*

[1] 2 Campbell, 372, 374. [2] 2 Campbell, 368, 374; 3 Howell State Trials, 824.

to be disputed."[1] Gentlemen, that was worthy of some judicial charges which you and I have heard.

Charles I. (1625–1659,) pursued the same course of tyranny by the same steps. Coventry could be implicitly relied on to do as commanded, and was made Lord Keeper in 1625. When the question of Ship-money was to be brought forward in 1636, Chief Justice Heath was thought not fit to be trusted with wielding the instrument of tyranny, and accordingly removed; "and Finch, well known to be ready to go all lengths, was appointed in his place." For he had steadfastly maintained that the King was absolute, and could dispense with law and parliament,—a fit person to be a Chief Justice, or a Lord Chancellor, in a tyrant's court, ready to enact iniquity into law. His compliance with the King's desire to violate the first principle of Magna Charta, "endeared him to the Court, and secured him further preferment as soon as any opportunity should occur." So he was soon made Lord Chancellor and raised to the peerage. Littleton had once been on the popular side, but deserted and went over to the Court—he was sure of preferment; and as he became more and more ready to destroy the liberties of the People, he was made Chief Justice, and finally Lord Chancellor in 1641. Lane was a "steady friend of the prerogative," and so was made Attorney-General to the Prince of Wales, and thence gradually elevated to the highest station.

Other Judicial appointments were continually made in the same spirit. Thus when Sir Randolf Crewe was Chief Justice of the King's Bench, the government questioned him to ascertain if he were "sound," and were shocked to hear him declare that the King had no right to levy taxes without consent of Parliament, or imprison his subjects without due process of law. He was "immediately dismissed from his office," (1626,) and Sir Nicolas Hyde appointed in his place. By such means the courts were filled with tools of the King or his favorites, and the pit digged for the liberties of the People, into which at last there fell—the head of the King!

Charles II. and James II., (1655–1686,) did not mend the evil, but appointed for judges "such a pack as had never before sat in Westminster Hall." Shaftesbury and Guildford had the highest judicial honors. Lord Chancellor Finch, mentioned already, had been accused by the Commons of High Treason and other misdemeanors, but escaped to the continent, and returned after the Restoration. He was appointed one of the Judges to try the Regicides. Thus he "who had been accused of high treason twenty years before by a full

[1] Speache in the Starre-Chamber, London, 1616.

parliament, and who by flying from their justice saved his life, was appointed to judge some of those who should have been his Judges."[1] He declared in Parliament that Milton, for services rendered to the cause of liberty while Latin Secretary to Cromwell, "deserved hanging."[2]

In these reigns such men as Saunders, Wright, and Scroggs, were made Judges, men of the vilest character, with the meanest appetites, licentious, brutal, greedy of power and money, idiotic in the moral sense, appointed solely that they might serve as tools for the oppression of the People. Among these infamous men was George Jeffreys, of whom Lord Campbell says,—"He has been so much abused that I began my critical examination of his history in the hope and belief that I should find that his misdeeds had been exaggerated, and that I might be able to rescue his memory from some portion of the obloquy under which it labors; but I am sorry to say that in my matured opinion his cruelty and his political profligacy have not been sufficiently exposed or reprobated; and that he was not redeemed from his vices by one single solid virtue."[3] But in consequence of his having such a character, though not well-grounded in law, he was made a Judge, a Peer, and a Lord Chancellor! Wright, nearly as infamous, miraculously stupid and ignorant, "a detected swindler, knighted and clothed in ermine, took his place among the twelve judges of England."[4] He also was made Chief Justice successively of the Common Pleas and the King's Bench! Lord Campbell, himself a judge, at the end of his history of the reign of Charles and James, complains of "the irksome task of relating the actions of so many men devoid of political principle and ready to suggest or to support any measures, however arbitrary or mischievous, for the purpose of procuring their own advancement."[5] It was the practice of the Stuarts "to dismiss judges without seeking any other pretence, who showed any disposition to thwart government in political prosecutions."[6] Nor was this dismissal confined to cases where the judge would obey the law in merely Political trials. In 1686 four of the judges denied that the king had power to dispense with the laws of the land and change the form of religion: the next morning they were all driven from their posts, and four others, more compliant, were appointed and the judicial "opinion was unanimous." Hereupon Roger Coke says well,—"the king . . . will make the judges in Westminster Hall to murder the common law, as well as the king and his brother desired to murder the parliament by itself; and to this end the king, when he would make any judges would make a bargain with them, that they should declare the king's'

[1] Ludlow, quoted in 2 Campbell, 470.
[2] 4 Parl. Hist. 162.
[3] 3 Campbell, 394.
[4] 2 Campbell Chief Justices, 86.
[5] 3 Campbell, 473.
[6] 3 Hallam, 142.

power of dispensing with the penal laws and tests made against recusants, out of parliament."[1]

Here, Gentlemen of the Jury, I must mention three obscure judges who received their appointments under Stuart kings. Before long I shall speak of their law and its application, and now only introduce them to you as a measure preliminary to a more intimate acquaintance hereafter.

1. The first is Sir William Jones, by far the least ignoble of the three. He was descended from one of the Barons who wrung the Great Charter from the hands of King John in 1618, and in 1628 dwelt in the same house which sheltered the more venerable head of his Welsh ancestor. In 1628 he was made judge by Charles I. He broke down the laws of the realm to enable the king to make forced loans on his subjects, and by his special mandate (Lettre de Cachet) to imprison whom he would, as long as it pleased him, and without showing any reason for the commitment or the detention! Yes, he supported the king in his attempt to shut up members of parliament for words spoken in debate in the house of commons itself; to levy duties on imports, and a tax of ship-money on the land. He was summoned before parliament for his offences against public justice, and finally deprived of office, though ungratefully, by the king himself.[2]

2. Thomas Twysden was counsel for George Coney in 1655, a London merchant who refused to pay an illegal tax levied on him by Cromwell — who followed in the tyrannical footsteps of the king he slew. Twysden was thrown into the Tower for defending his client — as Mr. Sloane, at Sandusky, has just been punished by the honorable court of the United States for a similar offence, — but after a few days made a confession of his "error," defending the just laws of the land, promised to offend no more, and was set at liberty, ignominiously leaving his client to defend himself and be defeated. This Twysden was made judge by Charles II. The reporters recording his decisions put down "*Twysden in furore*," thinly veiling the judicial wrath in modest Latin. He was specially cruel against Quakers and other dissenters, treating George Fox, Margarett Fell, and John Bunyan with brutal violence.[3]

3. Sir John Kelyng is another obscure judge of those times. In the civil war he was a violent cavalier, and "however fit he might be to *charge* the Roundheads under Prince Rupert, he was very unfit to

[1] 8 St. Tr. 195, note.

[2] Account of him in Preface to his Reports, (1675); 3 St. Tr. 162, 293, 844, 1181 2 Parl. Hist. 869; 1 Rushworth, 661, *et al.*; Whitlocke, 14, *et al.*

[3] 6 St. Tr. 634; 1 Campbell Justices, 442.

charge a jury in Westminster Hall." In 1660 he took part in the trial of the Regicides and led in the prosecution of Colonel Hacker, who in 1649 had charge of the execution of Charles I. In 1662 he took part in the prosecution of Sir Henry Vane, and by his cruel subtlety in constructing law, that former governor of Massachusetts, — one of the most illustrious minds of England, innocent of every crime, was convicted of high treason and put to death.[1] For this service, in 1663 Kelyng was made a judge; and then, by loyal zeal and judicial subserviency, he made up "for his want of learning and sound sense.". But he was so incompetent that even the court of Charles II. hesitated to make him more than a puny judge. But he had been a "valiant cavalier," and had done good service already in making way with such as the king hated, and so after the death of Sir Nicolas Hyde, he was made Lord Chief Justice in his place. "In this office," says Judge Campbell, he "exceeded public expectation by the violent, fantastical, and ludicrous manner in which he conducted himself."[2] But I will not now anticipate what I have to say of him in a subsequent part of this defence.

Gentlemen of the Jury, we shall meet these three together again before long, and I shall also speak of them "singly or in pairs." In the mean time I will mention one similar appointment in the reign of George the III. — the last king of New England.

In 1770 Sergeant Glynn, in Parliament, moved for an inquiry into the administration of criminal justice. Edmund Thurlow, a rough venal man, then recently appointed solicitor-general, proposed that a severe censure should be passed on him for the motion. Thurlow wanted the trial by jury abolished in all cases of libel, so that the liberty of the people should be in the exclusive care of government attorneys and judges appointed by the crown. Hear him speak on the 6th of December, 1770.

"In my opinion no man should be allowed with impunity to make a wanton attack upon such venerable characters as the judges of the land. We award costs and damages to the aggrieved party in the most trifling actions. By what analogy, then, can we refuse the same justice in the most important cases, to the most important personages? If we allow every pitiful patriot thus to insult us with ridiculous accusations, without making him pay forfeit for his temerity, we shall be eternally pestered with the humming and buzzing of these stingless wasps. Though they cannot wound or poison, they will tease and vex. They will divert our attention from the important affairs of State to their own mean antipathies, and passions, and prejudices. Did they not count upon the spirit of the times and imagine that the same latitude which is taken by the libellers is here allowable, they would not have dared to offer so gross an outrage. I hope we shall now handle them so roughly as to make this the last of such

[1] 6 St. Tr. 161.

[2] 1 Campbell Justices, 401.

audacious attempts. They are already ridiculous and contemptible. To crown their disgrace, let us inflict some exemplary punishment. Else none of us is safe. Virtue and honor, you see from this instance, are no safeguard from their attacks."

"The nature, the direct effect, and the remote consequences of a State libel, are so complicated and involved with various considerations of great pith and moment, that few juries can be adequate judges. So many circumstances are at once to be kept in view, so many ponderous interests are to be weighed, so many comparisons to be made, and so many judgments formed, that the mind of an ordinary man is distracted and confounded, and rendered incapable of coming to any regular conclusion. None but a judge, a man that has from his infancy been accustomed to decide intricate cases, is equal to such a difficult task. If we even suppose the jury sufficiently enlightened to unravel those knotty points, yet there remains an insuperable objection. In State libels, their passions are frequently so much engaged, that they may be justly considered as parties concerned against the crown."

"In order, therefore, to preserve the balance of our constitution, *let us leave to the judges*, as the most indifferent persons, *the right of determining the malice or innocence of the intention*."

"It is not that I think the intention a matter of fact; no, in the sense put upon it by the judges, it is a matter of law."

"Much dust has been raised about civil and criminal actions. But to what purpose? Is not reparation to be made to the public for any injury which it may have sustained, as much as to an individual? Is the welfare of the nation in general, of less consequence than that of a single person? Where then is the propriety of making such a bustle about the malice or innocence of the intention? The injury done is the only proper measure of the punishment to be inflicted, as well as of the damage to be assessed. Since you cannot plead the intention as a mitigation in the latter case, neither can you in the former."[1]

What followed? On the 23d of July, 1771, he was made Attorney-General. His subsequent history did not disappoint the prophecy uttered above by his former conduct and his notorious character. "In truth his success was certain, with the respectable share he possessed of real talents and of valuable requirements — strongly marked features, piercing eyes, bushy eyebrows, and a sonorous voice, all worked to the best effect by an immeasurable share of self-confidence — he could not fail."[2] He hated America with the intense malignity of a low but strong and despotic nature, and "took a most zealous part and uttered very violent language against the colonists. He scorned the very notion of concession or conciliation; he considered 'sedition' and 'treason,' (like *tobacco* and *potatoes*,) the peculiar plants of the American soil. The natives of these regions he thought were born to be taxed."[3] He favored the Stamp Act, the Coercion Bill, — quartering soldiers upon us, sending Americans beyond seas for trial, — the Boston Port Bill, and all the measures against the colonies. "To say that we have a right to tax America and never exercise that right, is ridiculous, and a man must abuse his

[1] 16 Parl. Hist. 1291, 1292, 1293. [2] 5 Campbell, 398. [3] 5 Campbell, 410.

understanding very much not to allow of that right;" "the right of taxing was never in the least given up to the Americans."[1] On another occasion he said, that "as attorney-general he had a right to set aside every charter in America."[2] What followed? Notwithstanding his youthful profligacy, the open profanity of his public and private speech, and his living in public and notorious contempt of matrimony, — he was made Lord Chancellor and elevated to the peerage in 1778! Him also we shall meet again.

Gentlemen of the Jury, I might as well try to bale all the salt water out of the sea as to mention every glaring and notorious instance where an oppressive government has appointed some discarder of all Higher Law for its servant in crushing the People. Come therefore to the next point.

(II.) The next step is by means of *such Judges to punish and destroy or silence men who oppose the wickedness of the party in power, and the encroachments of despotism.* Let me describe the general mode of procedure, and then illustrate it by special examples.

1. In the Privy Council, or elsewhere, it is resolved to punish the obnoxious men, — and the business is intrusted to the law-officers of the crown, appointed for such functions.

2. They consult and agree to pervert and twist the law — statute or common — for that purpose. By this means they gratify their master, and prepare future advancement for themselves.

3. The precedent thus established becomes the basis for new operations in the future, and may be twisted and perverted to serve other cases as they occur.

Now, Gentlemen, look at some examples taken from British history, in times of the same Kings mentioned before.

1. In 1610 two Puritans for refusing the *ex officio* oath, were clapped in Jail by the commissioners. They were brought on *habeas corpus* before a court, and Mr. Fuller, their counsel, a learned lawyer, insisted that they were imprisoned without due process of law. For this "contempt of court" he was thrown into jail by Archbishop Bancroft, whence he was rescued only by death.[3]

2. In 1613 there were many murmurs among the People of England at the tyranny of James. Fine and imprisonment did not quell the disturbance; so a more dreadful example was thought needful. The officials of Government broke into the study of Rev. Edmund Peacham, a Protestant minister, sixty or seventy years old. In an

[1] 17 Parl. Hist. 1313. [2] 18 St. Tr. 999. [3] Peirce's Vindication, (1717,) 174.

uncovered cask they found a manuscript sermon, never preached, nor designed for the pulpit or the press, never shown to any one. It contained some passages which might excite men to resist tyranny. He was arrested, and thrown into Jail, all his papers seized. The Government resolved to prosecute him for high treason. Francis Bacon, the powerful and corrupt Attorney-General, managed the prosecution. Before trial was ventured upon, he procured an extra-judicial opinion of the Judges appointed for such services, — irregularly given, out of court, that they would declare such an act high treason.

But a manuscript sermon, neither preached nor designed for the public, was hardly evidence enough of treason even for such Judges — so purchased, for such an Attorney — so greedy of preferment, with such a Cabinet and such a King. For all those, like the Pharisees of old, "feared the People." So their victim was tortured on the rack, and twelve leading questions prepared by the Government officials, were put to him there. I quote Secretary Winwood's record — still extant in his own handwriting — "He was this day examined before torture, in torture, between torture, and after torture; notwithstanding nothing could be drawn from him, he still persisting in his obstinate and insensible denials and former answers." Bacon was present at the torture, which took place in the Tower, Jan. 19, 1614, O. S. (30th Jan. 1615, N. S.). In August he was tried for high treason — "compassing and imagining the King's death" — before a packed jury; against law, and without legal evidence. He was of course found guilty under the ruling of the Court! But public opinion, even then making tyrants "tremble in their capitals," was so indignant at the outrage that the execution was not ventured on, and he was left to languish in Jail, till on the 27th of March, 1616, a King more merciful took the old minister where the wicked cease from troubling.[1]

In this case, Gentlemen of the Jury, you will notice three violations of the law.

(1.) The opinion of the Judges before the trial was extrajudicial and illegal.

(2.) The application of torture was contrary to law.

(3.) The statute of Treason was wrested to apply to this case — and a crime was constructed by the servants of the court.

It is curious to read the opinion of James himself. "The British Solomon" thus wrote: —

"So the only thing the Judges can doubt of is of the delinquent's intention, on his bare denial to clear him [himself], since nature teaches every man to defend his life as he may; and whether in case there was a doubt herein, the Judges should not rather incline to that side [namely, the side of the Government,] wherein all proba-

[1] 2 St. Tr. 869; 16 Montagu's Bacon, clxvi.; 2 Campbell, 291.

bility lies: but if Judges will needs trust rather the bare negative of an *infamous delinquent*— then all the probabilities, or rather infallible consequences upon the other part, caring more for the safety of *such a monster* than the preservation of a crown in all ages following, whereupon depend the lives of many millions, happy then are all *desperate and seditious knaves*, but the fortune of this crown is more than miserable. Which God forefend."[1]

3. In 1633, Laud, a tyrannical, ambitious man, and a servile creature of the King, mentioned before, was made Archbishop of Canterbury, continuing Bishop of London at the same time. Charles I. was strongly inclined to Romanism, Laud also leaned that way, aiming to come as near as possible to the Papal and not be shut out of the English Church. He made some new regulations in regard to the Communion Table and the Lord's Supper. John Williams, before mentioned, Dean of Westminster and Bishop of Lincoln, who had been Lord Keeper under King James, wrote a book against those innovations; besides, in his episcopal court he had once spoken of the Puritans as "good subjects," and of his knowing "that the King did not wish them to be harshly dealt with." In 1637 Laud directed that he should be prosecuted in the Star-Chamber for "publishing false news and tales to the scandal of his Majesty's government;" and "for revealing counsels of State contrary to his oath of a Privy Counsellor." He was sentenced to pay a fine of £10,000,—equal to $50,000, or thrice the sum in these times; to be suspended from all offices, and kept a close prisoner in the Tower during the King's pleasure—whence the Revolution set him at liberty. Besides he wrote private letters to Mr. Osbalderston, and called Laud "the little great man," for this he, in 1639, was fined £5,000 to the King, and £3,000 to the Archbishop. Osbalderston in his letters had spoken of the "great Leviathan" and the "little Urchin," and was fined £5,000, to the King, and the same to the Archbishop, and sentenced also to stand in the pillory with his ears nailed to it![2]

4. In 1629 Richard Chambers, a merchant of London, complained to the Privy Council of some illegal and unjust treatment, and declared "that the merchants in no part of the world are so screwed and wrung as in England; that in Turkey they have more encouragement." Laud, who hated freedom of speech and liberal comments on the government as much as "eminent citizens" nowadays, is said to have told the king, "If your majesty had many such Chambers, you would soon have no Chamber left to rest in." The merchant was tried before the "commissioners" at the Star-Chamber, and fined £2,000, and condemned to make a "submission for his great offence,"[3] which the stout Puritan refused to do, and was kept in

[1] 2 St. Tr. 879.

[2] 3 St. Tr. 769; 2 Campbell, 400.

[3] 3 St. Tr. 373; Frankyn, 361; 2 Hallam (Paris, 1841), 6 *ac etiam* 13; 2 Mrs. Macaulay, 16, 45, 65.

prison till the Court of King's Bench, faithful to the law, on Habeas Corpus, admitted him to bail: for which they were reprimanded. Laud and all the ecclesiastical members of the "commission" wished his fine £3,000.

5. In his place in Parliament in 1629, Sir John Eliot, one of the noblest men in England's noblest age, declared that "the Council and Judges had all conspired to trample underfoot the liberties of the subject." Gentlemen, the fact was as notorious as the advance of the Slave Power now is in America. But a few days after the king (Charles I.) had dismissed his refractory Parliament, Eliot, with Hollis, Long, Selden, Strode, and Valentine, most eminent members of the commons, and zealous for liberty and law, was seized by the king's command and thrown into prison. The Habeas Corpus was demanded—it was all in vain, for Laud and Strafford were at the head of affairs, and the priests and pliant Judges in Westminster Hall—Jones was one of them—clove down the law of the land just as their subcatenated successors did in Boston in 1851. The court decreed that they should be imprisoned during the king's pleasure, and not released until making submission and giving security for good behavior. Eliot was fined £2,000, Hollis and Valentine in smaller sums. Eliot—the brave man—refused submission, and died in the Tower. Thus was the attack made on all freedom of speech in Parliament![1]

6. In 1630, the very year of the first settlement of Boston, on the 4th of June, Rev. Dr. Alexander Leighton was brought before the Court of High Commission, in the Star-Chamber, to be tried for a seditious libel. He had published "An Appeal to the Parliament, or a Plea against Prelacy," a work still well known, remonstrating against certain notorious grievances in church and State, "to the end the Parliament might take them into consideration and give such redress as might be for the honor of the king, the quiet of the people, and the peace of the church," the court of commissions accounted it "a most odious and heinous offence, deserving the most serious punishment the court could inflict, for framing a book so full of such pestilent, devilish, and dangerous assertions." The two Chief Justices declared if the case had been brought to their courts, they would have proceeded against him for Treason, and it was only "his majesty's exceeding great mercy and goodness" which selected the milder tribunal. His sentence was a fine of £10,000, to be set in the pillory, whipped, have one ear cut off, one side of his nose slit, one cheek branded with S. S., Sower of Sedition, and then at some convenient time be whipped again, branded, and mutilated on the other

[1] 3 St. Tr. 293; 1 Rushworth; 2 Hallam, 2; 2 Parl. Hist. 488, 504; Foster's Eliot, 100; 2 Mrs. Macaulay, ch. i. ii.

side, and confined in the Fleet during life! Before the punishment could be inflicted he escaped out of prison, but was recaptured and the odious sentence fully executed. Those who "obstructed" the officer in the execution of that "process" were fined £500 a piece.[1] Gentlemen of the Jury, which do you think would most have astonished the Founders of Massachusetts, then drawing near to Boston, that trial on the 4th of June, 1630, or this trial, two hundred and twenty-five years later? At the court of Charles it was a great honor to mutilate the body of a Puritan minister.

But not only did such judges thus punish the most noble men who wrote on political matters, there was no freedom of speech allowed — so logical is despotism!

7. William Prynn, a zealous Puritan and a very learned lawyer, wrote a folio against theatres called "a Scourge for Stage-Players," dull, learned, unreadable and uncommon thick. He was brought to the Star-Chamber in 1632–3, and Chief Justice Richardson — who had even then "but an indifferent reputation for honesty and veracity" — gave this sentence: "Mr. Prynn, I do declare you to be a Schism-Maker in the Church, a Sedition-Sower in the Commonwealth, a wolf in sheep's clothing; in a word 'omnium malorum nequissimus' — [the wickedest of all scoundrels]. I shall fine him £10,000, which is more than he is worth, yet less than he deserveth; I will not set him at liberty, no more than a plagued man or a mad dog, who though he cannot bite, yet will he foam; he is so far from being a sociable soul that he is not a rational soul; he is fit to live in dens with such beasts of prey as wolves and tygers like himself; therefore I do condemn him to perpetual Imprisonment, as those monsters that are no longer fit to live among men nor to see light." "I would have him branded in the forehead, slit in the nose, and his ears cropped too." The sentence was executed the 7th and 10th of May, 1633.[2] But nothing intimidated, the sturdy man committed other offences of like nature, "obstructing" other "officers," and was punished again, and banished. But on the summoning of Parliament returned to England, and became powerful in that Revolution which crushed the tyrants of the time.

8. In 1685, James II. was in reality a Catholic. He wished to restore Romanism to England and abolish the work of the Reformation, the better to establish the despotism which all of his family had sought to plant. He was determined to punish such as spoke against the Papal Church, though no law prohibited such speaking. Judge

[1] 3 St. Tr. 383; Laud's Diary, 4th November; 2 Hallam, 28.

[2] 3 St. Tr. 561; 2 Hallam, 28, and his authorities. See also 2 Echard, 109, *et seq.*, 124, *et seq.*, 202, 368, 510; the remarks of Hume, Hist. ch. lii., remind me of the tone of the fugitive slave bill Journals of Boston in 1850–54.

Jeffreys, a member of the cabinet and favorite of the king, was at that time chief justice — abundantly fit for the work demanded of him. The pious and venerable Richard Baxter was selected for the victim. Let Mr. Macaulay tell the story.

"In a Commentary on the New Testament, he had complained, with some bitterness, of the persecution which the Dissenters suffered. That men, who, for not using the Prayerbook, had been driven from their homes, stripped of their property, and locked up in dungeons, should dare to utter a murmur, was then thought a high crime against the State and Church. Roger Lestrange, the champion of the government, and the oracle of the clergy, sounded the note of war in the Observator. An information was filed. Baxter begged that he might be allowed some time to prepare for his defence. It was on the day on which Oates was pilloried in Palace Yard that the illustrious chief of the Puritans, oppressed by age and infirmities, came to Westminster Hall to make this request. Jeffreys burst into a storm of rage. 'Not a minute,' he cried, 'to save his life. I can deal with saints as well as with sinners. There stands Oates on one side of the pillory; and if Baxter stood on the other, the two greatest rogues in the kingdom would stand together."

"When the trial came on at Guildhall, a crowd of those who loved and honored Baxter, filled the court. At his side stood Doctor William Bates, one of the most eminent Nonconformist divines. Two Whig barristers of great note, Pollexfen and Wallop, appeared for the defendant."

"Pollexfen had scarce begun his address to the jury, when the chief justice broke forth: 'Pollexfen, I know you well. I will set a mark on you. You are the patron of the faction. This is an old rogue, a schismatical knave, a hypocritical villain. He hates the Liturgy. He would have nothing but longwinded cant without book;' and then his lordship turned up his eyes, clasped his hands, and began to sing through his nose in imitation of what he supposed to be Baxter's style of praying, 'Lord, we are thy people, thy peculiar people, thy dear people.' Pollexfen gently reminded the court that his late majesty had thought Baxter deserving of a bishopric. 'And what ailed the old blockhead then,' cried Jeffreys, 'that he did not take it?' His fury now rose almost to madness. He called Baxter a dog, and swore that it would be no more than justice to whip such a villain through the whole city."

"Wallop interposed, but fared no better than his leader. 'You are in all these dirty causes, Mr. Wallop,' said the judge. 'Gentlemen of the long robe ought to be ashamed to assist such factious knaves.' The advocate made another attempt to obtain a hearing, but to no purpose. 'If you do not know your duty,' said Jeffreys, 'I will teach it you.'

"Wallop sat down, and Baxter himself attempted to put in a word; but the chief justice drowned all expostulation in a torrent of ribaldry and invective, mingled with scraps of Hudibras. 'My lord,' said the old man, 'I have been much blamed by Dissenters for speaking respectfully of bishops.'

"'Baxter for bishops!' cried the judge; 'that 's a merry conceit indeed. I know what you mean by bishops — rascals like yourself, Kidderminster bishops, factious, snivelling Presbyterians!'

"Again Baxter essayed to speak, and again Jeffreys bellowed, 'Richard, Richard, dost thou think we will let thee poison the court? Richard, thou art an old knave. Thou hast written books enough to load a cart, and every book as full of sedition as an egg is full of meat. By the grace of God, I 'll look after thee. I see a great many of your brotherhood waiting to know what will befall their mighty Don. And there,' he continued, fixing his savage eye on Bates, 'there is a doctor of the party at your elbow. But, by the grace of God Almighty, I will crush you all!'

"Baxter held his peace. But one of the junior counsel for the defence made a last effort, and undertook to show that the words of which complaint was made, would not bear the construction put on them by the information. With this view he began to read the context. In a moment he was roared down. 'You sha'n't turn the court into a conventicle!' The noise of weeping was heard from some of those who surrounded Baxter. 'Snivelling calves!' said the judge."[1]

He was sentenced to pay a fine of 500 marks, to lie in prison till he paid it, and be bound to good behavior for seven years. Jeffreys, it is said, wished him also to be whipped at the tail of a cart.[2] But the King remitted his fine.

Throughout the reign of James II. the courts of law became more and more contemptible in the eyes of the people. "All the three common law courts were filled by incompetent and corrupt Judges."[3] But their power to do evil never diminished.

9. James II. wished to restore the Catholic form of religion, rightly looking on Protestantism as hostile to his intended tyranny; so he claimed a right to dispense with the laws relating thereto, put a Jesuit into his Privy Council, expelled Protestants from their offices, and filled the vacancy thus illegally made with Papists; he appointed Catholic bishops.[4] In 1688 he published a proclamation. It was the second of the kind,—dispensing with all the laws of the realm against Catholicism; and ordered it to be read on two specified Sundays during the hours of service in all places of public worship. This measure seemed to be a special insult to the Protestants. The declaration of indulgence was against their conscience, and in violation of the undisputed laws of the land, but Chief Justice Wright declared from the bench his opinion that it was "legal and obligatory," and on the day appointed for reading the decree attended church "to give weight to the solemnity," and as it was not read—for the clerk "had forgot to bring a copy,"—he "indecently in the hearing of the congregation abused the priest, as disloyal, seditious, and irreligious."

But the clergy thought differently from the Chief Justice—Episcopalians and Dissenters agreeing on this point. Seven bishops petitioned the King that they might not be obliged to violate their conscience, the articles of their religion, and the laws of the realm, by reading the declaration. They presented their petition in person to the King, who treated it and them with insolence and wrath.

"The king, says Kennet, was not contented to have this declaration published in the usual manner, but he was resolved to have it solemnly read in all churches as the

[1] 1 Macaulay, (Harper's Ed.) 456–8.
[2] 1 Macaulay, 456; 11 St. Tr. 493.
[3] 2 Campbell's Justices, 87.
[4] See 2 Brewster's Newton, 108.

political gospel of his reign. The bishops and clergy were, of all others the most averse to the subject-matter of the declaration, as being most sensible of the ill design and ill effects of it; and therefore the court seemed the more willing to mortify these their enemies, and make them become accessory to their own ruin; and even to eat their own dung, as father Petre proudly threatened, and therefore this order of council was made and published."[1]

The petition was printed and published with great rapidity, the bishops were seized, thrown into the Tower, and prosecuted in the court for a "false, feigned, malicious, pernicious, and seditious" libel.

Judge Allybone thus addressed the Jury.

"And I think, in the first place, that *no man can* take upon him to *write against the actual exercise of the government, unless he have leave from the government*, but he makes a libel, be what he writes true or false; for if once we come to impeach the government by way of argument, it is the argument that makes it the government, or not the government. So that I lay down that, in the first place, *the government ought not to be impeached by argument*, nor the exercise of the government shaken by argument; because I can manage a proposition, in itself doubtful, with a better pen than another man; this, say I, is a libel.

"Then I lay down this for my next position, that *no private man can take upon him to write concerning the government at all; for what has any private man to do with the government*, if his interest be not stirred or shaken? It is the business of the government to manage matters relating to the government; it *is the business of subjects to mind only their own properties and interests.* If my interest is not shaken, *what have I to do with matters of government?* They are not within my sphere. If the government does come to shake my particular interest, the law is open for me, and I may redress myself by law; and when I intrude myself into other men's business that does not concern my particular interest, I am a libeller.

"These I have laid down for plain propositions; now, then, let us consider further, whether, if I will take upon me to contradict the government, any specious pretence that I shall put upon it, shall dress it up in another form and give it a better denomination? And truly I think it is the worse, because it comes in a better dress; for by that rule, every man that can put on a good vizard, may be as mischievous as he will, to the government at the bottom, so that, whether it be in the form of a supplication, or an address, or a petition, if it be what it ought not to be, let us call it by its true name, and give it its right denomination — it is a libel."

"The government here has published such a declaration as this that has been read, relating to matters of government; and *shall*, or ought *anybody* to come and *impeach that as illegal, which the government has done?* Truly, in my opinion, I do not think he should, or ought; for by this rule may every act of the government be shaken, when there is not a parliament *de facto* sitting.

"When the house of lords and commons are in being, it is a proper way of applying to the king; there is all the openness in the world for those that are members of parliament, to make what addresses they please to the government, for the rectifying, altering, regulating, and making of what law they please; but if every private man shall come and interpose his advice, I think there can never be an end of advising the government.

[1] 12 St. Tr. 239.

"*We are not to measure things from any truth they have in themselves, but from that aspect they have upon the government; for there may be every tittle of a libel true, and yet it may be a libel still;* so that I put no great stress upon that objection, that the matter of it is not false; and for sedition, it is that which every libel carries in itself; and as every trespass implies *vi and armis*, so every libel against the government carries in it sedition, and all the other epithets that are in the information. This is my opinion as to law in general. I will not debate the prerogatives of the king, nor the privileges of the subject; but as this fact is, I think these venerable bishops did meddle with that which did not belong to them; they took upon them, in a petitionary, to contradict the actual exercise of the government, which I think no particular persons, or singular body, may do."[1]

Listen, Gentlemen of the Jury, to the words of Attorney-General Powis: —

"And I cannot omit here to take notice, that *there is not any one thing that the law is more jealous of*, or does more carefully provide for the prevention and punishment of, *than all accusations and arraignments of the government. No man is allowed to accuse even the most inferior magistrate of any misbehavior in his office*, unless it be in a legal course, *though the fact is true.* No man may say of a justice of the peace, to his face, that he is unjust in his office. *No man may tell a judge, either by word or petition, you have given an unjust, or an ill judgment*, and I will not obey it; *it is against the rules and law of the kingdom, or the like.* No man may say of the great men of the nation, much less of the great officers of the kingdom, that they do act unreasonably or unjustly, or the like; least of all may any man say any such thing of the king; for these matters tend to possess the people, that the government is ill administered; and the consequence of that is, to set them upon desiring a reformation; and what that tends to, and will end in, we have all had a sad and too dear bought experience."[2]

Hearken to the law of Solicitor-General Williams: —

"If any person have slandered the government in writing, you are *not to examine the truth of that fact* in such writing, but the slander which it imports to the king or government; and *be it never so true*, yet if slanderous to the king or the government, *it is a libel and to be punished;* in that case, *the right or wrong* is *not to be examined, or if what was done by the government be legal, or no;* but whether the party have done such an act. If the king have a power (for still I keep to that), to issue forth proclamations to his subjects, and to make orders and constitutions in matters ecclesiastical, if he do issue forth his proclamation, and make an order upon the matters within his power and prerogative; and if any one would come and bring that power in question otherwise than in parliament, that the matter of that proclamation be not legal, I say that is sedition, and you are not to examine the legality or illegality of the order or proclamation, but the slander and reflection upon the government."

"If a person do a thing that is libellous, you shall not examine the fact, but the consequence of it; whether it tended to stir up sedition against the public, or to stir up strife between man and man, in the case of private persons; as if a man should say of a judge, he has taken a bribe, and I will prove it.

"They tell the king it is inconsistent with their honor, prudence, and conscience, to do what he would have them to do. And if these things be not reflective upon the king and government, I know not what is.

[1] 12 St. Tr. 427, 428, 429.

[2] 12 St. Tr. 281.

"I'll tell you what they should have done, Sir. If they were commanded to do any thing against *their consçiences, they should have acquiesced till the meeting of the parliament.* [At which some people in the court hissed.]

"*If the king will impose upon a man what he cannot do, he must acquiesce*; but shall he come and fly in the face of his prince? Shall he say it is illegal? and the prince acts against prudence, honor, or conscience, and throw dirt in the king's face? Sure that is not permitted; that is libelling with a witness."[1]

Here, however, there was a JURY — the seven bishops were acquitted amid the tumultuous huzzas of the people, who crowded all the open spaces in the neighborhood of Westminster Hall, and rent the air with their shouts, which even the soldiers repeated.[2]

Two of the Judges — Sir John Powell and Sir Richard Holloway — stood out for law and justice, declaring such a petition to the King was not a libel. They were presently thrust from their offices.

Gentlemen of the Jury, the Stuarts soon filled up the measure of their time as of their iniquity, and were hustled from the throne of England. But, alas, I shall presently remind you of some examples of this tyranny in New England itself. Now I shall cite a few similar cases of oppression which happened in the reign of the last King of New England.

I just now spoke of Edmund Thurlow, showing what his character was and by what means he gained his various offices, ministerial and judicial. I will next show you one instance more of the evil which comes from putting in office such men as are nothing but steps whereon despotism mounts up to its bad eminence.

10. On the 8th of June, 1775, — it will be eighty years on the first anniversary of Judge Curtis's charge to the grand-jury, — John Horne, better known by his subsequent name John Horne Tooke, formerly a clergyman but then a scholarly man devoting himself to letters and politics — published the following notice in the *Morning Chronicle and London Advertiser*, as well as other newspapers: —

"King's-Arms Tavern, Cornhill, June 7, 1775. At a special meeting this day of several members of the Constitutional Society, during an adjournment, a gentleman proposed that a subscription should be immediately entered into by such of the members present who might approve the purpose, for raising the sum of £100, to be applied to the relief of the widows, orphans, and aged parents of our beloved American fellow-subjects, who, faithful to the character of Englishmen, preferring death to slavery, were for that reason only inhumanly murdered by the king's troops at or near Lexington and Concord, in the province of Massachusetts, on the 19th of last April; which sum being immediately collected, it was thereupon resolved that Mr. Horne do pay to-morrow into the hands of Mess. Brownes and Collinson, on account of Dr. Franklin, the said sum of 100*l.* and that Dr. Franklin be requested to apply the same to the above-mentioned purpose."

[1] 12 St. Tr. 415, 416, 417.

[2] See 2 Campbell's Justices, 95.

At that time Thurlow, whom I introduced to you a little while ago, was Attorney-General, looking for further promotion from the Tory Government of Lord North. Mansfield was Chief Justice, a man of great ability, who has done so much to reform the English law, but whose hostility to America was only surpassed by the hatred which he bore to all freedom of speech and the rights of the Jury. The Government was eager to crush the liberty of the American Colonies. But this was a difficult matter, for in England itself there was a powerful party friendly to America, who took our side in the struggle for liberty. The city of London, however, was hostile to us, wishing to destroy our merchants and manufacturers, who disturbed the monopoly of that commercial metropolis. The government thought it necessary to punish any man who ventured to oppose their tyranny and sympathize with America. Accordingly it was determined that Mr. Horne should be brought to trial. But as public opinion, stimulated by Erskine, Camden and others, favored the rights of the Jury, it seems to have been thought dangerous to trust the case to a Grand-Jury. Perhaps the Judge had no brother-in-law to put on it, or the Attorney-General — though famous also for his profanity, — doubted that any *swearing* of his would insure a bill; nay, perhaps he did not venture to "bet ten dollars that I will get an indictment against him." Be that as it may, the Attorney-General dispensed with the services of the Grand-Jury and filed an information *ex officio* against Mr. Horne, therein styling him a "wicked, malicious, seditious, and ill-disposed person;" charging him, by that advertisement, with "wickedly, maliciously, and seditiously intending, designing, and venturing to stir up and excite discontents and sedition;" "to cause it to be believed that divers of his Majesty's innocent and deserving subjects had been inhumanly murdered by . . . his Majesty's troops; and unlawfully and wickedly to encourage his Majesty's subjects in the said Province of Massachusetts to resist and oppose his Majesty's Government." He said the advertisement was "a false, wicked, malicious, scandalous, and seditious libel;" "full of ribaldry, Billingsgate, scurrility, balderdash, and impudence;" "wicked is a term too high for this advertisement;" "its impudence disarmed its wickedness." In short, Mr. Horne was accused of "resisting an officer," obstructing the execution of the "process" whereby the American Provinces were to be made the slave colonies of a metropolitan despotism. The usual charge of doing all this by "force and arms," was of course thrown in. The publication of the advertisement was declared a "crime of such heinousness and of such a size as fairly called for the highest resentment which any court of justice has thought proper to use with respect to crimes of this denomination;" "a libel such that it is impossible by any artifice to aggravate it;" "It will be totally impossible for the imagination of any man, however shrewd, to state a libel more scandalous and base in the fact imputed, more malignant and hostile to the country in which the libeller is born, more dangerous in the example if it were suffered to pass unpunished, than this:" "It is in language addressed to the lowest and most miserable mortals, . . . it is addressed to the lowest of the mob, and the bulk of the people, who it is fit should be otherwise taught, who it is fit should be otherwise governed in this country."

Mr. Horne was brought to trial on the 4th of July, 1777. He defended himself, but though a vigorous writer, he was not a good speaker, and was in a strange place, while "Thurlow fought on his own dunghill," says Lord Campbell, "and throughout the whole day had the advantage over him." There was a special jury packed for the purpose by the hireling sheriff, — a "London jury" famous for corruption, — a tyrannical and powerful judge, ready to turn every weapon of the court against the defendant and to construct law against the liberty of speech. Of course Mr. Horne was convicted.

But how should he be punished? Thurlow determined.

"My Lords, the punishments to be inflicted upon misdemeanors of this sort, have usually been of three different kinds; fine, corporal punishment by imprisonment, and infamy by the judgment of the pillory. With regard to the *fine*, it is impossible for justice to make this sort of punishment, however the infamy will always fall upon the offender; because it is well known, that men who have more wealth, who have better and more respectful situations and reputations to be watchful over, employ men in desperate situations both of circumstances and characters, in order to do that which serves their party purposes; and when the punishment comes to be inflicted, this court must have regard to the apparent situation and circumstances of the man employed, that is, of the man convicted, with regard to the punishment.

"With regard to *imprisonment*, that is a species of punishment not to be considered alike in all cases, but . . . , that it would be proper for the judgment of the court to state circumstances which will make the imprisonment fall lighter or heavier, . . . that would be proper, if I had not been spared all trouble upon that account, by hearing it solemnly avowed . . . by the defendant himself, that imprisonment was no kind of inconvenience to him; for that certain employments, . . . would occasion his confinement in so close a way, that it was mere matter of circumstance whether it happened in one place or another; and that the longest imprisonment which this court could inflict for punishment, was not beyond the reach of accommodation which those occasions rendered necessary to him. In this respect, therefore, imprisonment is not only, . . . not an adequate punishment to the offence, but the public are told, . . . that it will be *no punishment*.

"I stated in the third place to your Lordships, *the pillory to have been the usual punishment for this species of offence.* I apprehend it to have been so, in this case, for above two hundred years before the time when prosecutions grew rank in the Star-Chamber . . . . the punishment of the pillory was inflicted, not only during the time that such prosecutions were rank in the Star-Chamber, but it also continued to be inflicted upon this sort of crime, and that by the best authority, after the time of the abolishing the Star-Chamber, after the time of the Revolution, and while my Lord Chief Justice Holt sat in this court.

"I would desire no better, no more pointed, nor any more applicable argument than what that great chief justice used, when it was contended before him that an abuse upon government, upon the administration of several parts of government, amounted to nothing, because there was no abuse upon any particular man. That great chief justice said, they amounted to much more; they are *an abuse upon all men.* Government cannot exist, if the law cannot restrain that sort of abuse. Government cannot exist, unless . . . the full punishment is inflicted which the most approved times have given to offences of much less denomination than these, of much less. I am sure it cannot be shown, that in any one of the cases that were punished in that manner, the aggravations of any one of those offences were any degree adequate to those which are presented to your Lordship now. If offences were so punished then, which are not so punished now, they lose that expiation which the wisdom of those ages thought proper to hold out to the public, as a restraint from such offences being committed again.

"I am to judge of crimes in order to the prosecution; your lordship is to judge of them ultimately for punishment. I should have been extremely sorry, if I had been induced by any consideration whatever, to have brought a crime of the magnitude which this was (of the magnitude which this was when I first stated it) into a court of justice, if I had not had it in my contemplation also that it would meet with an adequate restraint, which I never thought would be done without affixing to it the *judgment of the pillory;* I should have been very sorry to have brought this man here, after all the aggravations that he has superinduced upon the offence itself, if I had not been persuaded that those aggravations would have induced the *judgment of the pillory.*" [1]

But Mansfield thought otherwise, and punished him with a fine of £200 and imprisonment for twelve months.[2]

"Thus," says Lord Brougham, "a bold and just denunciation of the attacks made upon our American Brethren, which nowadays would rank among the very mildest and tamest effusions of the periodical press, condemned him to prison for twelve months." [3]

Thurlow was a man of low intellect, of a fierce countenance, a saucy, swaggering, insolent manner, debauched in his morals beyond the grossness of that indecent age,—ostentatiously living in public concubinage,—a notorious swearer in public and private. But he knew no law above the will of the hand that fed and could advance him, no justice which might check the insolence of power. And in less than a month after Mr. Horne was sent to jail, Thurlow was made Lord Chancellor of England, and sat on the woolsack in the House of Lords. His chief panegyrist can only say, "in worse times there have been worse chancellors." "But an age of comparative freedom and refinement has rarely exhibited one who so ill understood, or at least so ill discharged, the functions of a statesman and legislator."

I will enrich this part of my argument with an example of the opinions of this Judge, which would endear him to the present ad-

[1] 20 St. Tr. 780–783.

[2] 20 St. Tr. 651; 5 Campbell, 415.

[3] Statesmen, 2 Series, 109.

ministration in America, and entitle him to a high place among southern politicians. In 1788 a bill was brought into Parliament to mitigate the horrors of the African slave-trade. The Lord Chancellor, Thurlow, opposed it and said: —

"It appears that the French have offered premiums to encourage the African [slave] trade, and that they have succeeded. The natural presumption therefore is, that *we ought to do the same*. For my part, my Lords, I have no scruple to say that if the 'five days' fit of philanthropy' [the attempt to abolish the slave-trade] which has just sprung up, and which has slept for twenty years together, were allowed to sleep one summer longer, it would appear to me rather more wise than thus to take up a subject piecemeal, which it has been publicly declared ought not to be agitated at all till next session of Parliament. Perhaps, by such imprudence, the slaves themselves may be prompted by their own authority, to proceed at once to a 'total and immediate abolition of the trade.' One witness has come to your Lordship's bar with a face of woe — his eyes full of tears, and his countenance fraught with horror, and said, '*My Lords, I am ruined if you pass this bill! I have risked* £30,000 *on the trade this year! It is all I have been able to gain by my industry, and if I lose it I must go to the hospital!*' I desire of you to think of such things, my Lords, in your *humane phrensy, and to show some humanity to the whites as well as to the negroes*."[1]

One measure of tyranny in the hands of such Judges is Constructive Crime, a crime which the revengeful, or the purchased judge distils out of an honest or a doubtful deed, in the alembic he has made out of the law broken up and recast by him for that purpose, twisted, drawn out, and coiled up in serpentine and labyrinthine folds. For as the sweet juices of the grape, the peach, the apple, pear, or plumb may be fermented, and then distilled into the most deadly intoxicating draught to madden man and infuriate woman, so by the sophistry of a State's Attorney and a Court Judge, well trained for this work, out of innocent actions, and honest, manly speech, the most ghastly crimes can be extorted, and then the "leprous distilment" be poured upon the innocent victim,

"And a most instant tetter barks about,
Most lazar-like, with vile and loathsome crust,
All his smooth body!"

Here is an example. In 1668 some London apprentices committed a riot by pulling down some houses of ill-fame in Moorfields, which had become a nuisance to the neighborhood; they shouted "Down with Bawdy Houses." Judge Kelyng had them indicted for High Treason. He said it was "an accroachment of royal authority." It was "levying war." He thus laid down the law. "The prisoners are indicted for levying war against the King. By levying

[1] 5 Campbell, 460; 27 Parl. Hist. 638.

war is not only meant when a body is gathered together as an army, but if a *company of people will go about any public reformation, this is high treason.* These people do pretend their design was against brothels; now let men to go about to pull down brothels, with a captain [an apprentice 'walked about with a green apron on a pole"] and an ensign and weapons, — if this thing be endured, *who is safe?* It is high treason because it doth betray the peace of the nation, and *every subject is as much wronged as the King;* for if every man may reform what he will, no man is safe; therefore the thing is of desperate consequence, and we must make this for a public example. There is reason why we should be very cautious; we are but recently delivered from rebellion [Charles I. had been executed nineteen years before, and his son had been in peaceable possession of the throne for eight years], and we know that that rebellion first began under the pretence of religion and the law; for the Devil hath always this vizard upon it. We have great reason to be very wary that we fall not again into the same error. Apprentices for the future shall not go on in this manner. It is proved that Beasly went as their captain with his sword, and flourished it over his head [this was the "weapons,"] and that Messenger walked about Moorfields with a green apron on the top of a pole [this was the "ensign"]. What was done by one, was done by all; in high treason all concerned are principals."[1]

Thereupon thirteen apprentices who had been concerned in a riot were found guilty of high treason, sentenced, and four hanged. All of the eleven Judges — Twysden was one of them — concurred in the sentence, except Sir Matthew Hale. He declared there was no treason committed; there was "but an unruly company of apprentices."[2]

This same Judge Kelyng, singularly thick-headed and ridiculous, loved to construct crimes where the law made none. Thus he declares, "in cases of high treason, if any one do any thing by which he showeth his *liking* and *approbation* to the Traitorous Design, this is in him High Treason. For all are Principals in High Treason, who contribute towards it by Action or Approbation."[3] He held it was an overt act of treason to print a "treasonable proposition," such as this, "The execution of Judgment and Justice is as well the people's as the magistrates' duty, and if the magistrates pervert Judgment, the people are bound by the law of God to execute judgment without them and upon them."[4] So the printer of the book, containing the "treasonable proposition," was executed. A man, by name Axtell, who commanded the guards which attended at the trial and execution of Charles I., was brought to trial for treason. He contended

[1] 1 Campbell's Justices, 404–5; Kelyng's Reports, 70. [2] 6 St. Tr. 879, note 911.
[3] Kelyng's Reports, 12. [4] Ibid. 22.

that he acted as a soldier by the command of his superior officer, whom he must obey, or die. But it was resolved that "that was no excuse, for his superior was a Traitor and all that joined with him in that act were Traitors, and did by that approve the Treason, and when the command is Traitorous, then the Obedience to that Command is also Traitorous." So Axtell must die. The same rule of course smote at the head of any private soldier who served in the ranks![1]

These wicked constructions of treason by the court, out of small offences or honest actions, continued until Mr. Erskine attacked them with his Justice, and with his eloquence exposed them to the indignation of mankind, and so shamed the courts into humanity and common sense.[2] Yet still the same weapon lies hid under the Judicial bench as well of England as of America, whence any malignant or purchased Judge, when it suits his personal whim or public ambition, may draw it forth, and smite at the fortune, the reputation, or the life of any innocent man he has a private grudge against, but dares not meet in open day. Of this, Gentlemen of the Jury, in due time.

The mass of men, busy with their honest work, are not aware what power is left in the hands of judges — wholly irresponsible to the people; few men know how they often violate the laws they are nominally set to administer. Let me take but a single form of this judicial iniquity — the Use of Torture, borrowing my examples from the history of our mother country.

In England the use of torture has never been conformable either to common or to statute law; but how often has it been practised by a corrupt administration and wicked judges! In 1549 Lord Seymour of Sudley, Admiral of England, was put to the torture;[3] in 1604 Guy Fawkes was "horribly racked."[4] Peacham was repeatedly put to torture as you have just now heard, and that in the presence of Lord Bacon himself in 1614.[5] Peacock was racked in 1620, Bacon and Coke both signing the warrant for this illegal wickedness, — "he deserveth it as well as Peacham did," said the Lord Chancellor, making his own "ungodly custom" stand for law.[6] In 1627 the Lord Deputy of Ireland wanted to torture two priests, and Charles I. gave him license, the privy council consenting — "all of one mind that he might rack the priests if he saw fit, and hang them if he found reason!"[7] In 1628 the judges of England solemnly decided that torture

[1] Kelyng's Reports, 13.
[2] See his Defence of Hardy, 24 St. Tr. 877.
[3] See 2 St. Tr. 774, note.
[4] 1 Jardine, Crim. Tr. 16.
[5] 2 St. Tr. 871.
[6] 1 Jardine, 19.
[7] Ibid.

was unlawful; but it had always been so,—and Yelverton, one of the judges, was a member of the commission which stretched Peacham on the rack.[1] Yet, spite of this decision, torture still held its old place, and a warrant from the year 1640 still exists for inflicting this illegal atrocity on a victim of the court.[2] Yet even so late as 1804, when Thomas Pictou, governor of Trinidad, put a woman to tortures of the most cruel character, by the connivance of the court he entirely escaped from all judicial punishment.[3] Yes, torture was long continued in England itself, though not always by means of thumbscrews and Scottish boots and Spanish racks; the monstrous chains, the damp cells, the perpetual irritation which corrupt servants of a despotic court tormented their victims withal, was the old demon under another name.[4] Nay, within a few months the newspapers furnish us with examples of Americans being put to the torture of the lash to force a confession of their alleged crime—and this has been done by the power which this court has long been so zealous to support—the Slave Power of America.

It has been well said:—

"It must be owned that the Guards and Fences of the law have not always proved an effectual security for the subject. The Reader will . . . find many Instances wherein they who hold the sword of Justice did not employ it as they ought to in punishment of Evil-Doers, but to the Oppression and Destruction of Men more righteous than themselves. Indeed it is scarce possible to frame a Body of Laws which a tyrannical Prince, influenced by wicked Counsellors and corrupt Judges, may not be able to break through. . . . The Law itself is a dead letter. Judges are the interpreters of it, and if they prove men of no Conscience nor Integrity, they will give what sense they will to it, however different from the true one; and when they are supported by superior authority, will for a while prevail, till by repeated iniquities they grow intolerable and throw the State into convulsions which may at last end in their own ruin. This shows how valuable a Blessing is an upright and learned Judge, and of what great concern it is to the public that none be preferred to that office but such whose Ability and Integrity may be safely depended on."[5]

Thus, Gentlemen of the Jury, is it that judges who know no law but the will of "the hand that feeds them," appointed for services rendered to the enemies of mankind and looking for yet higher rewards, have sought to establish the despotism of their masters on the ruin of the People. But the destruction of obnoxious individuals is not the whole of their enormity; so I come to the next part of the subject.

[1] 3 St. Tr. 371. See 30 St. Tr. 892.

[2] 1 Jardine, 20. See Emlyn, Preface to St. Tr. in 1 Hargrave, p. iii.

[3] 30 St. Tr. 225.

[4] See case of Huggins in 17 St. Tr. 297, 309.

[5] 1 Hargrave's St. Tr. 6.

(III.) The next step is for such judges to interpret, wrest, and pervert the laws so as to prepare for prospective Acts of Tyranny.

Here, Gentlemen of the Jury, I shall have only too many examples to warn you with.

Early in his reign James I. sought to lay burthensome taxes on the people without any act of Parliament; this practice was continued by his successors.

1. In 1606 came "the great Case of Impositions," not mentioned in the ordinary histories of England. The king assumed the right to tax the nation by his own prerogative. He ordered a duty of five shillings on every hundred pounds of currants imported into the kingdom to be levied in addition to the regular duty affixed by Act of Parliament. This was contrary to law, nay, to the Constitution of England, her Magna Charta itself provided against unparliamentary taxation. Sir John Bates, a London merchant, refused to pay the unlawful duty, and was prosecuted by information in the Star-Chamber. "The courts of justice," says Mr. Hallam, "did not consist of men conscientiously impartial between the king and the subject; some corrupt with hopes of promotion, many more fearful of removal, or awe-struck by the fear of power." On the "trial" it was abundantly shown that the king had no right to levy such a duty. "The accomplished but too pliant judges, and those indefatigable hunters of precedents for violations of constitutional government, the great law-officers of the crown," decided against the laws, and Chief Justice Fleming maintained that the king might lay what tax he pleased on imported goods! The corrupt decision settled the law for years — and gave the king absolute power over this branch of the revenue, involving a complete destruction of the liberty of the people, — for the Principle would carry a thousand measures on its back.[1] The king declared Fleming a judge to his "heart's content." Bacon's subserviency did not pass unrewarded. Soon after James issued a decree under the great seal, imposing heavy duties on almost all merchandise "to be for ever hereafter paid to the king and his successors, on pain of his displeasure."[2] Thus the Measure became a Principle.

2. James, wanting funds, demanded of his subjects forced contributions of money, — strangely called "Benevolences," though there was no "good-will" on either side. It was clearly against the fundamental laws of the kingdom. Sir Oliver St. John refused to

[1] 2 St. Tr. 371, and 11 Hargrave, 29; 1 Campbell's Justices, 204.

[2] 1 Hallam, 231. See 1 Parl. Hist. 1030, 1132, 1150; Baker's Chronicle, 430.

pay what was demanded of him, and wrote a letter to the mayor of Marlborough against the illegal exaction. For this he was prosecuted in the Star-Chamber in 1615 by Attorney-General Bacon. The court, with Lord Chancellor Ellesmere at its head, of course decided that the king had a right to levy Benevolences at pleasure. St. John was fined five thousand pounds, and punished by imprisonment during the king's pleasure. This decision gave the king absolute power over all property in the realm,—every private purse was in his hands![1] With such a court the king might well say, "Wheare any controversyes arise, my Lordes the Judges chosene betwixte me and my people shall discide and rulle me."[2]

3. Charles I. proceeded in the steps of his father: he levied forced loans. Thomas Darnel and others refused to pay, and were put in prison on a General Warrant from the king which did not specify the cause of commitment. They brought their writs of *habeas corpus*, contending that their confinement was illegal. The matter came to trial in 1627. Sir Randolf Crewe, a man too just to be trusted to do the iniquity desired, was thrust out of office, and Sir Nicolas Hyde appointed chief justice in his place. The actual question was, Has the king a right to imprison any subject forever without process of law? It was abundantly shown that he had no such right. But the new chief justice, put in power to oppress the people, remembering the hand that fed him, thus decreed,—"Mr. Attorney hath told you that the *king hath done it, and we trust him in great matters*, and he is bound by law, and he bids us proceed by law; . . . and we make no doubt but *the king*, if you look to him, he knowing the cause why you are imprisoned, *he will have mercy;* but that we believe that . . . he cannot deliver you, but *you must be remanded*." Thus the judges gave the king absolute power over the liberties of any subject.[3]

But the matter was brought up in Parliament and discussed by men of a different temper, who frightened the judge by threats of impeachment, and forced the king to agree to the PETITION OF RIGHT designed to put an end to all such illegal cruelty. Before Charles I. would sign that famous bill, he asked Judge Hyde if it would restrain the king "from committing or restraining a subject *without showing cause*." The crafty judge answered, "*Every law, after it is made, hath its exposition, which is to be left to the courts of justice to determine;* and although the Petition be granted *there is no fear of* [*such a*] *conclusion as is intimated in the question!*" That is, the court will interpret the plain law so as to oppress the subject and please the

[1] 2 St. Tr. 899; 1 Hallam, 251; 2 Campbell, 291. [2] 1 Parl. Hist. 1156.

[3] 3 St. Tr. 1. See also 2 Parl. Hist. 288; 1 Rushworth and 1 Mrs. Macaulay, 341.

king! As the judges had promised to annul the law, the king signed it.[1] Charles dissolved Parliament and threw into jail its most noble and powerful members — one of whom, Eliot, never left the prison till death set him free.[2] The same chief justice gave an extrajudicial opinion justifying the illegal seizure of the members, — "that a parliament man committing an offence against the King in Parliament not in a parliamentary course, may be punished after the Parliament is ended;" "that by false slanders to bring the Lords of the Council and the Judges, not in a parliamentary way, into the hatred of the people and the government into contempt, was punishable out of Parliament, in the Star-Chamber, as an offence committed in Parliament beyond the office, and beside the duty of a parliament man."[3] Thus the judges struck down freedom of speech in Parliament.

4. In 1634 Charles I. issued a writ levying ship-money, so called, on some seaport towns, without act of Parliament. London and some towns remonstrated, but were forced to submit, all the courts being against them. Chief Justice Finch, "a servile tool of the despotic court," generalized this unlawful tax, extending it to inland towns as well as seaboard, to all the kingdom. All landholders were to be assessed in proportion to their property, and the tax, if not voluntarily paid, collected by force. The tax was unpopular, and clearly against the fundamental law of the kingdom. But if the government could not get the law on its side it could control its interpreters, for "every law hath its exposition." So the Judges of Assize were ordered in their circuits to tell the people to *comply with the order and pay the money!* The King got an extrajudicial opinion of the twelve Judges delivered irregularly, out of court, in which they unanimously declared that in time of danger the *King might levy such tax as he saw fit, and compel men to pay it.* He was the sole judge of the danger, and of the amount of the tax.[4]

John Hampden was taxed twenty shillings — he refused to pay, though he knew well the fate of Richard Chambers a few years before. The case came to trial in 1637, in the Court of Exchequer before Lord Chancellor Coventry, a base creature, mentioned before. It was "the great case of Ship-money." The ablest lawyers in England showed that the tax was contrary to Magna Charta, to the fundamental laws of the realm, to the Petition of Right and to the practice of the kingdom. Hampden was defeated. Ten out of the twelve Judges sided with the King. Croke as the eleventh had made up his mind to do the same, but his noble wife implored him not to

[1] 1 Campbell, Justices, 311; 2 Parl. Hist. 245, 350, 373, 408, *et al.*; 3 St. Tr. 59.

[2] See above, p. 29.

[3] 1 Campbell's Justices, 315.

[4] 3 St. Tr. 825. See the opinion of the Judges with their twelve names, 844, and note †.

sacrifice his conscience for fear of danger, and the Woman, as it so often happens, saved the man.[1] Attorney-General Banks thus set forth the opinion of the Government, and the consequent "decision" of the Judges. He rested the right of levying Ship-money on the "intrinsic, absolute authority of the King." There was no Higher Law in Old England in 1634! Banks said, "this power [of arbitrary and irresponsible taxation] is innate in the person of an absolute King, and in the persons of the Kings of England. All-magistracy it is of nature; and obedience and subjection [to] it is of nature. This power is not anyways derived from the people, but reserved unto the King when positive laws first began. For the King of England, he is an absolute monarch; nothing can be given to an absolute prince but what is inherent in his person. He can do no wrong. He is the sole judge and we ought not to question him, whom the law trusts we ought not to distrust." "The Acts of Parliament contain no express words to take away so high a prerogative; and the King's prerogative, even in lesser matters, is always saved, where express words do not restrain it."[2]

It required six months of judicial labor to bring forth this result, which was of "infinite disservice to the crown." Thereupon Mr. Hallam says:—

> "Those who had trusted to the faith of the judges were undeceived by the honest repentance of some, and looked with indignation on so prostituted a crew. That respect for courts of justice which the happy structure of our Judicial administration has in general kept inviolate, was exchanged for distrust, contempt, and a desire of vengeance. They heard the speeches of some of the Judges with more displeasure than even their final decision. Ship-money was held lawful by Finch and several other Judges, not on the authority of precedents which must in their nature have some bounds, but on principles subversive of every property or privilege in the subject. Those paramount rights of monarchy, to which they appealed to-day in justification of Ship-money, might to-morrow serve to supersede other laws, and maintain more exertions of despotic power. It was manifest by the whole strain of the court lawyers that no limitations on the King's authority could exist but by the King's sufferance. This alarming tenet, long bruited among the churchmen and courtiers, now resounded in the halls of justice."[3]

Thus by the purchased vote of a corrupt Judiciary all the laws of Parliament, all the customs of the Anglo-Saxon tribe, Magna Charta itself with its noble attendant charters, were at once swept away, and all the property of the kingdom put into the hands of the enemy of the People. These four decisions would make the King of England as absolute as the Sultan of Turkey, or the Russian Czar. If the opinion of the Judges in the case of Impositions and Ship-money were

[1] Whitelocke, Memor. 25. [2] 2 Hallam, 16. [3] 2 Hallam, 18.

accepted in law, — then all the Property of the People was the King's; if the courts were correct in their judgments giving the King the power by his mere will to imprison any subject, during pleasure, and also to do the same even with members of Parliament and punish them for debates in the House of Commons, then all liberty was at an end, and the King's Prerogative extended over all acts of Parliament, all property, all persons.

5. One step more must be taken to make the logic of despotism perfect, and complete the chain. That work was delegated to clergymen purchased for the purpose — Rev. Dr. Robert Sibthorpe and Rev. Dr. Roger Mainwaring. The first in a sermon "of rendering all their dues," preached and printed in 1627, says, "the Prince who is the Head, and makes his Court and Council, it is his duty to direct and make laws. 'He doth whatsoever pleaseth him;' 'where the word of the King is there is power, and who may say unto him, What doest thou?'" And again, "If Princes command any thing which subjects may not perform, because it is against the Laws of God, or of Nature, or impossible; yet Subjects are bound to undergo the punishment, without either resisting, or railing, or reviling, and are to yield a Passive Obedience where they cannot exhibit an Active one, . . . but in all others he is bound to active obedience."[1]

Mainwaring went further, and in two famous sermons — preached, one on the 4th of July, 1628, the other on the 29th of the same month — declared that "the King is not bound to observe the Laws of the Realm concerning the Subject's Rights and Liberties, but that his *Royal will and Command*, in imposing Loans, and Taxes, without consent of Parliament, *doth oblige the subject's conscience upon pain of eternal damnation.* That those who refused to pay this Loan offended against the Law of God and the King's Supreme Authority, and became guilty of Impiety, Disloyalty, and Rebellion. And that the authority of Parliament is not necessary for the raising of Aid and Subsidies; and that the slow proceedings of such great Assemblies were not fitted for the Supply of the State's urgent necessities, but would rather produce sundry impediments to the just designs of Princes." "*That Kings partake of omnipotence with God.*"[2]

The nation was enraged. Mainwaring was brought before Par-

[1] Cited in Franklyn, 208; 1 Rushworth, 422, 436, 444.

[2] Franklyn, 208, 592. These two Sermons were published in a volume with the title "Religion and Allegiance." . . . "Published by his Majesty's special command." (London, 1628.) Prof. Stuart seems inspired by this title in giving a name to his remarkable publication — written with the same spirit as Dr. Mainwaring's — "Conscience and the Constitution." (Andover, 1851.) See 3 St. Tr. 335; 1 Rushworth, 422, 436, 585, *et al.*; 1 Hallam, 307; 2 Parl. Hist. 388, 410.

liament, punished with fine and imprisonment and temporary suspension from office and perpetual disability for ecclesiastical preferment. But the King who ordered the publication of the sermons, and who doubtless had induced him to preach them, immediately made him Rector of Stamford Parish, soon appointed him Dean of Worcester, and finally in 1645 made him Bishop of St. David's. A few years ago such clerical apostasy would seem astonishing to an American. But now, Gentlemen of the Jury, so rapid has been the downfal of public virtue, that men filling the pulpits once graced and dignified by noblest puritanic piety, now publicly declare there is no law of God above the fugitive slave bill. Nay, a distinguished American minister boldly proclaimed his readiness to send his own Mother (or "Brother") into eternal bondage! Thus modern history explains the old; and the cheap bait of a republican bribe can seduce American dissenters, as the wealthy lure of royal gifts once drew British churchmen into the same pit of infamy. Alas, hypocrisy is of no sect or nation.

Gentlemen, the Government of England once decreed "that every clergyman, four times in the year, should instruct his parishioners in the Divine right of Kings, and the damnable sin of resistance."[1] No Higher Law! America has ministers who need no act of Parliament to teach them to do the same; they run before they are sent.

6. After the head of one Stuart was shorn off and his son had returned, no wiser nor better than his father, the old progress of despotism began anew. I pass over what would but repeat the former history, and take two new examples to warn the nation with, differing from the old only in form.

In 1672, Charles II. published a proclamation denouncing rigorous penalties against all such as *should speak disrespectfully of his acts*, or *hearing others thus speak should not immediately inform the magistrates!* Nay, in 1675, after he had sold himself to the French king, and was in receipt of an annual pension therefrom, he had this test-oath published for all to sign: "I do solemnly declare that *it is not lawful upon any pretence whatever to take up arms against the king*, ... and that *I will not*, at any time to come, *endeavor the alteration of the government*, either in Church or State."[2]

An oath yet more stringent was enforced in Scotland with the edge of the sword, namely, to defend all the prerogatives of the crown, *never without the king's permission to take part in any deliberations upon ecclesiastical or civil affairs; and never to seek any reform in Church or State.*"

[1] 2 Campbell, 460; 1 Rushworth, 1205.

[2] Carroll's Counter Revolution (Lond. 1846), 99, *et seq.*

Notwithstanding all that the Charleses had done to break down the liberty of Englishmen, still the great corporate towns held out, intrenched behind their charters, and from that bulwark both annoyed the despot and defended the civil rights of the citizen. They also must be destroyed. So summons of *quo warranto* were served upon them, which frightened the smaller corporations and brought down their charters. Jeffreys was serviceable in this wicked work, and on his return from his Northern Circuit, rich with these infamous spoils, as a reward for destroying the liberties of his countrymen, the king publicly presented him with a ring, in token of "acceptance of his most eminent services." This fact was duly blazoned in the Gazette, and Jeffreys was "esteemed a mighty favorite," which, "together with his lofty airs, made all the charters, like the walls of Jericho, fall down before him, and he returned, laden with surrenders, the spoil of towns."[1]

London still remained the strong-hold of commerce, of the Protestant Religion, and of liberal Ideas in domestic Government; for though subsequently corrupted by lust of gain, which sought a monopoly, the great commercial estates and families of England were not then on the side of Despotism, as now strangely happens in America.

When the king sought to ruin Shaftesbury,— a corrupt man doubtless, but then on the side of liberty, the enemy of encroaching despotism,— a London Grand-Jury refused to find a bill, and was warmly applauded by the city. Their verdict of IGNORAMUS was a "personal liberty bill" for that time, and therefor was the king's wrath exceeding hot, for "Ignoramus was mounted in Cathedra," and there was a stop put to such wickedness. So London must be brought down. She refused to surrender her Charter. In 1682 the king proceeded to wrest it from her by the purchased hand of the courts of law. But even they were not quite adequate to the work. So Chief Justice Pemberton was displaced, and Saunders,— a man as offensive in his personal habit of body as he was corrupt in conduct and character— was put in his office. Dolbin, too just for the crime demanded of him, was turned out, and Withins made to succeed him. For "so great a weight was there at stake as could not be trusted to men of doubtful principles," says North. Saunders, who had plotted this whole matter, was struck with an apoplexy when sentence was to be given, but sent his opinion in writing. Thus on the judgment given by only two judges, who assigned no reasons for their decision, it was declared that the Charter of London was forfeit,

[1] 8 St. Tr. 1038, and the quotations from North (Examen.) Sprat, and Roger Coke, in note on p. 1041, *et seq.* See, too, Fox, James II. p. 48, 54, and Appendix, Barillon's Letter of Dec. 7th, 1684.

and the liberties and franchises of the city should "be seized into the king's hands."[1]

Thus fell the charter of London! Gentlemen of the Jury, the same sword was soon to strike at the neck of New England; the charter of Massachusetts could not be safe in such a time.

In 1686 James II. wished to destroy Protestantism, — not that he loved the Roman form of religion, but that tyranny which it would help him get and keep. So he claimed the right by his royal prerogative to dispense with any laws of the land. Of the twelve Judges of England eight were found on his side, and the four unexpectedly proven faithful were at once dismissed from office and their places filled with courtiers of the king, and the court was unanimous that the king had a constitutional right to destroy the constitution. Then he had not only command of the purses of his subjects and their bodies, but also of their mind and conscience, and could dictate the actual Religion of the People as well as the official "religion" of the priests.[2]

One State-secret lay at the bottom of the Stuarts' plans, — to appoint base men for judges, and if by accident a just man came upon the bench, to keep him in obscurity or to hustle him from his post. What names they offer us — Kelyng, Finch, Saunders, Wright, Jeffreys, Scroggs![3] infamous creatures, but admirable instruments to destroy generous men withal and devise means for the annihilation of the liberties of the people. Historians commonly dwell on the fields of battle, recording the victories of humanity, whereof the pike and gun were instruments; but pass idly over the more important warfare which goes on in the court house, only a few looking on, where lawyers are the champions of mankind, and the battle turns on a sentence; nay, on a word which determines the welfare of a nation for ages to come. On such little hinges of law do the great gates hang, and open or shut to let in the happiness or the ruin of millions of men! Naseby and Worcester are important places truly, venerable for great deeds. Cromwell and Blake are names not likely to perish while men can appreciate the heroism which sheds blood. But Westminster Hall has rung with more important thunder than cannon ever spoke, and Pym and Selden, St. John and Hampden — nay, Penn, Bunyan, Fox, Lilburne — have done great service for mankind. Gentlemen of the Jury, it is a matter of great magnitude which hinges on the small question of fact and law to-day. You are to open or shut for Humanity. If the People make themselves sheep there will be wolves enough to eat you up.

[1] 2 Hallam, 333; Burnet, Own Times (London, 1838), 350; 8 St. Tr. 1039, 1081 note, 1267, *et seq.*; 2 Campbell, Justices, 63; North's Examen. 626; Fox, 54.

[2] 11 St. Tr. 1165; 12 Ibid. 358.

[3] This last name is thought to be extinct in Great Britain, but I find one Thomas Scruggs *in Massachusetts* in 1635 *et post*, 1 Mass. Records (1628–1641), index.

It is difficult to calculate the amount of evil wrought by such corrupt judges as I have spoken of; they poison the fountains of society. I need not speak of monsters like Scroggs and Jeffreys, whose names rot in perpetual infamy, but creatures less ignoble, like Wright, Saunders, Finch, Kelyng, Thurlow, Loughborough, and their coadjutors, must be regarded as far more dangerous than thieves, murderers, or pirates. A cruel, insolent Judge selecting the worst customs, the most oppressive statutes, and decisions which outrage human nature — what an amount of evil he can inflict on groaning humanity!

Gentlemen of the Jury, in this long sad history of judicial tyranny in England there is one thing particularly plain: such judges hate freedom of speech, they would restrict the Press, the Tongue, yes, the Thought of mankind. Especially do they hate any man who examines the actions of the government and its servile courts, and their violation of justice and the laws. They wish to take exemplary and malignant vengeance on all such. Let me freshen your knowledge of some examples.

1. In 1410 the government made a decree "that whatsoever they were that should rede the Scriptures in the mother tongue, they should forfeit land, catel, body, lif, and godes from their heyres forever, and so be condempned for heretykes to God, enemies to the crowne, and most errant traiters to the land." The next year, in *one day thirty-nine persons were first hanged and then burned for this "crime."*[1]

2. In 1590, Mr. Udall, a Puritan minister, published a book, "Demonstrations of Discipline," not agreeable to the authorities. He was brought to a trial for a Felony, — not merely a "misdemeanor." The jury were ordered by the judge to find him guilty of that crime if they were satisfied that he published the book, — for the court were to judge whether the deed amounted to that crime! He was found "guilty," and died in jail after nearly three years of cruel confinement.[2]

3. In 1619 one Williams of Essex wrote a book explaining a passage in the book of Daniel as foretelling the death of James I. in 1621. He inclosed the manuscript in a box, sealed it, and secretly conveyed it to the king. For this he was tried for high treason, and of course executed. "*Punitur Affectus, licet non sequatur Effectus,*" said the court, for "*Scribere est agere,*" "Punish the wish though the object be not reached," for "writing is doing!"[3]

[1] 1 St. Tr. 252.

[2] 1 St. Tr. 1271; 1 Neal's Puritans (N. Y. 1844), 190. See 16 Parl. Hist. 1276, where Mr. Dunning says this is the first example of such a charge to a jury.

[3] 2 St. Tr. 1085.

4. In 1664 Mr. Keach, a Baptist, published a "Childs' Instructer, or a New and Easy Primmer," in which he taught the doctrines of his sect, "that children ought not to be baptized" but only adults; "that laymen may preach the gospel." He was brought before Lord Chief Justice Hyde, who after insulting the prisoner, thus charged the grand-jury: — "He is a base and dangerous fellow; and if this be suffered, children by learning of it will become such as he is, and therefore I hope you will do your duty." Of course such a jury indicted him. The "trial" took place before Judge Scroggs; the Jury were at first divided in opinion. "But," said the Judge, "you must agree!" So they found him guilty. He was fined "£20, twice set in the pillory, and bound to make public submission."[1]

5. In 1679 George Wakeman and others were tried for high treason before Scroggs, whose conduct was atrocious, and several pamphlets were published commenting on the ridiculous and absurd conduct of this functionary, "Lord Chief Justice Scroggs." One Richard Radley in a bantering talk had bid another man "Go to Weal Hall, to my Lord Scroggs, *for he has received money enough of Dr. Wakeman!*" Radley was indicted for "speaking scandalous words of Chief Justice Scroggs." Whereupon at the opening of the court that eminent officer, who did not disdain to wreak public and judicial vengeance on heads that wrought his private and personal grief, made a speech setting forth his magisterial opinions on the liberty of the press. Doubtless this court knows original authority for the opinions they follow; but for your instruction, Gentlemen of the Jury, I will give you the chief things in the judicial speech of Scroggs, Lord Chief Justice of the Supreme Court of England in 1679.[2]

"For these hireling scribblers who traduce it [the fairness and equality of the trial in which he had been notoriously unfair and unequal], who write to eat, and lie for bread, I intend to meet with them another way; for they are only safe while they can be secret; but so are vermin, so long as they can hide themselves. . . . . They shall know that the law wants not the power to punish a libellous and licentious press, nor I a resolution to exact it. And this is all the answer is fit to be given (besides a whip) to these hackney writers." "However, in the mean time, the *extravagant boldness of men's pens and tongues is not to be endured, but shall be severely punished;* for if once causes come to be tried with complacency to particular opinions, and shall be innocently censured if they go otherwise, public causes shall all receive the doom as the multitude happen to be possessed; and at length any cause shall become public . . . . at every session the Judges shall be arraigned, the Jury condemned, and the verdicts overawed to comply with popular wish and indecent shouts."

"There are a set of men . . . . that too much approve and countenance such vulgar ways, ... that embrace all sorts of informations, true or false, likely or impossible, nay though never so silly and ridiculous, they refuse none; so shall all addresses be made to them, and they be looked on as the only patrons of religion and government!"

[1] 7 St. Tr. 687.

[2] 6 St. Tr. 701; see Dunning in 16 Parl. Hist. 1276, *et seq.*

His associates chimed in with accordant howl. Puny Judge Jones declared, —

"We have a particular case here before us, as a matter of scandal against a great Judge, the *greatest Judge in the kingdom*, in criminal causes [the Lord Chancellor Nottingham was greater in *civil* causes]; and it is a great and an high charge upon him. And certainly there was never any age, I think, more licentious than this in aspersing governors, scattering of libels and *scandalous speeches against those that are in authority;* and without all doubt *it doth become the court to show their zeal in suppressing it*." [It was 'resisting an officer.'] "That trial [of Dr. Wakeman] was managed with *exact justice and perfect integrity*. And therefore I do think it very fit that this person be proceeded against by an information, that he may be made *a public example* to all such as shall presume to scandalize the government, and the governors, with any false aspersions and accusations."

Accordingly Mr. Radley, for that act, was convicted of speaking "scandalous words against the Lord Chief Justice Scroggs" and fined £200.[1]

Mr. Hudson says of the Star-Chamber, "So tender the court is of upholding the honor of the sentence, as they will punish them who speak against it with great severity." [2]

6. In 1680 Benjamin Harris, a bookseller, sold a work called "An Appeal from the country to the city for the Preservation of his Majesty's Person, Liberty, Property, and the Protestant Religion." He was brought to trial for a libel, before Recorder Jeffreys and Chief Justice Scroggs who instructed the jury they were only to inquire *if Harris sold the book*, and if so, find him "guilty." It was for the court to determine what was a libel. He was fined five hundred pounds and placed in the pillory; the Chief Justice wished that he might be also whipped.[3]

7. The same year Henry Carr was brought to trial. He published a periodical — "the Weekly Packet of advice from Rome, or the History of Popery" — hostile to Romanism. Before the case came to court, Scroggs prohibited the publication on his own authority. Mr. Carr was prosecuted for a libel before the same authority, and of course found guilty. The character of that court also was judgment against natural right. Jane Curtis and other women were in like manner punished for speaking or publishing words against the same "great judge."[4] And it was held to be a "misdemeanor" to publish a book reflecting on the justice of the nation — the truer the book the worse the libel! It was "obstructing an officer," and of course it was a greater offence to "obstruct" him with Justice and Truth than with wrong and lies. The greater the justice of the act the more

[1] 7 St. Tr. 701.
[2] In 2 Collectanea Juridica, 228.
[3] 7 St. Tr. 925.
[4] 7 St. Tr. 1111, 959; 4 Parl. Hist. 1274.

dangerous the "crime!" If the language did not hit any one person it was "malice against all mankind."

8. In 1684 Sir Samuel Barnardiston was brought to trial charged with a "High Misdemeanor." He had written three private letters to be sent — it was alleged — by post to his friend, also a private man. The letters do not appear designed for any further publication or use; they related to matters of news, the events of the day and comments thereon, and spoke in praise of Algernon Sidney and Lord Russell who were so wickedly beheaded about the time the letters were written. It would require a microscopic eye to detect any evil lurking there. Jeffreys presided at the trial, and told the jury: —

"The letters are *factious, seditious, and malicious letters, and as base as the worst of mankind could ever have invented.*" "And if he be guilty of it — the greater the man is the greater the crime, and the more understanding he has, the more malicious he seems to be; for your little ordinary sort of people, that are of common mean understanding, they may be wheedled and drawn in, and surprised into such things; but men of a public figure and of some value in the world that have been taken to be men of the greatest interest and reputation in a party, it cannot be thought a hidden surprise upon them; no, it is a work of time and thought, it is a thing fixed in his very nature, and it *shows so much venom as would make one think the whole mass of his blood were corrupt.*" "Here is the matter he is now accused of, and here is in it malice against the king, malice against the government, malice against both Church and State, malice against any man that bears any share in the government, indeed malice against all mankind that are not of the same persuasion with these bloody miscreants." "Here is . . . the sainting of two horrid conspirators! Here is the Lord Russell sainted, that blessed martyr; Lord Russell, that good man, that excellent Protestant, he is lamented! And here is Mr. Sidney sainted, what an extraordinary man he was! Yes, surely he was a very good man — and it is a shame to think that such bloody miscreants should be sainted and lamented who had any hand in that horrid murder [the execution of Charles I.] and treason . . . who could confidently bless God for their being engaged in that good cause (as they call it) which was the rebellion which brought that blessed martyr to his death. It is high time for all mankind that have any Christianity, or fear of Heaven or Hell, to bestir themselves, to rid the nation of such caterpillars, such monsters of villany as those are!"

Of course the packed jury found him guilty; he was fined £10,000.[1]

Gentlemen of the Jury, such judges, with such kings and cabinets, have repeatedly brought the dearest rights of mankind into imminent peril. Sad indeed is the condition of a nation where Thought is not free, where the lips are sewed together, and the press is chained! Yet the evil which has ruined Spain and made an Asia Minor of Papal Italy, once threatened England. Nay, Gentlemen of the Jury, it required the greatest efforts of her noblest sons to vindicate for you and me the right to print, to speak, to think. Milton's "Speech for

[1] 7 St. Tr. 1333.

the Liberty of unlicensed Printing" is one monument of the warfare which lasted from Wicliffe to Thomas Carlyle. But other monuments are the fines and imprisonment, the exile and the beheading of men and women! Words are "sedition," "rebellion," "treason;" nay, even now at least in New England, a true word is a "Misdemeanor," it is "obstructing an officer." At how great cost has our modern liberty of speech been purchased! Answer John Lilburne, answer William Prynn, and Selden, and Eliot, and Hampden, and the other noble men who

——— "in the public breach devoted stood,
And for their country's cause were prodigal of blood."

Answer Fox and Bunyan, and Penn and all the host of Baptists, Puritans, Quakers, martyrs, and confessors — it is by your stripes that we are healed! Healed! are we healed? Ask the court if it be not a "misdemeanor" to say so!

A despotic government hates implacably the freedom of the press. In 1680 the Lord Chief Justice of England declared the opinion of the twelve judges "indeed all subscribe that to *print or publish any news-books, or pamphlets of news whatsoever, is illegal; that it is a manifest intent to the breach of the peace*, and they may be proceeded against by law for an illegal thing." "And that is for a public notice to all people, and especially printers and booksellers, that *they ought to print no book or pamphlet of news whatsoever without authority;*" "*they shall be punished if they do it without authority*, though there is nothing reflecting on the government."[1] Judge Scroggs was right — it was "resisting an officer," at least "obstructing" him in his wickedness. In England, says Lord Campbell, the name and family of Scroggs are both extinct. So much the worse for you and me, Gentlemen. The Scrogges came over to America; they settled in Massachusetts, they thrive famously in Boston; only the name is changed.

In 1731 Sir Philip Yorke, attorney-general, solemnly declared that an editor is "*not to publish any thing reflecting on the character and reputation and administration of his Majesty or his Ministers;*" "if he breaks that law, or exceeds that liberty of the press he is to *be punished for it.*" Where did he get his law — in the third year of Edward I., in A. D. 1275! But that statute of the Dark Ages was held good law in 1731; and it seems to be thought good law in 1855! And the attorney who affirmed the atrocious principle, soon became Chief Justice, a "consummate judge," a Peer, Lord Hardwicke, and Lord Chancellor![2] Lord Mansfield had not a much higher opinion of the liberty of the press; indeed, in all libel cases, he assumed it was exclusively the

[1] 7 St. Tr. 1127. [2] 17 St. Tr. 674; 5 Campbell, 57; Hildreth's Despotism, 199.

function of the judges to determine whether the words published contained malicious or seditious matter, the jury were only to find the fact of publication.[1] Thus the party in power with their Loughboroughs, their Thurlows, their Jeffreys, their Scroggs — shall I add also American names — are the exclusive judges as to what shall be published relating to the party in power — their Loughboroughs, their Thurlows, their Jeffreys and their Scroggs, or their analogous American names! It was the free press of England — Elizabeth invoked it — which drove back the "invincible Armada;" this which stayed the tide of Papal despotism; this which dyked the tyranny of Louis XIV. out from Holland. Aye, it was this which the Stuarts, with their host of attendants, sought to break down and annihilate for ever;[2] which Thurlow and Mansfield so formidably attacked, and which now in America — but the American aspect of the matter must not now be looked in the face.

But spite of all these impediments in the way of liberty, the voice of humanity could not be forever silenced. Now and then a virtuous and high-minded judge appeared in office — like Hale or Holt, Camden or Erskine. Even in the worst times there were noble men who lifted up their voices. Let me select two examples from men not famous, but whose names, borne by other persons, are still familiar to this court.

In 1627 Sir Robert Phillips, member for Somersetshire, in his place in Parliament, thus spoke against the advance of despotism:[3] —

"I read of a custom among the old Romans, that once every year they had a solemn feast for their slaves; at which they had liberty, without exception, to speak what they would, thereby to ease their afflicted minds; which being finished, they severally returned to their former servitude. This may, with some resemblance and distinction, well set forth our present state; where now, after the revolution of some time, and grievous sufferance of many violent oppressions, we have, as those slaves had, a day of liberty of speech; but shall not, I trust, be hereafter slaves, for we are free: yet what new illegal proceedings our estates and persons have suffered under, my heart yearns to think, my tongue falters to utter. They have been well represented by divers worthy gentlemen before me; yet one grievance, and the main one, as I conceive, hath not been touched, which is our Religion: religion, Mr. Speaker, made vendible by commission, and men, for pecuniary annual rates, dispensed withal; Judgments of law against our liberty there have been three; each latter stepping forwarder than the former, upon the Rights of the Subject; aiming, in the end, to tread and trample underfoot our law, and that even in the form of law."

"The first was the Judgment of the Postnati, (the Scots,) . . . The second was the Judgment upon Impositions, in the Exchequer Court by the barons; which hath been the source and fountain of many bitter waters of affliction unto our merchants." "The

1 20 St. Tr. 900. But see 28 St. Tr. 595, and 16 Parl. Hist. 1211.

2 For the frequency of trials for words spoken in Charles II.'s reign of terror, see the extracts from Narcissus Luttrel's Brief Historical Relation, 10 St. Tr. 125.

3 1 Rushworth, 502.

third was that fatal late Judgment against the Liberty of the Subject imprisoned by the king, argued and pronounced but by one judge alone." "I can live, although another who has no right be put to live with me; nay, I can live although I pay excises and impositions more than I do; but to have my liberty, which is the soul of my life, taken from me by power; and to have my body pent up in a gaol, without remedy by law, and to be so adjudged: O improvident ancestors! O unwise forefathers! To be so curious in providing for the quiet possession of our lands, and the liberties of Parliament; and to neglect our persons and bodies, and to let them lie in prison, and that *durante bene placito*, remediless! If this be law, why do we talk of liberties? Why do we trouble ourselves with a dispute about law, franchises, property of goods, and the like? What may any man call his own, if not the Liberty of his Person? I am weary of treading these ways."[1]

In 1641 Sir Philip Parker, Knight of the Shire for Suffolk, in his place in Parliament, thus spoke:—

"The cries of the people have come up to me; the voice of the whole nation tingles in my ears." "'T is true, I confess, we have tormented ourselves with daily troubles and vexations, and have been very solicitous for the welfare of the Commonwealth; but what have we performed, what have we perfected? Mr. Speaker, excuse my zeal in this case; for my mouth cannot imprison what my mind intends to let out; neither can my tongue conceal what my heart desires to promulge. Behold the Archbishop [Laud], that great incendiary of this kingdom, lies now like a firebrand raked up in the embers; but if ever he chance to blaze again I am afraid that what heretofore he had but in a spark, he will burn down to the ground in a full flame. Wherefore let us begin, for the kingdom is pregnant with expectation on this point. I confess there are many more delinquents, for the judges and other knights walk *in querpo;* but they are only thunderbolts forged in Canterbury's fire."[2]

Six of the wicked judges were soon brought to trial.[3]

This same threefold experiment of despotism which was attempted in England, was tried also in America by the same tyrannical hand. Here, also, the encroaching power put creatures of its arbitrary will in judicial offices; they then by perverting the laws, punished the patriots, and next proceeded to destroy the best institutions of the land itself. Here I shall take but a few examples, selected from the colonial history of our own New England.

After capturing the great fortress of freedom at home, by taking away the charter of London, Charles proceeded to destroy the freedom of the colonies; the Charter of Massachusetts was wrested from us on a *quo warranto* in 1683,[4] and the colony lay at the feet of the

[1] 2 Parl. Hist. 232. See also 441, 471. He had been thrown into the Tower by James in 1624. Cabbala (3d Ed.), 311.

[2] Parl. Hist. 867.

[3] 1 Rushworth, 502.

[4] See the steps of the process in 1 Hutchinson, (Salem, 1795,) 297; 8 St. Tr. 1068, note.

monarch. In privy council it had already been determined that our rights should be swept into the hands of some greedy official from the court.[1] In 1686 James II. sent Sir Edmund Andros to New England as a "Commissioner" to destroy the liberty of the people. He came to Boston in the "Kingfisher, a fifty gun ship," and brought two companies of British soldiers, the first ever stationed in this town to dragoon the people into submission to an unrighteous law. Edward Randolph, the most determined enemy of the colony, greedily caressing the despotic hands that fed him, was his chief coadjutor and assistant, his secretary, in that wicked work. Andros was authorized to appoint his own council, and with their consent enact laws, levy taxes, to organize and command the militia. He was to enforce the hateful "Acts of Trade." He appointed a council to suit the purpose of his royal master, to whom no opposition was allowed. Dudley, the new Chief Justice, told the people who appealed to Magna Charta, "they must not think the privileges of Englishmen would follow them to the end of the world." Episcopacy was introduced; no marriages were to "be allowed lawful but such as were made by the minister of the Church of England." Accordingly, all must come to Boston to be married, for there was no Episcopal minister out of its limits. It was proposed that the Puritan Churches should pay the Episcopal salary, and the Congregational worship be prohibited. He threatened to punish any man "who gave two pence" toward the support of a Non-conformist minister. All fees to officers of the new government were made exorbitantly great. Only one Probate office was allowed in the Province, that was in Boston; and one of the creatures of despotic power was, prophetically, put in it. Andros altered the old form of oaths, and made the process of the courts to suit himself.

He sought to wrest the charters from the Colonies; that of Rhode Island fell into his hands; Connecticut escaped by a "miracle:"

> "The Charter-Oak — it was the tree
> That saved our sacred Liberty."

The Charter government of Plymouth was suspended. Massachusetts was put under arbitrary despotism. Towns were forbidden to meet, except for the choice of officers; there must be no deliberation; "discussion must be suppressed." He was to levy all the taxes; he

[1] Barillon to Louis XIV. in Fox's Appendix, p. vii., *et seq.* In 1685 Halifax, who had been friendly to the rights of the colonies, was dismissed from his office; Sunderland, their enemy, had a pension from Louis XIV. of £5,000 or £6,000 a year; p. cxxvii., cxxx. *et seq.*, cxliii., cxlviii. Not the last instance of a high functionary pensioned by a foreign hand!

assessed a penny in the pound in all the towns. Rev. John Wise, one of the ministers of Ipswich, advised the people to resist the tax. "Democracy," said he, "is Christ's government in Church and State; we have a good God and a good king; we shall do well to stand to our privileges." One of the Council said, "*You have no privileges left you, but not to be sold as slaves.*" Even that was not likely to last long. The town of Ipswich refused to pay the tax, because invalid; the governor having no authority to tax the people: "they will petition the King for liberty of an assembly before they make any rates." The minister and five others were arrested; they had "obstructed an officer." The Rev. Mr. Wise was guiltiest of all; he did it with a word, an idea. They were brought to Boston, and thrown into jail, "for contempt and high misdemeanors." They claimed the *habeas corpus;* Chief Justice Dudley refused it, on the ground that it did not extend to America! They were tried before a packed jury, and such a court as James II. was delighted to honor. The patriots plead the laws of England and Magna Charta. It was all in vain. "I am glad," said the judge to his packed jury, "there be so many worthy gentlemen of the jury, so capable to do the king service; and we expect a good verdict from you, seeing the matter hath been so sufficiently proved against the *criminals.*" The jury of course found them guilty. They were fined from £15 to £50 a piece. The whole cost to the six was over £400. "It is not for his majesty's interest that you should thrive," said one of those petty tyrants,—a tide-water of despotism.[1]

Andros denied the colonial title to lands, claiming that as the charter was declared void, all the lands held under its authority escheated to the crown,—"The calf died in the cow's belly." A deed of purchase from the Indians was "worth no more than the scratch of a bear's paw." "The men of Massachusetts did much quote Lord Coke" for their titles: but Rev. John Higginson, minister of the first church in Salem, the son of the first minister ever ordained in New England,—and ancestor of this noble-hearted man [Rev. T. W. Higginson] who is now also indicted for a "misdemeanor,"—found other laws for their claim, and insisted on the citizens' just and natural right to the lands they had reclaimed from the wilderness.[2] Andros said, "You are either subjects, or else you are rebels;" and in either case, their lands would be forfeit.

Andros hated freedom of speech and of thought. He was to allow no unlicensed printing. Randolph was appointed censor of

[1] 1 Hutch. 316; 2 Hildreth, Hist. 108; 2 Bancroft, 425; Washburn, Judicial Hist. of Mass. 105; Drake's Boston, ch. L.

[2] 1 Felt's Salem, 24; 2 Ib. 542; Felt's Ipswich, 123, *et seq.*; Gage's Rowley, 157, *et seq.;* Sullivan's Land Titles, 54.

the press, and ordered the printer to publish nothing without his approbation, nor "any almanac whatever." There must be but one town meeting in a year, and no "deliberation" at that; no "agitation," no discussion of grievances. There must be no preaching on the acts of the government. Rev. Dr. Increase Mather, one of the ablest men in the Colonies, was the special object of his hate. Randolph advised the authorities to forbid any non-conformist minister to land in New England without the special consent of the governor, and that he should restrain such as he saw fit to silence. The advice was not lost on such willing ears. John Gold, of Topsfield, was tried for "treasonable words," and fined fifty pounds — a great deal more at Topsfield in 1687, than "three hundred dollars" is now in Boston. Rev. Increase Mather had opposed the surrender of the Charter of Massachusetts, and published his reasons; but with such prudence, for he was careful how he "evinced an express liking" for justice, that it was difficult to take hold of him. So the friends of government forged a letter with his name, to a person in Amsterdam. Randolph showed the letter to persons whom he wished to prejudice against the alleged writer. When Mr. Mather learned the facts, he wrote a letter to a friend, clearing himself, and charging the forgery on Randolph or his brother. Randolph brought his action for a libel, claiming £500 damages. But it came to nothing — then. Now times are changed!

Col. Pynchon, of Springfield, one of the officers in this new state of things, was empowered to bind over all persons suspected of riots, "outrageous or abusive *reflecting words and speeches against the government.*" "The spirit of justice was banished from the courts that bore the name."[1]

But notwithstanding the attempt to stifle speech, a great tall minister at Rowley, called Andros "a wicked man!" For that offence he was seized and put in prison! He, also, like Higginson, is represented in this court by one of his own name; and the same inextinguishable religious fire which burned in the bosom of Robert in Old England, and from Samuel in New England flashed into the commissioned face of Andros, now lightens at this bench from the eyes of WENDELL PHILLIPS, who confers new glory on his much-honored ancestor.

Gentlemen of the Jury, you know how this wickedness was brought to an end. If the courts would not decree Justice, there was a rougher way of reaching it, and having it done. Civil war, revolution by violence, came in place of the simple forms of equity, which

[1] 1 Hutch. 327; Washburn, ibid.

the judges had set at nought. William of Orange, a most valiant son-in-law, drove the foul tyrant of Old England from that Island, where the Stuarts have ever since been only "Pretenders;" and on the 19th of April, 1689, the people of Massachusetts had the tyrant of New England put solemnly in jail! We were rid of that functionary for ever, and all such "commissioners" have been held odious in New England ever since the days of Andros. Eighty-six years later came another 19th of April, also famous. Well said Secretary Randolph, "Andros has to do with a perverse people," — they would not bow to such tyranny in 1689. But he afterwards became a quite acceptable governor in Virginia, — where, I doubt not, he has descendants in African bondage at this day.

Catholic James II. sought to establish arbitrary power in America, as in England, by his prerogative — the Omnipotence of the King; he failed; the high-handed despotism of the Stuarts went to the ground. The next attempt at the same thing was by the legislature — the Omnipotence of Parliament — for a several-headed despotism took the place of the old, and ruled at home with milder sway. It tried its hand in America; there were no more requisitions from a king hostile to the Colonies, but acts of Parliament took their place. After the French power in North America had given way, the British government sought to tame down and break in the sturdy son, who had grown up in the woods so big and rough, as obstinate as his father. Here are three measures of subjugation, all flowing from the same fountain of Principle — vicarious government by a feudal superior.

1. All the chief colonial officers were to be appointed by the king, to hold office during his pleasure, to receive their pay from him. Such was the tenure of the executive officers who had a veto on all colonial legislation, and of the judicial officers. Thus the power of making and administering the laws fell from the people distributed everywhere, into the hands of the distant government centralized in the King.

2. A standing army of British soldiers must be kept in the Colonies to overawe the people, and enforce the laws thus made and administered.

3. A revenue was to be raised from the Colonies themselves — from which the King would pay his officers and provide for his army that enforced his laws. The eagle is to feather the arrow which shoots him in mid heaven.

Thus law was a threefold cord wherewith to bind the strong Puritan. But his eyes were not put out — not then. Blindness came at a later day — when he had laid his head in the lap of a not attractive Delilah. With such judges and governors, backed by a standing army of hirelings — how soon would her liberty go down, and the Anglo-American States resemble Spanish America!

In 1760 Francis Bernard was made governor of Massachusetts, and thus officially put at the head of the Judiciary, a man wholly devoted to the Crown, expecting to be made a baronet! He did not wish an annual election of councillors, but wanted the sovereign power to enforce its decrees by violent measures. Thus Thomas Hutchinson was made Chief Justice in 1760, and afterwards Lieutenant-Governor, — continually hostile to the constitution of his native land. Thus Andrew Oliver — "Governor Oliver," "hungry for office and power," was appointed Secretary, Commissioner of Stamps and Lieutenant-Governor; and Peter Oliver — "Judge Oliver" — though not bred a lawyer, was made Chief Justice, the man who refused to receive his salary from the treasury of Massachusetts, preferring the money of the crown which owned him. In the revolutionary times of the *five Judges of Massachusetts four were Tories!*

Accordingly, when the Stamp Act was passed — 22d March, 1765 — there were Judicial officers in the Colonies ready to declare it "constitutional;" executive magistrates ready to carry out any measures intrusted to them. "I will cram the stamps down their throat with the end of my sword," said an officer at New York. Governor Bernard wanted soldiers sent to Boston to enforce submission; so did Hutchinson and "Governor Oliver." The Governor of New York thought, "if *Judges be sent from England*, with an able attorney-general and solicitor-general to *make examples of some very few*, the Colony will remain quiet."[1]

In 1768 John Hancock was arrested at Boston — for a "misdemeanor;" I suppose, "obstructing an officer," or some such offence.[2] The government long sought to procure indictments against James Otis — who was so busy in fencing out despotism — Samuel Adams, and several other leading friends of the colony. But I suppose the judge did not succeed in getting his brother-in-law put on the grand-jury, and so the scheme fell through. No indictment for that "misdemeanor" then. Boston had the right men to do any thing for the crown, but they did not contrive to get upon the grand-jury.

The King, it was George III., in his parliament, spoke of the Patriots of Boston, as "those turbulent and seditious persons." In the House of Commons, Stanley called Boston an "insolent town;" its inhabitants "must be treated as aliens;" its "charter and laws

[1] 5 Bancroft, 358. [2] 6 Bancroft, 213.

must be so changed as to give the King the appointment of the Council, and to the *sheriffs the sole power of returning jurors;*" then the Stamp Act could be carried out, and a revenue raised without the consent of the people. The plan was admirably laid; an excellent counsel! Suppose, as a pure conjecture, an hypothesis of illustration — that there were in Boston a fugitive slave bill court, eager to kidnap men and so gain further advancement from the slave power, which alone distributes the federal offices; suppose the court should appoint its creatures, relatives, nay, its uterine brother — its brother in birth — as fugitive slave bill commissioners to hunt men; and then should get its matrimonial brother — its brother-in-law — on the grand-jury to indict all who resisted the fugitive slave bill! You see, gentlemen, what an admirable opportunity there would be to accomplish most manifold and atrocious wickedness. This supposed case exactly describes what was contemplated by the British authorities in the last century! Only, Gentlemen, it was so unlucky as not to succeed; nay, Gentlemen, as to fail — then! Such accidents will happen in the best of histories!

It was moved in Parliament to address the king "to bring to condign punishment" such men as Otis and Adams and Hancock. Chief Justice Hutchinson declared Samuel Adams "*the greatest incendiary in the king's dominions.*" Hutchinson was right for once. Samuel Adams lit a fire which will burn on Boston Common on the Fourth day of next July, Gentlemen, and on many other commons besides Boston. Aye, in the heart of many million men — and keep on burning long after Hutchinson ceases to be remembered with hate, and Adams with love. "The greatest incendiary!" so he was. Hutchinson also thought there must be "an Abridgment of what are called English Liberties," doubtless the liberty of speaking in Faneuil Hall, and other meeting-houses was one "of what are called English Liberties" that needed speedy abridgment. He wished the law of treason to be extended so that it might catch all the patriots of Boston by the neck. He thought it treasonable to deny the authority of Parliament.[1] Men suspected of "misdemeanors" were to be sent to England for trial! What a "trial" it would have been — Hancock and Adams in Westminster Hall with a jury packed by the government; Thurlow acting as Attorney-General, and another Thurlow growling on the bench and expecting further office as pay for fresh injustice! Truly there would have been an "abridgment of English Liberties." Gentlemen of the Jury, Mr. Phillips and Mr. Higginson in this case are charged with "obstructing an officer." Suppose they were sent to South Carolina to be tried by a jury of Slave-holders, or

[1] 6 Bancroft, 250, 251, 291; Sabine's Loyalists, 207, *et al.*

still worse, without change of place, to be tried by a court deadly hostile to freedom, — wresting law and perverting justice and "enlarging testimony," personally inimical to these gentlemen; suppose that the Slave-hunter whose "process" was alleged to be resisted, was kinsman to the court, and the judge had a near relation put on the jury — what opportunity would there be for justice; what expectation of it? Gentlemen of the Jury, that is the state of things which the despots of England wanted to bring about by sending Hancock and Adams over seas for trial! Bernard, Oliver, and Hutchinson were busy in getting evidence against the Patriots of New England, especially against Adams. Affidavits were sent out to England to prove that he was a fit subject to be transported for "trial" there. And an old statute was found from the enlightened reign of Henry VIII. authorizing that mode of trial in case of such "misdemeanor." Commissary Chew wished that two thirds of the lawyers and printers were shipped off to Africa "for at least seven years." Edes and Gill, patriotic printers in Boston, and "all the authors of numberless treasonable and seditious writings," were to go with them.[1] They were all guilty, very guilty! Gentlemen of the Jury, they committed "misdemeanors," they "obstructed officers," they resisted the process of despotism! But alas —

"The Dog it was that died."

Edes and Gill never saw Africa; the patriotic lawyers and printers made no reluctant voyage to England.

"The Dog it was that died."

Bernard, Hutchinson, Oliver, and their coadjutors went over the seas for punishment after being tried at home by a Law older than the statute of Henry VIII.; a law not yet repealed, Gentlemen, the Higher Law which God wrote ineffaceably in the hearts of mankind; and indignant America pronounced sentence — Tories, Traitors! Commissary Chew learned a lesson at Saratoga in 1777. And the Franklins, the Mayhews, the Hancocks, the Adamses, they also were tried at home, and not found wanting; and the verdict! Gentlemen of the Jury, you know what verdict America has pronounced on these men and their kinsfolk! There is only one spot in the United States where the Hutchinsons, the Olivers, the Bernards are honored, — that is where the Adamses, the Hancocks, the Mayhews, and the Franklins, with the principles of justice they gave their lives to, are held in contempt! Where is the one spot, that speck of foreign dirt

[1] 6 Bancroft, 250, 251, 291; Sabine's Loyalists, 207, *et al.*

in the clean American garden? It is where the Democratic Herod and the Whig Pilate are made friends that they may crucify the Son of Man, the Desire of all nations, the Spirit of Humanity — it is the court of the Fugitive Slave Bill judges, the Gabbatha of the Kidnappers. Look there!

In 1765 it was too late to conquer America. What Andros and Randolph could accomplish in 1686 with their sixty soldiers, could not be done in 1768 with all the red coats Britain could send out: nor in 1778 with all the Hessians she could purchase. The 19th of April, 1689, foretold another 19th of April — as that many to-morrows after to-day! In the House of Lords Camden and Pitt thought Parliament not omnipotent.[1] Samuel Adams declared "Acts of Parliament against natural equity are void;" prayed that "Boston might become a Christian Sparta," and looked to the Law of an Omnipotence somewhat higher than a king or a court. He not only had Justice, but also the People on his side. What came of that last attempt of the last king of New England to establish a despotism here? The same, Gentlemen, which will ultimately come of all such attempts.

Gentlemen of the Jury, there is one great obstacle which despotism has found in Anglo-Saxon lands, steadily opposing its steady attempts to destroy the liberties of the People. It is easy for the controlling power, which represents the Centripetal Tendency of the Nation, to place its corrupt and servile creatures in judicial offices, vested with power to fine, to imprison, and to kill; it is then easy for them to determine on the destruction of all such friends of Justice and Humanity as represent the Centrifugal Tendency of the Nation; and with such judicial instruments it is not difficult to wrest and pervert law in order to crush the Patriots, and construct a word into "Treason," or "evincing express approbation" into a "Misdemeanor," "resisting an officer." And if the final decision rested with such a court, it would be exceeding easy to make way with any man whom the judge's private malignity or the public vengeance of his master, wished to smite and kill. But in the Anglo-Saxon people there is one institution, old, venerable, and well-beloved, which has stood for two thousand years, the great Fortress of Freedom. Thank God, Gentlemen, it still stands. Neither British Kings nor American Slave-drivers have yet brought it to the ground. Of this I must now say a word.

[1] 16 Parl. Hist. 168, 195, 658.

III. Of the Great Safeguard which has been found serviceable in protecting Democratic Institutions and the Rights of Man they are designed to defend. — Of the Trial by Jury.

This is an invaluable protection against two classes of foes to the welfare of mankind.

1. Against such as would commit offences upon the property or persons of men, without law and contrary to the form of law, — against common criminals of all denominations. Against such it is a sword — to resist and punish.

2. Against such as would commit offences upon the property or persons of men, with the form of law and by means of its machinery, — against unjust legislators, corrupt Judges, and wicked magistrates; against such it is a shield defending the public head.

In all the States of Anglo-Saxon origin there are two great popular institutions — Democratic Legislation and Democratic Administration of Law.

In the process of its historical development the first has come to the representative form of democratic legislation, — popular law-making by a body of sworn delegates met in an Assembly, local or federal, subject to a constitution, written or only traditional, which is the People's Power of Attorney, authorizing them to do certain matters and things pertinent to law-making. These are a Jury of general Law-makers.

In its process of historical development, the second has also come to a representative form, that of democratic application of law, popular law-applying, by a body of sworn delegates, that is a Court, subject to a constitution and laws, written or only traditional, which are the People's Power of Attorney authorizing them to do certain matters and things pertinent to law-applying. These are a Jury of special Law-appliers.

Neither of them as yet has reached its perfect and ultimate form; both are still in a state of transition. These two are the most valuable institutional safeguards against unorganized selfishness in the community, — against thieves, robbers, murderers, traitors, and the like; against the organized selfishness which gets into places of delegated power, and would misuse the Form of law so as to prevent the People from attaining the Purpose of law.

There is also a body of men intermediate between the two, — the Law-Explainers, the Judges. Speaking theoretically they are not ultimately either Law-makers or Law-appliers, yet practically, in their legitimate function, they certainly have much to do with both the making and applying of laws. For it is their business, not only to preside at all trials, and determine many subordinate questions of mere form to expedite the process, but also from the whole mass of laws, oral or written, statutes and customs, to select such particular laws as they think require special attention, — this is like the work of law-makers; and also, in their charges to the grand and petty Juries, to suggest the execution thereof in such cases as the times may bring, — this is like the work of the law-appliers.

The good judge continually modifies the laws of his country to the advantage of mankind. He leaves bad statutes, which aim at or would promote injustice, to sleep till themselves become obsolete, or parries their insidious thrusts at humanity; he selects good statutes which enact natural Justice into positive law; and mixes his own fresh instincts of humanity with the traditional institutions of the age. All this his official function requires of him — for his oath to keep and administer the laws binds him to look to the Purpose of Law — which is the Eternal Justice of God, — as well as to each special statute. Besides, after the Jury declares a man guilty, the Judge has the power to fix the quantity and sometimes the quality of his punishment. And the discretion of a great noble man will advance humanity.

In this way a good Judge may do a great service to mankind, and correct the mistakes, or repel the injustice of the ultimate makers and appliers of law, and supply their defects. Thus in England those eminent Judges, Hale, Somers, Hobart, Holt, Camden, Mansfield, and Brougham, have done large service to mankind. Each had his personal and official faults, some of them great and glaring faults of both kinds, but each in his way helped enact natural Justice into positive law, and so to promote the only legitimate Purpose of human legislation, securing Natural Rights to all men. To such Judges mankind owes a quite considerable debt.

But in America the Judge has an additional function; he is to determine the Constitutionality of a law. For while the British King and Parliament claim to be legislatively omnipotent, supreme, the Ultimate human source of law, the Living Constitution of the realm, and therefore themselves the only Norm of law, — howsoever ill-founded the claim may be, — in America it is the People, not their elected servants, who are the Ultimate human source of law, the Supreme Legislative power. Accordingly the People have prepared a written Constitution, a Power of Attorney authorizing their servants to do certain matters and things relating to the government of the nation. This constitution is the human Norm of law for all the servants of the people. So in administering law the Judge is to ask, Is the statute constitutional? does it square with the Norm of law which the People have laid down; or have the legislative servants exceeded their Power of Attorney, and done matters and things which they were not empowered to do? In deciding this question, the Judge is to consider not merely the Provisional Means which the Constitution designates, but also the Ultimate Purpose thereof, the Justice and Liberty which, as its preamble declares, it expressly aims at, and which are also the ideal End of all sound legislation.

There is no country in the world where a great man has so noble a place and opportunity to serve mankind as in America.

But a wicked Judge, Gentlemen, may do great harm to mankind, as I have already most abundantly shown. For we have inherited a great mass of laws, — customary or statutory; the legislature repeals, modifies, or adds to them; the Judge is to expound them, and suggest their application to each special case. The Jury is to apply or refuse to apply the Judge's "law." In all old countries, some of these laws have come from a barbarous, perhaps even from a savage period; some are the work of tyrants who wrought cruelly for their own advantage, not justly, or for the good of mankind; some have been made in haste and heat, the legislature intending to do an unjust thing. Now an unjust Judge has great power to select wicked statutes, customs, or decisions; and in no country has he more power for evil than in the federal courts of the United States. For as in England, when the King-power makes a wicked law, the Judge, who is himself made by that same power, may declare it just, and execute the heinous thing; so in America, when the Slave power enacts a wicked statute, contrary to the purpose of the constitution and to the natural justice of God, the Judge, who is the creature of that same power, may declare it constitutional and binding on all the People who made the constitution as their Power of Attorney. Thus all the value of the constitution to check despotism is destroyed, and the Fortress of Freedom is betrayed into the hands of the enemies of liberty!

But barbarous laws must not be applied in a civilized age; nor unjust laws enforced by righteous men. While left unrepealed, a fair and conscientious Jury will never do injustice, though a particular statute or custom demand it, and a wicked Judge insist upon the wrong; for they feel the moral instinct of human nature, and look not merely to the letter of a particular enactment, but also to the spirit and general purpose of law itself, which is justice between man and man. The wicked Judge, looking only to the power which raised him to his place, and may lift him higher still, — not to that other Hand which is over all, — or consulting his own meanness of nature, selects the wicked laws, and makes a wicked application thereof. Thus in America, under plea of serving the people, he can work most hideous wrong.

Besides, the Judges are lawyers, with the technical training of lawyers, with the disposition of character which comes from their special training and profession, and which marks the manners, the language and looks of a lawyer. They have the excellence of the lawyer, and also his defects. Commonly they are learned in their profession, acute and sharp, circumspect, cautious, skilful in making nice technical distinctions, and strongly disposed to adhere to historical precedents on the side of arbitrary power, rather than to obey the instinctive promptings of the moral sense in their own consciousness. Nay, it seems sometimes as if the moral sense became extinct, and the legal letter took the place of the spirit of Justice which gives life to the People. So they look to the special statute, its technical expositions and applications, but not to Justice, the ultimate Purpose of human law ; they preserve the means and miss the end, put up the bars in the nicest fashion, and let the cattle perish in their pen. Like the nurse in the fable, they pour out the baby, and carefully cherish the wooden bath-tub! The Letter of the statute is the Idol of the Judicial Den, whereunto the worshipper offers sacrifices of human blood. The late Chief Justice Parker, one of the most humane and estimable men, told the Jury they *had nothing to do with the harshness of the statute !* but must execute a law, however cruel and unjust, because somebody had made it a law! How often Juries refuse to obey the statute and by its means to do a manifest injustice; but how rarely does a Judge turn off from the wickedness of the statute to do Justice, the great Purpose of human law and human life! Gentlemen, I once knew a democratic judge — a man with a noble mind, and a woman's nicer sense of right — who told the Jury, " Such is the law, such the decisions; such would be its application to this particular case. But it is unjust; — it would do a manifest and outrageous wrong if thus applied. You as Jurors are to do Justice by the law, not injustice. *You will bring in a verdict according to your conscience.*" They did so. Gentlemen, I should not dare tell you that Judge's name. It would greatly injure his reputation. God knows it — for there is a Higher Law.

When the New York Convention assembled in 1846 to revise the constitution of that State, some powerful men therein felt the evil of having the Court of last Appeal consist wholly of lawyers. Mr. Ruggles thought the judges who reëxamine the decisions and pronounce the final judgment in disputed cases, and determine the constitutionality of laws, should be men who are "brought into direct contact with the people and their business." He wished that of the eight judges of this appellate Court, four should be Justices of the Supreme Court, and four more should be elected by the people on a general ballot, thus securing a popular element in that highest Court.

By this popular element, representing the instinctive Justice of Humanity, he hoped to correct that evil tendency of professional men which leads them away "from the just conclusions of natural reason into the track of technical rules inapplicable to the circumstances of the case, and at variance with the nature and principles of our social and political institutions."[1] "Such judges," said another lawyer, "would retain more of the great general principles of moral justice, . . . the impulses of natural equity, such as . . . would knock off the rough corners of the common law and loosen the fetters of artificial and technical equity."[2]

Commonly in America, as in England, for judges the Federal Government appoints lawyers who have done some party service, or are willing to execute the designs of the great ruling Power, the Slaveholders, regardless alike of the interests of the People and the protestations of the Conscience of Mankind.[3] You know how Hardwicke and Thurlow got their office in England, how they filled it, and what additional recompense followed each added wickedness. Need I mention the name of Americans with a similar history? Gentlemen, I pass it by for the present.

Still further, these judges thus appointed become familiar with fraud, violence, cruelty, selfishness, — refined or brutal, — which comes before them; they study the technicalities of the statutes, balance the scruples of advocates; they lose their fresh intuitions of justice, becoming more and more legal, less and less human, less natural and more technical; their eye is microscopic in its niceness of discrimination, microscopic also in its narrowness of range. They forget the universality of justice, — the End which laws should aim at; they direct their lynx-eyed attention to the speciality of the statutes which is only the Means, of no value save as conducing to that end. Their understanding is sharp as a mole's eye for the minute distinctions of the technicalities of their craft; but, as short-sighted as the mole, they cannot look at justice. So they come to acknowledge no obligation but the legal, and know no law except what is written in Black Letter on parchment, printed in statute-books, reported in decisions; the Law written by God on the soul of man they know not, only the statute and decision bound in pale sheepskin. In the logic of legal deduction — technical inference — they forget the intuition of conscience: not What is right? but What is law? is the question, and they pay the same deference to a wicked statute as a just one. So

[1] Debates in New York Convention, 371, *et al.*

[2] Jordan's Speech, *ibid.*, 447, *et al.* See also Mr. Stow's Remarks, 473, and Mr. Stephens', 474, *et al.* Yet all these four speakers were lawyers.

[3] Hildreth's Despotism in America (1854), 263, *et al.*

the true Mussulman values the absurdities of the Koran as much as its noblest wisdom and tenderest humanity.

Such a man so appointed, so disciplined, will administer the law fairly enough in civil cases between party and party, where he has no special interest to give him a bias — for he cares not whether John Doe or Richard Roe gain the parcel of ground in litigation before him. But in criminal cases he leans to severity, not mercy; he suspects the People; he reverences the government. In political trials he never forgets the hand that feeds him, — Charles Stuart, George Guelph, or the Slave Power of America.

These things being so, in such trials you see the exceeding value of the jury, who are not Office-holders, under obligation to the hand that feeds them; not Office-seekers, willing to prostitute their faculties to the service of some overmastering lust; not lawyers wonted to nice technicalities; not members of a class, with its special discipline and peculiar prejudices; but men with their moral instincts normally active, and unsophisticated humanity in their hearts. Hence the great value of the jury in criminal trials.

Gentlemen, you are the jurors in this case, to decide between me and the government. Between the government and ME! no, Gentlemen, between the Fugitive Slave Bill and Humanity. You know the Function of the court — the manner of the Judges' appointment — the services they are expected to render in cases like this, the services they have already rendered.

Let me speak of the Function of the Jury. To do that, I must say a few words of its Historical Development. I must make it very brief and sketchy. Here I shall point out six several steps in the successive development of popular Law-making and Law-applying.

1. In the barbarous periods of the Teutonic Family,[1] it seems the "whole People" came together at certain regular seasons to transact the business of the nation. There was also a meeting of the inhabitants of each district or neighborhood at stated times, — a "regular meeting;" and sometimes a special meeting to provide for some emergency — a "called meeting." If one man had wronged another the matter was inquired into at those popular meetings. One man presided — chosen for the occasion. In the early age it appears he was a priest, afterwards a noble, or some distinguished man, selected on the spot. The whole people investigated the matter, made the law — often an *ex post facto* law, — applied it to the special case, and

[1] By this term I mean all the nations with language akin to the German.

on the spot administered the punishment — if corporeal, or decreed the recompense — if pecuniary. The majority carried the day. Thus at first the Body of People present on the occasion were the law-makers, the law-appliers, and law-executors. Each law was special — designed for the particular case in hand, retrospective for vengeance more than prospective for future welfare.

2. Then in process of time, there came to be a body of laws — fixed and understood by the People. Partly, these came from the customs of the People, and represented past life already lived; but partly, also, from the decrees of the recognized authorities — theocratic, monarchic, aristocratic, democratic — representing the desire for a better life, a rule of conduct for the future. Then at their meetings, to punish an offender the people did not always make a new law, they simply used what they found already made. They inquired into the fact, the deed done, the law, and applied the general law to the special fact, made their decree and executed it. Thus extemporaneous Making of law for the particular case, gradually passed away, and was succeeded by the extemporaneous Declaration of the law previously made, and its Application to the matter in hand.

3. By and by it was found inconvenient for a multitude to assemble and make the laws, so a body of select men took a more special charge of that function. Sometimes a chief, or king, usurped this for himself; or men were chosen by the people, and took an oath for the faithful discharge of their trust. Thus came popular law-making by sworn delegates, representatives of the people, who had a certain special power of attorney, authorizing them to make laws. These might be Priests — as at the beginning; or Nobles of priestly stock, as at the next stage; or Military Chiefs — as in all times of violence; or powerful Private men, — summoned from the nation, of their own accord undertaking the task, or chosen by the various neighborhoods, — the whole process seems to have been irregular and uncertain, as indeed it must be amongst rude people.

So at that time there were two sources of law-making.

(1.) The unorganized People — the primary source, whose unconscious life flows in certain channels and establishes certain customs, rules of conduct, obeyed before they are decreed, without any formal enactment. These were laws *de facto*.

(2.) The organized Delegates — priestly, kingly, nobilitary, or warlike — the secondary source. These made statute laws. As this was a self-conscious and organized body, having an object distinctly set before its mind and devising means for its purposes, it easily appropriated to itself the chief part of the business of law-making. Statute laws became more and more numerous and important; they were the principal — the customs were only subsidiary, laws *de Jure*, enacted before they are obeyed by the People. Still new customs continued to flow from the primitive source of legislation, the People, and of course took new forms to suit the conditions of national life.

4. Still the people came together to apply the laws — customary or enacted, — to the special cases which occurred. There were fixed periods when they assembled without notice given, — "regular law-days;" and if an emergency occurred, they were summoned on "extraordinary law-days." Here wrongs between party and party, and offences against the public, were set right by the "Country," the "Body of the county," that is, by the bulk of the population. The majority carried the day.

5. At length it was found inconvenient for so large a body to investigate each particular case, or to determine what cases should be presented for investigation.

(1.) So this preliminary examination was delegated to a smaller body of men, sworn to discharge the trust faithfully, who made inquiry as to offences committed, and reported the criminals for trial to the full meeting, the actual "Body of the country." Here, then, is the first organized and sworn "Jury;" "the grand inquest;" — here is popular Indictment by delegates.

(2.) Then it was found inconvenient for a large body — the whole country — to investigate the cases presented. Men were busy with their own work, and did not wish to appear and consume their time. So a smaller body of men was summoned to attend to any special case which was presented by the Grand Inquest. These also were sworn to do their duty. They were to try the men indicted. Here is Trial by sworn delegates, who represent the Body of the People. They were still called the "Country," as any spot of the Atlantic is the "Ocean." Here is the "Trial by Jury." They must be taken from the neighborhood of the parties concerned — for at this stage the jurors were also the witnesses, and other sworn witnesses were not then known. All the Jurors must concur in the vote of condemnation before the magistrate could hurt a hair of the accused's head.

Still after the people had delegated their law-making to one body of sworn representatives, and the twofold function of law-applying, by Indictment and Trial, to other sworn representatives, there was yet a a great concourse of people attending the court on the "law-days;" especially when important matters came up for adjudication; then the crowd of people took sides with Plaintiff or Defendant; with the authorities which accused, or with the man on trial, as the case might be. Sometimes, when the Jury acquitted, the people tore the suspected man to pieces; sometimes when the Jury condemned, they showed their indignation — nay, rescued the prisoner. For the old tradition of actual trial by the "Body of the Country" still prevailed.

6. At length the Jurors are no longer the witnesses in the case.

Others testify before them, and on the evidence which is offered, the Grand-Jury indict or not, and the Trial Jury acquit or condemn. Then the Jurors are no longer taken from the immediate neighborhood of the party on trial, only from his district or county. But sworn witnesses from the neighborhood, depose to the facts. There is no longer a great concourse of people in the open air, but the trial is carried on in a small court house, yet with open doors, in the face of the people, *coram populo* — public opinion still influences the Jury.

As most of the Jurors were unlearned men, not accustomed to intricate questions, it became necessary for the presiding judge, a man of nicer culture, to prepare rules of evidence which should prevent the matter from becoming too complicated for the rustic judgment. Thence came the curious and strange "rules of evidence" which prevail in all countries where trial by Jury is established, but are unknown in lands where the trial is conducted solely by experts, educated men. But as the mass of the people, as in America, become well informed, the old rules appear ridiculous, and will perish.

The number of sworn judges varies in different tribes of the Teutonic family, but as twelve has long been a sacred number with the Anglo-Saxons, that was gradually fixed for the Jury. Twelve consenting voices are indispensable for the indictment or the condemnation.

Such is the form of the Jury as we find it at this day. The other officers have also undergone a change. So, Gentlemen, let me give you a brief sketch of the Historical Formation of the Function of the Judge in nations of the same ethnological origin. Here I shall mention four steps.

1. At the meetings of the people to make, apply, and execute the law, some one must preside to keep order, put the question, and declare the vote. He was the Moderator of the meeting. At first it would seem that some important man, a priest, or a noble, or some other wise, distinguished, or popular man, performed that function. The business over, he dropped into his private place again. A new one was chosen at each meeting.

2. If the former moderator had shown skill and aptness, he was chosen the next time; again and again; at length it was a matter of course that he should preside. He studied the matter, and became "expert in all the manners and customs of his nation." This happens in most of the New England towns, where the same man is Moderator at the town-meetings for many years in succession. Men love to walk in the path they have once trodden, even if not the shortest way to their end.

3. When the nation is organized more artificially and the laws chiefly proceed from the secondary source, the government, — elective or usurpatory — a judge is appointed by the central authority to visit

the districts (counties) and assist at the administration of justice. As the law is now made by the distant delegates, the judge they send down declares and explains it to the people, for they have not made it as before directly, nor found it ready-made, an old inherited custom, but only receive it as the authorities send it down from the Capitol. The law is *written* — the officer can read while they have no copy of the law, or could not read it had they the book. Hence the necessity of a judge learned in the law. Still the people are to apply the written law or apply it not.

Besides, the old customs remain, the unwritten laws of the people, which the judge does not understand so well as they. He represents the written law, the assembly the unwritten custom or tradition. The judge is appointed that he may please the central power; the people are only to satisfy such moral convictions as they have. There is often a conflict between the statute and the custom, a conflict of laws; and still more between the judge and the jury — a conflict in respect to the application of the law.

4. Then comes the critical period of the Trial by Jury. For the deputed judge seeks to enlarge his jurisdiction, to enforce his law, often against the customs and the consciences of the People, the jury, who only seek to enlarge Justice. He looks technically at the statute, the provisional Means of law, not at Justice the ultimate Purpose of law. To the "Country," the "Body of the People," or to the jury of inquest and of trial, he assumes not to suggest the law and its application, but absolutely to *dictate* it to them. He claims the exclusive right to decide on the Law and its Application; the jury is only to determine the Fact — whether the accused did the deed charged or not.

If the judge succeeds in this battle, then tyranny advances step by step; the jury is weakened; its original function is curtailed; certain classes of cases are taken from its jurisdiction; it becomes only the tool of the government, and finally is thrown aside. Popular law-making is gone; popular law-applying is also gone; local self-government disappears and one homogeneous centralized tyranny takes the place of the manifold Freedom of the people. So the trial by jury faded out of all the South-Teutonic people, and even from many regions of the German and Scandinavian North. But the Anglo-Saxon, mixing his blood with Danes and Normans, his fierce kinsfolk of the same family, has kept and improved this ancient institution. When King or Parliament made wicked laws, or appointed corrupt and cruel men for judges, the People have held this old ancestral shield between the tyrant and his victim. Often cloven through or thrust aside, the Saxon Briton never abandons this. The Puritan swam the Atlantic with this on his arm — and now all the Anglo-

Saxon tribe reverences this defence as the Romans their twelve AONCILIA, the mythic shield which "fell from Heaven."[1]

After so much historic matter, Gentlemen, it is now easy to see what is —

THE FUNCTION OF THE JURY AT THIS TIME. Here I make three points.

I. They are to decide the QUESTION OF FACT, the matter charged, and determine whether the accused did the deed alleged to be done. That is the first step — to determine the Fact.

II. They are to decide the QUESTION OF LAW, the statute or custom supposed to apply to the Deed done, and determine whether there is such a statute or custom, and whether it denounces such a Deed as a Crime assigning thereto a punishment. That is the second step — to determine the Law.

III. They are to decide the QUESTION OF THE APPLICATION OF THE LAW TO THE FACT, and to determine whether that special statute shall be applied to the particular person who did the deed charged against him. That is the third step — to determine the Application of the Law.

Gentlemen, I shall speak a few words on each of these points, treating the matter in the most general way. By and by I shall apply these general doctrines to this special case.

I. The jury is to DECIDE THE QUESTION OF FACT; to answer, Did the accused do the deed alleged, at the time and place alleged, with the alleged purpose and producing the alleged result? The answer will be controlled by the Evidence of sworn witnesses, who depose under a special oath to "tell the truth, the whole truth, and nothing but the truth." Their Evidence is the Testimony as to the Fact, — the sole testimony; the jury is the ultimate arbiter to decide on the credibility of the evidence, part by part, and its value as a whole.

Sometimes it is an easy matter to answer this Question of Fact; sometimes exceedingly difficult. If there be doubts they must weigh for the accused, who is held innocent until proven guilty.

With us the theory that the jury is the exclusive judge of the Question of Fact is admitted on all sides. But in England it has often happened that the judge instructs the jury to "*find the facts*" so and so; that is — he undertakes to decide the Question of Fact.

[1] In this brief sketch I do not refer to the authorities, but see, who will, the classic passages and proof-texts in the well-known works of Grimm, Rogge, Biener, Michelsen, Möser, Phillips, Eichhorn, Maurer, and others.

In libel cases it is very common for New England judges to undertake to determine what constitutes a libel, and to decide on the intentions of the accused; that is to decide the most important part of the complex and manifold Question of Fact. For it is as much a question of fact to determine what constitutes a libel, as what constitutes theft, the *animus libellandi* as much as the *animus furandi*. Sometimes juries have been found so lost to all sense of manhood, or so ignorant of their duties, as to submit to this judicial insolence and usurpation.

If the Jury decide the Question of Fact in favor of the accused, their inquiry ceases at that step, they return their verdict, "NOT GUILTY;" and the affair is ended. But if they find he did the deed as charged, then comes the next function of the Jury.

II. The Jury are to DECIDE THE QUESTION OF LAW. Is there a statute or custom denouncing a penalty on that special deed? is the statute constitutional? To determine this matter, there are three sources of evidence external to their own knowledge.

1. *The Testimony of the Government's Attorney.* The Government itself is his client, and he gives such a statement of the law as suits the special purposes of the rulers and his own private and particular interest, selects such statutes, customs, and decisions, as will serve this purpose, and declares, Such is the law. Nay, he makes inferences from the law, and thereby infers new customs, and constructs new statutes, invents new crimes. He treats the law as freely as he treats the facts — making the most that is possible against the party accused. You have seen already what tricks Government attorneys have played, how they pervert and twist the law — making it assume shapes never designed by its original makers. He gives his opinion as to the law, as he gave an opinion as to the fact. This is not necessarily his personal and actual, but only his official and assumed opinion — what he wishes the Jury to think is law in this particular case.

2. *The Testimony of the Defendant's Attorney.* The accused is his client. He is to do all he can to represent the law as favorable as possible to the man on trial. He gives an opinion of the law, not his personal and actual, but his official and assumed opinion — what he wishes the Jury to think is law in this particular case.

3. *The Testimony of the Judge on the Bench.* But in the English courts, and the Federal courts of the United States, he is commonly no more than a government attorney in disguise; I speak only of the general rule, not the exceptions to it. He has received his office as the reward for party services — was made a judge because he was one-sided as a lawyer. In all criminal cases he is expected to twist the law to the advantage of the hand that feeds him. Especially is this so in all Political trials — that is, prosecutions for opposition to

the party which the judge represents. The judge may be impartial, or partial, just or unjust, ignorant or learned. He gives an opinion of the law, — not his personal and actual, but his official and assumed opinion — what he wishes the jury to think is law in this particular case. For the court also is a stage, and the judges, as well as the attorneys, may be players,

"And one man in his time play many parts."

Of these three classes of witnesses, no one gives evidence under special oath to tell the law, the whole law, and nothing but the law — or if it be so understood, then all these men are sometimes most grossly and notoriously perjured; but each allows himself large latitude in declaring the law. The examples I have already cited, show that the judge often takes quite as wide a range as the attorney-general, or the prisoner's counsel.

As the jury hears the manifold evidence as to the facts, and then makes up its mind thereon and decides the Question of Fact, often rejecting the opinion of various witnesses, as ignorant, partial, prejudiced, or plainly false and forsworn; so will the jury hear the manifold and often discrepant evidence as to the law, and then make up their mind thereon and decide the Question of Law, often rejecting the opinion of various witnesses thereupon as ignorant, partial, prejudiced, or plainly false and forsworn.

In regard to the Fact, the jury is limited to the evidence adduced in court. What any special juror knows from any other source is not relevant there to procure conviction. But in regard to the Law there is no such restriction; for if the jury know the law better than these three classes of witnesses for it in court, then the jury are to follow their better knowledge. At any rate, the jury are to make up their minds on this question of Law, and for themselves determine what the special Law is.

Every man is to be held innocent until proved guilty — until the special Deed charged is proved against him, and until that special deed is proved a Crime. The jury is not to take the government attorney's opinion of the Fact, nor the prisoner's counsel's opinion of the Fact, nor yet the judge's opinion thereon; but to form their own opinion, from the evidence offered to make up their own judgment as to the Fact. So likewise they are not to take the government attorney's opinion of the Law, or the prisoner's counsel's opinion of the Law, nor yet the judge's opinion thereon; but from all the evidence offered, not otherwise known to them, to make up their own judgment as to the Law. After they have done so — if they decide the Law in favor of the accused, the process stops there. The man goes free; for it does not appear that his deed is unlawful. But if the jury find the Law against the deed, they then proceed to their third function.

III. The jury is to decide the QUESTION OF THE APPLICATION OF THE LAW TO THE FACT. Here is the question: "Ought the men who have done this deed against the form of Law to be punished thereby?" The government attorney and the judge are of the opinion that the law should be thus applied to this case, but they cannot lay their finger on him until the jury, specially sworn "well and truly to try and true deliverance make," have unanimously come to that opinion, and say, "Take him and apply the law to him."

The Deed may be clear and the Statute clear, while the Application thereof to the man who did the deed does not follow, and ought not to follow. For

1. It is not designed that the full rigor of every statute shall be applied to each deed done against the letter thereof. The statute is a great sleeping Lion, not to be roused up when everybody passes that way. This you see from daily practice of the courts. It remains in the Discretion of the Attorney to determine what offences he will present to the Grand-Jury,—he passes by many, and selects such as he thinks ought to be presented. It remains in the Discretion of the Grand-Jury to determine whom they will indict, for sometimes when the Fact and Law are clear enough to them, they yet find "no bill" or *ignore* the matter. And after the man is indicted, it still remains in the Discretion of the Attorney to determine whether he will prosecute the accused, or pass him by. Indeed I am told that the very Grand-Jury who found the bills which have brought you and me face to face, hesitated to indict a certain person on account of some circumstances which rendered his unlawful act less deserving of the legal punishment: the Attorney told them he thought they had better find a bill, and he would enter a *nolle prosequi* in court,—plainly admitting that while the Law and the Fact were both clear, that the Grand-Jury were to determine in their Discretion whether they would apply the law to that man, whether they would indict or not; and the Attorney whether he would prosecute or forbear. It remains equally in the Discretion of the Trial Jury to determine whether the man who did the unlawful deed shall be punished—whether the spirit of that statute and the Purpose of Law requires the punishment which it allows.

2. Besides, in deciding this question—the jurors are not only to consider the one particular statute brought against the prisoner, but the whole Complex of Customs, Statutes, and Decisions, making up the Body of Law, and see if that requires the application of this special statute to this particular deed. Here are two things to be considered.

(1.) The general Purpose of the whole Body of Laws, the Object aimed at; and

(2.) The Means for attaining the end. Now the Purpose of Law being the main thing, and the statute only subsidiary to that purpose, the question comes — "Shall we best achieve that Purpose by thus applying the statute, or by not applying it?" This rests with the Jury in their Discretion to determine.

3. Still more, the Jury have consciences of their own, which they must be faithful to, which no official position can ever morally oblige them to violate. So they are to inquire, "Is it right in the sight of God, in the light of our consciences, to apply this special statute to this particular case and thus punish this man for that unlawful deed?" Then they are to ask, also, "Was the deed *naturally wrong;* done from a wrong motive, for a wrong purpose?" If not, then be the statute and the whole complex of laws what they may, it can never be right for a jury to punish a man for doing a right deed, however unlawful that deed may be. No oath can ever make it right for a man to do what is wrong, or what he thinks wrong — to punish a man for a just deed!

But if the twelve men think that the Law ought not to be applied in this case — they find "not guilty," and he goes free; if otherwise, "guilty," and he is delivered over to the judges for sentence and its consequences, and the judge passes such sentence as the Law and his Discretion point out.

The judge commonly, and especially in political trials, undertakes to decide the two last Questions himself, determining the Law and the Application thereof, and that by his Discretion. He wishes to leave nothing to the Discretion of the jury, who thus have only the single function of deciding the Question of Fact, which is not a Matter of Discretion — that is, of moral judgment, — but only a logical deduction from evidence, as the testimony compels. He would have no moral element enter into their verdict. The judge asks the jury to give him a deed of the ground on which he will erect such a building as suits his purpose, and then calls the whole thing the work of the jury, who only granted the land!

But this assumption of the judges ultimately and exclusively to decide the question of Law and its Application, is a tyrannous usurpation.

(1.) It is contrary to the fundamental Idea of the Institution of Trial by jury.

(2.) It leads to monstrous tyranny by putting the Property, Liberty, and Life of every man at the mercy of the government officers, who determine the Law and its Application, leaving for the jury only the bare question of Fact, which the judge can so manage in many cases as to ruin most virtuous and deserving men.

(3.) Not only in ancient times did the jury decide the three questions of Fact, of Law, and of its special Application, but in cases of great magnitude they continue to do so now, in both America and England, and sometimes in direct contradiction to the commands of the judges.

Gentlemen of the Jury, if you perform this threefold function, then you see the exceeding value of this mode of trial,

1. For the punishment of wrong deeds done against the law, done by the unorganized selfishness of thieves, housebreakers, murderers, and other workers of unrighteousness;

2. And also for the prevention of wrong deeds attempted in the name of law, by the organized selfishness of the makers and officers thereof.

For in each special case brought to trial, the jury are judges of the Law and of its Application. They cannot make a law — statute or custom — nor repeal one; but in each particular case they must demand or forbid its execution. These Tribunes of the Saxon People have no general veto on law-making, and can efface no letter from the statute-book, but have a special and imperative veto on each case for the Application of the law.

Justice, the point common to the interests of all men, yes, the point common to God and our Conscience, is the Aim and Purpose of Law in general; if it be not that the law is so far unnatural, immoral, and of no obligation on the conscience of any man. The special Statute, Custom, or Decision, is a provisional Means to that end; if just, a moral means and adequate in kind; if unjust, an immoral means, inadequate in kind, and fit only to defeat the attainment of that Justice which is the Purpose of all Law. Accordingly, if by an accident, a special statute is so made that its application in a particular case would do injustice and so defeat the Design and Purpose of Law itself, then the function of the jury under their oath requires them to preserve the End of law by refusing to apply the provisional statute to an unjust use. And if by design a statute is made in order to do injustice to any man — as it has very often happened in England as well as America, — then the jury will accomplish their function by refusing to apply that statute to any particular case. So will they fulfil their official oath, and conserve the great ultimate Purpose of Law itself.

Gentlemen, you will ask me where shall the jury find the Rule of Right, and how know what is just, what not? In your own Conscience, Gentlemen; not in the conscience of the Attorney for the

Plaintiff-Government, or the accused Defendant; not in the conscience of the community; still less in the technical "opinion" of the lawyers, or the ambition, the venality, the personal or purchased rage of the court. Of course you will get such help as you can find from judges, attorneys, and the public itself, but then decide as you must decide — each man in the light of his own conscience, under the terrible and beautiful eyes of God. How does the juror judge of the Credibility of Evidence? By the "opinion" of the lawyers on either side? by the judge's "opinion," or that of the community? No one would dare determine thus. He decides personally by his own common sense, not vicariously by another's opinion. And as you decide the Matter of Fact by your own Discretion of Intellect, so will you decide the Matter of Right by your own Discretion of Conscience.

Gentlemen, when the jury do their official duty it becomes impossible to execute a statute, or custom, or to enforce a decision which the jury — "the country" — think unjust and not fit to be applied.

But if the judge usurps these two functions of the jury, and himself decides the Question of Law and its Application, you see what follows — consequences the most ghastly, injustice in the name of Law, and with the means of Law! Yes, tyranny spins and weaves with the machinery of Freedom, and a Nessus-shirt of bondage is fixed on the tortured body of the People. The power of the judge will be especially dangerous in times of political excitement, and in political trials.

Gentlemen, this matter is so important, and the danger now so imminent that you will pardon me a few words while I set forth the mode by which this wickedness goes to work, and what results it brings to pass. Follow me in some details.

I. As to the judges dealing with the Grand-Jury.

Here let me take the examples from the circuit court of the United States in a supposed case where a man is to be tried for violating the fugitive slave bill. You will see this is a case which may actually happen.

1. The judge challenges the whole body summoned as grand-jurors and catechizes them after this fashion.

(1.) "Have you formed an opinion that the law of the United States, known as the Fugitive Slave Law of 1850, is Unconstitutional, so that you cannot indict a person under it for that reason, although the court holds the statute to be Constitutional?"

This is riddling No. 1. Such as think the fugitive slave bill unconstitutional are at once set aside. The judge proceeds to ask such as have no doubt that it is constitutional,

(2.) "Do you hold any opinions on the subject of Slavery in

general, or of the Fugitive Slave Law in special, which would induce you to refuse to indict a man presented to you for helping his brother to freedom?"

This is riddling No. 2; other "good men and true" are rejected, but some are found "faithful" to the purposes of the court; and the judge puts his next question,

(3.) "Will you accept for Law whatever the court declares such?"

This is riddling No. 3. Still the judge finds three-and-twenty men small enough to pass through all these sieves. They are to be "the jury." All the men who deny the constitutionality of the wicked statute; all who have such reverence for the unalienable Rights of man and for the Natural Law of God that they would not prevent a Christian from aiding his brother to escape from bondage; all who have such respect for their own manhood that they will not swear to take a judge's word for law before they hear it — are shut out from the "grand inquest;" they are no part of the "Country," or the "Body of the county," are not "good men and true."

Gentlemen of the Jury, consider the absurdity of swearing to take for law what another man will declare to be law, and before you hear it! Suppose the judge should be drunk and declare the fugitive slave bill in perfect harmony with the Sermon on the Mount, those noble words "Whatsoever ye would that men should do unto you, do ye even so unto them," — are jurors to believe him? What if the judge should be sober, and declare it a "misdemeanor" to call the fugitive slave bill a wicked and hateful statute, and all who thus offended should be put in jail for twelve months! Are honest men to take such talk for American law?

The jurors then take this oath which the clerk reads them: —

"You, as a member of this Inquest for the District of Massachusetts, shall diligently inquire and true presentment make of all such matters and things as shall be given you in charge; the counsel of the United States, your fellows', and your own you shall keep secret; you shall present no man for envy, hatred, or revenge; neither shall you leave any man unpresented — for love, fear, favor, affection, or hope of reward; but you shall present things truly as they come to your knowledge, according to the best of your understanding. So help you God!"[1]

Then the judge appoints the most pliant member of the jury as "foreman" — selecting, if possible to find him, some postmaster or other official of the government, or some man marked for his injustice or venality, who may have the desirable influence with his fellows.

2. The next thing is to moisten this material thus trebly sifted, and

[1] See other forms of Oath in 8 St. Tr. 759, 772.

mould it into such vessels of tyranny as he can fill with his private or judicial wrath and then empty on the heads of his personal foes or such as thwart his ambitious despotism or the purposes of his government. So he delivers his CHARGE TO THE GRAND-JURY.

By way of introduction, he tells them —

(1.) That they are not the Makers of Law. Legislation is the function of Congress and the President; even the COURT, the "SUPREME COURT OF THE UNITED STATES" itself cannot make a law, or repeal one!

(2.) That they are not the Declarers, or Judges of Law. To know and set forth the Law is the function of the COURT. It is true every man in his personal capacity, as private citizen, is supposed to know the law, and if he violates it, of his own presumption, or by the persuasion of some others who falsely tell him about the law, he must be punished; for "*ignorantia nemini excusat*," ignorance excuseth none; the private advice of the full bench of judges would be held no excuse. But in their official capacity of jurors they are supposed to know nothing of the Law whatsoever.

It seems taken for granted that though one of the Jurors may be an old judge of the Supreme Court of the United States, and have sat on the bench for twenty years; nay, though he may be also an old legislator of twenty years' standing, and as legislator have made the very statute in question, and also as judge subsequently have explained and declared it, yet the moment he takes the oath as Grand-Juror, all this knowledge is "gone from him" as completely as Nebuchadnezzar's dream. The court is the assembly of magicians, astrologers, sorcerers, and Chaldeans to restore it. Congress might pass a law compelling ex-judges, ex-senators, and ex-representatives — who are so numerous now-a-days, and continually increasing and likely to multiply yet more, — to serve as grand-jurors; soon as they take their oath, they are in law held and accounted to be utterly ignorant of law, and bound to accept as law whatsoever the court declares such. The acting judge may be young, blind, ignorant, ambitious, drunk with brandy or rage, he may have a personal interest in promoting the law, and may notoriously twist it so as to gratify his peculiar or familistic spleen, still the jury is to accept the court's opinion for the nation's law. Any political ignoramus, if hoisted to the "bench," has judicial authority to declare the law, — it is absolute. If he errs, "he is responsible to the proper authorities — he may be removed by impeachment;" but the jury must not question the infallibility of his opinion. For though the grand-jury is "the country," the judge is not only all that, and more so; but is "the rest of mankind" besides.

Then the judge goes further — talks *solemnly*, yet familiar; to wheedle jurors the better, he mixes himself with them, his "WE" embracing both judge and jury. I shall now quote actual language used in this very court, by the late Hon. Judge Woodbury: —

"One of the peculiar dangers . . . to which jurors, as well as judges, are exposed, is the *unpopularity, or obnoxiousness* . . . of any particular law, which has been violated, leading *us* . . . to be timid or unfaithful in enforcing it . . . the subject-matter being a delicate or offensive one." "While we . . . are holding the scales as well as the sword of Justice, in *humble imitation of the Divine Judge* on high," it is our duty to "*let law, as law,* [that is, whether it is just or unjust] *reign supreme,* reign equally over all, and as to *all things,* no less than persons; and till it is changed by the proper authorities, *not to interpose our individual caprices or fancies or speculations* [that is, our *convictions of justice*] *to defeat its due course and triumph.*" We must *not* "*disregard laws,* when disliked, *because we can,* under the universal suffrage enjoyed here, *otherwise help* legally *to change or annul them* by our votes." "As jurors *you have sworn to obey them till so changed,* and ought to stand by them faithfully, to the last moment of their existence." "We are safest in our capacity of public officers . . . to execute the laws as they are [right or wrong], *while others* who may make or retain bad laws in the statute-book, *are answerable for their own wrong.* If they preserve laws on the statute-book, which are darkness rather than light and life to the people, theirs is the fault, [that is, if a blacksmith make a dagger, and tell us to stab an innocent man with it, we must obey, and the blame will rest on the blacksmith who made the dagger, not on the assassin who murdered with it!] In some cases, also, when we think the *existing laws and punishments are wrong,* and hence venture to encourage others in disobedience by neglecting to indict and punish offenders, it should make us pause and halt when it is remembered, it may turn out that *we* ourselves *may not be exactly Solons or Solomons* in these respects, nor quite so much wiser than the laws themselves, as sometimes we are hastily induced to suppose." "Miserable must be the fate of that community where the ministers of the law are themselves disposed to disregard it;" "government will become a curse;" "and this whether such a *betrayal of public trust* springs from the *delusions of false philanthropy or fanatical prejudices, no less than when it comes from unbridled licentiousness.*"

"We must not lay the flattering unction to our souls, that because by some *possibility there may not be guilt,* we can rightfully discharge as if there were no guilt." "It is sometimes urged against agreeing to indict, convict, or punish, that we have *conscientious scruples on the subject;*" "if sincere tenderness of conscience presses on the heart and mind against executing some of the laws, *it should lead us to decline office or resign;* not to neglect or disobey, while in office, what we have promised and sworn to perform;" [as if the juror swore to do injustice!] "or if a majority prove unaccommodating or inflexible against us, then it behooves those differing from them . . . *to withdraw entirely from such a government, and emigrate.*" [So the juror must not try to do justice at home, but seek it in exile.] "But in all such cases we must take special care not to indulge ourselves in considering an act as a sin which *is only disagreeable,* or the result of only some *prejudice or caprice.*" "*The presumptions are that all laws,* sanctioned by such intelligent, numerous, and respectable members of society as compose our legislative bodies, *are constitutional,* and until pronounced otherwise by the proper tribunal, the judiciary, *it is perilous for jurors to disobey them,*" [that is, to refuse to execute them] "and it is trifling with their solemn obligations to *disregard them in any way and on any occasion, from constitutional doubts,* unless of the clearest and strongest character." [1]

1 The above extracts are from Judge Woodbury's charge to the Grand-Jury, in Circuit Court of United States, at Boston, taken from the *Evening Traveller,* copying the reprint of Boston Daily Advertiser, of October 25, 1850.

He then tells them that *no feeling of Humanity* must be allowed to prevent them from executing any law which the court declares to them, "whether the statute is a harsh one, is not for us to determine."[1] *A cruel law is to be enforced as vigorously as a humane one; an unjust law* as a *just one;* a statute which aims to defeat the purpose of Law itself, just as readily as one which aims to secure the dearest rights of humanity. If the statute is notoriously wicked, as in the case supposed, then the Judge says: "It is to be observed that this statute [the fugitive slave bill] subjects no person to arrest who was not before liable to be seized and carried out of the State;" "Congress has enacted this law. *It is imperative, and it will be enforced.* Let no man mistake the mildness and forbearance with which the criminal code is habitually administered, [as in cases of engaging in the slave-trade] for weakness or timidity. *Resistance [to the fugitive slave bill] must make it sternly inflexible.*" "As great efforts have been made to convince the public that the recent law [the fugitive slave bill] cannot be enforced with a good conscience, but may be conscientiously resisted . . . I deem it proper to advert, briefly, to *the moral aspects* of the subject." "The States without the constitution would be to each other foreign nations." "Those, therefore, who have the strongest convictions of the *immorality of the institution of slavery*, are not thereby authorized to conclude that the *provision for delivering up fugitive slaves is morally wrong*, [that is, if it be wrong to hold man in bondage, it is also not wrong,] or that our Fathers . . . did not act wisely, justly, and humanely in acceding to the compacts of the Constitution." "Even those who go to the extreme of condemning the Constitution and the laws made under it, as *unjust and immoral*, cannot . . . justify resistance. In their view, such laws are inconsistent with the justice and benevolence and against the will of the Supreme Lawgiver, and they emphatically ask, '*Which shall we obey, the law of man, or the Will of God?*' I answer, 'OBEY BOTH!' The *incompatibility* which the question assumes [between *Right and Wrong, or Good and Evil, or God and the Devil*] *does not exist!* Unjust and oppressive laws *may indeed be passed* by human governments. But if *Infinite and Inscrutable Wisdom permits political society*, having the power of human legislation, *to establish such laws, may not the same Infinite and Inscrutable Wisdom permit and require an individual*, who has no such power, *to obey them?*" [So "if Infinite and Inscrutable Wisdom permits" a Blacksmith

[1] Words of Chief Justice Parker, in *Commonwealth* vs. *Griffith*, 2 Pickering's Reports, 19, cited with approbation by Chief Justice Shaw, in the Sims case, 7 Cushing's Reports, 705, and also cited from him and acted on by fugitive slave bill Commissioner Loring, in the Burns case.

"having the power" to forge steel and temper it, to make daggers, "may not the same Infinite and Inscrutable Wisdom permit and require the individual" carpenter or tailor, who has no such power, to use the dagger for the purpose intended!] "Conscience, indeed, is to be reverenced, and obeyed; but still we must remember that it is *fallible*, especially when the rights of others are concerned, [that is, the right to kidnap men] *and may lead us to do great injustice*, [by refusing to punish a man who helps his brother enjoy his self-evident, natural, and unalienable right to life, liberty, and the pursuit of happiness]. The annals of the world abound with enormities committed by a narrow and darkened conscience." A *statute* "is the moral judgment, the *embodied conscience of the political community*, [the fugitive slave bill the 'embodied conscience' of New England]. To this not only is each individual bound to submit, [right or wrong,] but it is a new and *controlling element in forming his own moral judgment;*" [that is, he must *think* the statute is just]. "Obedience is a *moral duty*, [no matter how immoral the law may be]. *This is as certain as that the Creator made man a social being;*" "to *obey the laws of the land* [no matter what laws, or how wicked soever] *is, then, to obey the Will of God!*"

Gentlemen of the Jury, you think I have imagined and made up this language out of my own fancy. No, Gentlemen, I could not do it. I have not the genius for such sophistry. I only quote the words of the Hon. Judge Peleg Sprague delivered to the grand-jury of this Circuit Court of United States at Boston, March 18, 1851.[1] Gentlemen, I showed you what Thurlow could say at Horne Tooke's trial on the 4th of July, 1777. Nay, I quoted the words of Powis and Allybone, and Scroggs and Jeffreys.[2] But, Gentlemen, the judge of New England transcends the judges of Old England.

3. Having made this general preparation for his work and shaped his vessel to the proper form, he proceeds to fill it with the requisite matter.

(1.) He practically makes the Law just as he likes, so as to suit the general purpose of the government, or the special purpose of his private vengeance or ambition. Thus,

a. Out of the whole complex of law — statutes, decisions, customs, charges, opinions of judicial men, since the Norman conquest or before it, — he selects that special weapon which will serve his present turn. And tells the jury, "that is the law which you are sworn to enforce. I have not made it — it is the *Lex terræ*, the Law of the

[1] See *Boston Daily Advertiser* of March 19, 1851.

[2] See above, p. 33, 37, *et al.*

Land." Or if in such an arsenal, so copious, he finds no weapon ready made, then

b. Out of that pile of ancient instruments he selects something which he forges over anew, and thus constructs a new form of law when he could not find one ready for his hand. If a straight statute will not catch the intended victims he perverts it to a hook and therewith lays hold. He thus settles the law.

(2.) He next practically determines what Deed constitutes the "offence" forbidden by the law he has just made. So he selects some act which it is notorious was done by the man he strikes at, and declares it is the "offence," the "crime." Here too he is aided by ancient precedent; whereof if our brief Republican annals do not furnish examples, he hies to the exhaustless treasury of Despotism in the English common law. He opens the "Reports," the "Statutes of the Realm," or goes back to the "Year-books." Antiquity is rich in examples of tyranny. "He readily finds a stick who would beat a dog." "Such are the opinions," quoth he, "of the venerable Chief Justice Jones," or "my Lord Chancellor Finch," or "Baron Twysden," or "my Lord Chief Justice Kelyng."

Thus the Judge constructs the Jury — out of such men as he wishes for his purpose; constructs the Law, constructs the Offence, the Crime: nay, he points out the particular Deed so plain that he constructs the Indictment. All that is left for the "Grand Inquest" is the mechanical work of listening to the "evidence" and signing the Bill — "*Billa Vera*," a true bill. That they may accomplish this work he delivers them over to the District Attorney; he may be also an agent of the government, appointed for his party services, looking for his reward, expecting future pay for present work, extra pay for uncommon zeal and "discretion." Gentlemen of the Jury, this *may* be the case — humanity is fallible, and it sometimes may happen even in the Circuit Court of the United States that such a man should hold the office of District Attorney. For it is not to be expected, nay, it is what we should not even ask — that this place should always be filled by such conspicuous talent, such consummate learning, and such unblemished integrity as that of the present attorney (Hon. Mr. Hallett). No, Gentlemen of the Jury, as I look round these walls I am proud of my country! Such a District Attorney, so bearing "his great commission in his look;" his political course as free from turning and winding as the river Missouri; high-minded, the very Cæsar's wife of democratic virtue, — spotless and unsuspected; never seeking office, yet alike faithful to his principles and his party; and with indignant foot spurning the Administration's bootless bribe, — the fact outtravels fancy. Nay, Gentlemen, it is something to be an American — I feel it as I look about me. For the honorable Attorney is perfectly suited to this Honorable Court; — yea, to the Administration which gives them both their dignity and their work and its pay. Happy country with such an Attorney, fortunate with such a Court, but thrice and four times fortunate when such several stars of justice unite in such a constellation of juridic fire!

But, Gentlemen, it is too much to ask of human nature that it should be always so. In my supposed case, the judge delivers the persons accused to the officers, restless, bellowing, and expecting some fodder to be pitched down to them from the national mow, already licking their mouths which drool with hungry anticipation. They will swear as the court desires. Then the Attorney talks with the most pliant jurors, coaxes them, wheedles them, stimulates them to do what he wants done. Some he threatens with the "displeasure of the government;" he swears at some. After all, if the jury refuse to find a bill, — a case, Gentlemen, which has happened, — they are discharged; and a new jury is summoned; some creature of the government is put on it, nay, perhaps some kinsman of the anxious judge, at least a Brother-in-Law, and at last twenty-three men are found of whom twelve consent to a "True Bill." Then great is the joy in the judge's heart, — it is corrupt judges I am speaking of, Gentlemen of the Jury, not of upright and noble men, may it please your Honors! There is great joy in the judge's heart, and great rejoicing *amongst his kinsfolk and intimate friends* who whinney and neigh over it in the public journals, and leer at the indicted man in the street, lolling out their tongues greedy for his vengeance!

II. Now, Gentlemen, look next at the judge's dealing with the Trial-Jury. He proceeds as before.

1. He sifts the material returned to him, through those three sieves of questioning, and gets a Jury with no hard individual lumps of solid personal independence. They take the oath which you have just taken, Gentlemen: "You shall well and truly try the issue between the United States and the Defendant at the Bar, according to the law, and the evidence given you, so help you God!"

The facts are then presented, and the case argued on both sides.

2. The Judge sums up, and charges the Jury. He explains their oath; to try the issue *according to the law* does not mean (a) according to the whole complex which is called "*Law*," or "*The Law*," but according only to that particular statute which forbids the deed charged, — for otherwise the Jury must judge of the Purpose of Law, which is Justice, and inquire into the rightfulness of the deed and of the statute which forbids it. Nor does it mean (b) by the Jurors' notion of that statute, but only by the Judge's opinion thereof. He

tells them — if they proceed to inquire into the natural Justice of the deed, or into the law which forbids it, then they transcend their office, and are guilty of "Perjury," and reads them the statute for the punishment of that offence, and refers to examples — from the times of the Stuarts, though he does not mention that — when Jurors were fined and otherwise severely dealt with for daring to resist a judge.

Then out of the facts testified to by the government witnesses, he selects some one which is best supported, of which there is no doubt. He then declares that the question of "Guilty or not guilty" turns on that point. If the accused did that deed — then he is Guilty. So the moral question, "Has the man done a wrong thing?" is taken from their consideration; the intellectual question, "Has he done a deed which amounts to the crime forbidden?" is not before them; only the mechanical question, "Did he do that particular act?" They are not to inquire as to the Justice of the law, its Constitutionality, or its Legality; nor the Justice or the Criminality of the deed — only of its Actuality, Did he do this deed? Nay, sometimes the Judge treats them as cattle, and orders them to *find the facts for the government.* If they refuse, he threatens them with punishment.

Thus he constructs the Trial-Jury, the Law, the Evidence, the Crime, and the Fact.

Now, Gentlemen, when this is done and done thoroughly, the Judge has kept all the Forms, Presentment by the Grand-Jury, and Trial by a Petty Jury; but the substance is all gone; the Jury is only a stalking horse, and behind it creeps the Judicial servant of Tyranny, armed with the blunderbuss of law, — made and loaded by himself, — and delivers his shot in the name of law, but against Justice, that purpose of all law. Thus can tyranny be established — while all the forms of law are kept.[1]

Gentlemen of the Jury, let me make this more clear by a special case wholly fictitious. — Thomas Nason, a "Non-Resistant" and a Quaker, is a colored citizen of Boston, the son and once the slave of Hon. James Nason of Virginia, but now legally become a free man by self-purchase; he has the bill of sale of himself in his pocket, and so carries about him a title deed which would perhaps satisfy your Honors of his right to liberty. But his mother Lizzie (Randolph) Nason, a descendant of both Mr. Jefferson and Mr. Madison, — for Virginia, I am told, can boast of many children descended from two Presidents, perhaps from three, who

> "Boast the pure blood of an illustrious race,
> In quiet flow from Lucrece to Lucrece" —

[1] See 1 Jardine, Criminal Trials, 110. 2 Parker's Sermons, 266 and note.

from Saxon master to African slave, — is still the bondwoman of the Hon. James, the father of her son Thomas. From the "Plantation manners" of her master, the concubine, "foolishly dissatisfied with slavery," flies to Boston, and takes refuge with her Quaker son, who conceals his mother, and shelters her for a time. But let me suppose that his Honor Judge Curtis, while at Washington, fired with that patriotism which is not only habitual but natural and indigenous to his Honor, informs Mr. Nason of the hiding-place of his female slave, thus betraying a "mistress" to her master, no longer, alas, her "keeper." It is no injurious imputation — it is an imaginary honor I attribute to the learned and honorable Judge. Mr. Nason sends the proper agent to Boston to save the Union of States by restoring the union of master and slave. Mr. George Ticknor Curtis, fugitive slave bill commissioner, and brother to the Hon. Judge, issues his warrant for kidnapping the mother; his coadjutor and friend, Mr. Butman, attempts to seize her in her son's house. Thomas, unarmed, resists the intruder, and with a child's pop-gun drives that valiant officer out of the house, and puts the mother in a place of safety, — beneath the flag of England, or the Pope, or the Czar. Commissioner Curtis telegraphs the news to Washington, — announcing a "NEW CASE OF TREASON — more 'levying war!'" The Secretaries of State and of War write dreadful letters, breathing fire and slaughter, and President Pierce, a man of most heroic courage, alike mindful of his former actual military exploits at Chapultepec, of his delegated triumph at Greytown, and of the immortal glory of Mr. Fillmore, issues his Proclamation, calling on all good citizens, and especially on the politicians of his party, to "Save the Union" from the treason of this terrible Thomas Nason, who will blow up the Constitution with a pop-gun!

At the next session of the Honorable Circuit Court of the United States in and for the first District, his Honor the Hon. Benjamin Robbins Curtis, Judge, constructs and charges the Grand-Jury in the manner already set forth. He instructs them that if any man, by force and arms, namely, with a pop-gun, does resist a body of United States officers, attempting to kidnap a woman, his own mother, that he thereby levies war against the United States, and accordingly commits the crime of "Treason" which consists in levying war against the United States — the "*amount* of force is not material." And it is their duty to indict all persons in that form offending. The Attorney, the Hon Benjamin Franklin Hallett, offers to "bet ten dollars that I will get" Nason "indicted," and urges the matter. But no bill is found, the Jury is discharged, a new Jury is summoned, and Mr. William W. Greenough, the Brother-in-law of the Judge is put on it, "drawn as Juror"—and then a "true bill" is found, Mr. Hallett actually making an indictment that cannot be quashed!

On the day before Thanksgiving Thomas Nason is arraigned; and is brought to trial for this new Boston Massacre on the anniversary of the old one—on the Fifth of March. The judge constructs a Trial-Jury as before. Mr. Hallett, assisted by Mr. Thomas, Mr. George T. Curtis, and Commissioner Loring, manage the case for the government, bringing out the whole strength of the kidnapping party, and directing this Macedonian phalanx of Humanity and Law and Piety against a poor friendless negro. Mr. Hale, Mr. Ellis, and Mr. Dana defend him. Officer Butman and his coadjutors—members of the "Marshal's guard"—testify that Mr. Nason attacked them with the felonious weapon above named, putting them in mortal bodily fear greater than that which in Mexico once overthrew the (future) President of all this land! Mr. Herrman, the dealer in toys, testifies that he sold the murderous weapon for twenty-five cents to Mr. Nason who declared that he "could frighten Butman with it;" that it is of German manufacture, and is called a Knallbüchse!

Judge Curtis sums up the matter. He tells the jury, (1.) That they are not to judge of the Law punishing treason, but to take it from the Court. (2.) Not to judge what Act constitutes the Crime of Treason, but take that also from the Court, and if the Court decides that offering a pop-gun at a rowdy's breast constitutes the crime of treason, they are to accept the decision as constitutional law. (3.) They are not to ask if it be just to hang a man for thus resisting a body of men who sought to kidnap his mother, for even if it be unjust and cruel it is none of their concern, for they must execute a cruel and unjust law with even more promptitude than a just and humane one, and in the language of the "Defender of the Constitution," "conquer their prejudices," and "do a disagreeable duty." (4.) If they think the Law commands one thing and the Will of God exactly the opposite, in the well-known words of Judge Sprague, they must "obey both" by keeping the law of man when it contradicts the law of God, for they can never be good Christians so long as they scruple to hang a Quaker for driving off a kidnapper; and obedience to the law is a moral duty, no matter how immoral the law may be, and "to obey the law of the land is to obey the will of God." (5.) But they have a simple question of fact to determine; namely, Did the Defendant resist officer Butman in the manner set forth? If satisfied of that, they must find him guilty. No mistaken notions of Justice must induce them to refuse their verdict—for they are not to make the law, but only help execute it; and their conscience is so "fallible, especially when the rights of others are concerned, and may lead them to do great injustice," for "the annals of the world abound with enormities committed by a narrow and darkened conscience." They must not ask if it be "religious" to do so—for to use the words of the most religious of all Americans, a man of most unspotted life in public and private, "Religion has nothing to do with politics," and this is a political trial. If there be any injustice in the law and its execution the blame lies with the makers thereof not with the jurors, and they may wash their hands as clean as Pilate's from the blood of Christ. Besides, if there be injustice the President can pardon the offender, and from his well-known religious character—which rests on the unbiased testimony of his *own minister* and the statement of several partisan newspapers published in the very heat of the election, when men, and especially politicians looking for office, never exaggerate,—he doubtless "will listen to petitions for a commutation of punishment!"

But there is no injustice in it—for slavery is part of the *lex terræ*, the law of the land, protected by the Constitution itself, which is the *Lex Suprema*—the Supreme Law of the Land, and nearly eighty years old! Besides, "Slavery is not immoral," not contrary to the public policy of Massachusetts; and, moreover, the "mother" whom the criminal actually rescued, was a "foreigner" and "whatever rights she had, she had no right *here*."[1]

But it is not a cruel or an unchristian thing to require a negro layman to allow his mother to be kidnapped in his own house—especially if she were a born slave, and so by the very law "a chattel personal to all uses, intents, and purposes whatever," and of course wholly divested of all natural rights, even if a colored person ever had any—for an eminent American minister, of one of the most enlightened sects in Christendom, has publicly offered to send his own freeborn mother into bondage for ever!

Moreover, if the jurors do not find a verdict of guilty, then they themselves are guilty of PERJURY!

So the jury, without leaving their seats, find him guilty; the judge sentences; the President signs the Death-warrant, and Marshal Freeman hangs the man—to the great joy of the Commissioner's and the Marshal's guard who vacate the brothels once more and attend on that occasion and triumph over the murdered Quaker.

But the mischief does not stop there; the Boston slave-hunters are not yet satisfied with blood; the judge constructs another grand-jury as before, only getting more of his kinsfolk thereon, and taking his law from the impeached Judges Kelyng and Chase, charges that all

[1] See Hon. Judge Curtis's Speech at the Union Meeting in Faneuil Hall, November 26, 1850.

persons who *advise* to an act of levying war, or evince an "*express liking*" for it, or "*approbation*" of it, are also guilty of treason; and "in treason all are Principals." Accordingly the jury must indict all who have evinced an "express liking" of the rescue, though they did not evince approval of the rescue by such means. It appears that Rev. Mr. Grimes in the meeting-house the Sunday before the treason was consummated, had actually prayed that God would "break the arm of the oppressor and let the oppressed go free;" that he read from a book called the Old Testament, "Bewray not him that wandereth," "Hide the outcast," and other paragraphs and sentences of like seditious nature. Nay, that from the New Testament he had actually read the Sermon on the Mount, especially the Golden Rule and the summing of the Law and the Prophets in one word, Love,—and had applied this to the case of fugitive slaves; moreover, that he had read the xxvth chapter of Matthew from the 31st to the 46th verse, with dreadful emphasis.

Nay, anti-slavery men—in lectures—and in speeches in the Music Hall, which was built by pious people—and in Faneuil Hall, which was the old Cradle of Liberty, had actually spoken against man-stealing,—and even against some of the family of kidnappers in Boston!

Still further, he adds, with great solemnity, a woman—a negro woman,—the actual wife of the criminal Nason—had brought intelligence—to her husband—that Mr. George T. Curtis,—the brother of the judge,—had issued his warrant—and Mr. Butman—"with a monstrous watch"—was coming to execute it—she told her husband,—and—incited him to his dreadful crime! If you find these facts you must convict the prisoners.

So thirty or forty more are hanged for treason.

Gentlemen of the Jury, these fictitious cases doubtless seem extravagant to you. I am glad they do. In peaceful times, in the majority of cases there is no disagreement between the law, the judge, and the jurors; the law is just, or at least is an attempt at justice, the judge wishes to do justice by means thereof, and the jurors aim at the same thing. In such cases there is no motive for doing wrong to any person: so the judge fairly interprets the righteous and wholesome law, the jurors willingly receive the interpretation and apply it to the special case, and substantial justice is done. This happens not only in civil suits between party and party, but also in most of the criminal cases between the Public and the Defendant. But in times of great political excitement, in a period of crisis and transition, when one party seeks to establish a despotism and deprive some other class of men of their natural rights, cases like those I have imagined actually happen. Then there is a disagreement between the judge and the jury; nay, often between the jury and the special statute wherewith the government seeks to work its iniquity. It is on such occasions that the great value of this institution appears, — then the jury hold a shield over the head of their brother and defend him from the malignity of the government and the Goliath of injustice, appointed its champion to defy the Law of the living God, is smote in the forehead by the smooth stone taken from a country brook, and lies there slain by a simple rustic hand; for in such cases the jury fall back on their original rights, judge of the Fact, the Law, and the Application of the Law to the Fact, and do justice in spite of the court, at least prevent injustice.

Now, Gentlemen of the Jury, I will mention some examples of this kind, partly to show the process by which attempts have been made to establish despotism, that by the English past you may be warned for the American present and future; and partly that your function in this and all cases may become clear to you and the Nation. The facts of history will show that my fancies are not extravagant.

1. In April, 1554, just three hundred and one years ago this very month, in England, Sir Nicolas Throckmorton, a gentleman of distinguished family, was brought to trial for high treason. He had held a high military office under Henry VIII. and Edward VI., but "made himself obnoxious to the Papists, by his adherence to some of the persecuted Reformers." With his two brothers he attended Anne Askew to her martyrdom when she was burnt for heresy, where they were told to "take heed to your lives for you are marked men." He was brought to trial April 17th, 1554, the first year of Bloody Mary. Of course he was allowed no counsel; the court was insolent, and demanded his condemnation. But the jury acquitted him; whereupon the *court shut the twelve jurors in prison!* Four of them made their peace with the judges, and were delivered: but eight were kept in jail till the next December, and then fined, — three of them £60 apiece, and five £225 apiece.

This is one of the earliest cases that I find, where an English jury in a political trial refused to return such a verdict as the tyrant demanded.[1]

2. In September, 1670, William Penn, afterwards so famous, and William Mead, were brought to trial before the Lord Mayor of Lon-

[1] See the case in 1 St. Tr. 869, and 1 Jardine, 40, also 115. The great juridical attacks upon English Liberty were directed against the Person of the Subject, and appear in the trials for Treason, but as in such trials the defendant had no counsel, the great legal battle for English Liberty was fought over the less important cases where only property was directly concerned. Hence the chief questions seem only to relate to money.

don, a creature of the king, charged with "a tumultuous assembly." For the Quaker meeting-house in Grace Church Street, had been forcibly shut by the government, and Mr. Penn had preached to an audience of Dissenters in the street itself. The court was exceedingly insolent and overbearing, interrupting and insulting the defendants continually. The jury found a special verdict—"guilty of speaking in Grace Church Street." The judge sent them out to return a verdict more suitable to the desire of the government. Again they substantially found the same verdict. "This both Mayor and Recorder resented at so high a rate that they exceeded the bounds of all reason and civility." The Recorder said, "You shall not be dismissed till we have a verdict that the court will accept; you shall be locked up without meat, drink, fire, and tobacco; you shall not think thus to abuse the court; we will have a verdict by the help of God, or you shall starve for it!" When Penn attempted to speak, the Recorder roared out, "Stop that prating fellow's mouth or put him out of court." The jury were sent out a third time, and kept all night, with no food, or drink, or bed. At last they returned a verdict of "not guilty," to the great wrath of the court. *The judge fined the jurors forty marks apiece*, about $140, *and put them in jail* until they should pay that sum. The foreman, Edward Bushel, refused to pay his fine and was kept in jail until he was discharged on *Habeas Corpus* in November. Here the attempt of a wicked government and a cruel judge was defeated by the noble conduct of the jurors, who dared be faithful to their duty.[1]

3. In 1681 an attempt was made to procure an indictment against the Earl of Shaftesbury, for High Treason. The Bill was presented to the Grand-Jury at London; Chief Justice Pemberton gave them the charge, at the king's desire—it was Charles II. They were commanded to *examine the evidence in public* in the presence of the court, in order that they might thus be overawed and forced to find a bill, in which case the court had matters so arranged that they were sure of a conviction. The court took part in examining the witnesses, attempting to make out a case against the Earl. But the jury returned the bill with IGNORAMUS on it, and so found no indictment. The spectators rent the air with their shouts. The court was in great wrath, and soon after the king seized the Charter of London, as I have already shown you, seeking to destroy that strong-hold of Liberty. Shaftesbury escaped—the jury was discharged. Why did not the court summon another jury, and the chief justice put his brother-in-law on it? Roger Coke says, "But as the knights of Malta could make knights of their order for eight pence a piece, yet

[1] 6 St. Tr. 951; Dixon's Life of Penn; 22 St. Tr. 925.

could not make a soldier or seaman; so these kings [the Stuarts] though *they could make what judges they pleased* to do their business, *yet could not make a grand-jury.*" For the grand-juries were returned by the Sheriffs, and the sheriffs were chosen by the Livery, the corporation of London. This fact made the king desire to seize the charter, *then he could make a grand-jury to suit himself*, out of the kinsfolk of the judge.[1]

4. Next comes the remarkable case of the Seven Bishops, which I have spoken of already.[2] You remember the facts, Gentlemen. The king, James II., in 1688, wishing to overturn Protestantism — the better to establish his tyranny — issued his notorious proclamation, setting aside the laws of the land and subverting the English Church. He commanded all Bishops and other ministers of religion to read the illegal proclamation on a day fixed. Seven Bishops presented to him a petition in most decorous language, remonstrating against the Proclamation, and asking to be excused from reading it to their congregations. The king consulted with Father Petre, — a Jesuit, his confessor — on the matter, and had the bishops brought to trial for a misdemeanor, for publishing "a seditious libel in writing against his majesty and his government." It was "obstructing an officer."

Then the question before the trial-jury was, Did the seven bishops, by presenting a petition to the king — asking that they might not be forced to do an act against the laws of England and their own consciences — commit the offence of publishing a seditious libel; and, Shall they be punished for that act? All the judges but two, Holloway and Powell, said "Yes," and the jury were so charged. But the jury said, "Not guilty." The consequence was this last of the Stuarts was foiled in his attempt to restore papal tyranny to England and establish such a despotism as already prevailed in France and Spain. Here the jury stood between the tyrant and the Liberties of the People.

Gentlemen of the Jury, let me show you how that noble verdict was received. Soon as the verdict was given, says Bishop Burnet, "There were immediately very loud acclamations throughout Westminster Hall, and the words 'Not guilty,' 'Not guilty,' went round with shouts and huzzas; thereat the King's Solicitor moved very earnestly that such as had shouted in the court might be committed. But the shouts were carried on through the cities of Westminster and London and flew presently to Hounslow Heath, where the soldiers in the camp echoed them so loud that it startled the king."[3] "Every man seemed transported with joy. Bonfires were made all

[1] 8 St. Tr. 759, see the valuable matter in the notes, also 2 Hallam, 330 and notes.
[2] See above, p. 32.
[3] 12 St. Tr. 430.

about the streets, and the news going over the nation, produced the like rejoicings all England over. The king's presence kept the army in some order. But he was no sooner gone out of the camp, than he was followed with an universal shouting, as if it had been a victory obtained."[1] "When the Bishops withdrew from the court, they were surrounded by countless thousands who eagerly knelt down to receive their blessing." Of course the two judges who stood out for the liberties of the citizens, were removed from office!

5. Here is another remarkable case, that of William Owen, in 1752. These are the facts. In 1750 there was a contested election of a member of Parliament for Westminster. Hon. Alexander Murray, an anti-ministerial member of the Commons, was denounced to the House for his conduct during the election, and it was ordered that he should be confined a close prisoner in Newgate, and that he receive his sentence on his knees. He refused to kneel, and was punished with great cruelty by the bigoted and intolerant House. Mr. Owen, who was a bookseller, published a pamphlet, entitled "The Case of Alexander Murray, Esq.," detailing the facts and commenting thereon. For this an information was laid against him, charging him with publishing a "wicked, false, scandalous, seditious, and malicious libel."

On the trial, the Attorney-General, Ryder, thus delivered himself: —

> "What! — shall a person appeal from that Court, who are the only judges of things belonging to them, the House of Commons I mean. An appeal! To whom? To a mob? Must Justice be appealed from? To whom? To injustice? Appeal to 'the good people of England,' 'particularly the inhabitants of Westminster'! The House of Commons are the good people of England, being the representatives of the people. The rest are — what? Nothing — unless it be a mob. But the clear meaning of this libel was an *appeal to violence*, in fact, and to stigmatize the House." "Then he charges the House with sinking material evidence; which in fact is accusing the House of injustice. This is a charge the most shocking; the most severe, and the most unjust and virulent, against the good, the tender House of Commons; that safeguard of our liberty, and guardian of our welfare."
>
> "This libel . . . will be found the most powerful invective that the skill of man could invent. I will not say the skill, but the wit, art, and false contrivance of man, instigated by Satan;" "to say that this is not a libel, is to say that there is no justice, equity, or right in the world."

The Solicitor-General told the Jury that they were only to inquire *if Mr. Owen published the pamphlet*, "*the rest follows of course;*" "you are upon your oaths; you judge of the facts . . . and *only them*." Chief Justice Lee summed up the evidence "and delivered it as his

[1] Burnet's Own Times, 470. See also 2 Campbell, Justices, 89, *et seq.*

opinion, that the *Jury ought to find the defendant guilty;* for he thought the *fact of publication was fully proved; and if so they could not avoid bringing in the defendant guilty.*"

The jury returned, "Not guilty;" but Ryder, the Attorney-General, put this question, Do you think the evidence is not sufficient to convince you that *Owen did sell the book?* The foreman stuck to his general verdict, "Not guilty," "Not guilty;" and several of the jurymen said, "that is our verdict, my lord, and we abide by it." "Upon which the court broke up, and there was a prodigious shout in the hall." Then "the Jury judged as to facts, law, and justice of the whole, and therefore did not answer the leading question which was so artfully put to them."[1] Of course the insolent Attorney-General was soon made "Lord Chief Justice," and *rode* the bench after the antiquated routine.

This was the third great case in which the Jury had vindicated the right of speech.

6. Here is another case very famous in its day, and of great value as helping to establish the rights of juries, and so to protect the natural right of the citizens — the Trial of John Miller for reprinting Junius's Letter to the King, in 1770.

Here are the facts. Mr. Miller was the publisher of a newspaper called the *London Evening Post*, and therein, on December 19, 1769, he reprinted Junius's celebrated Letter to the King. For this act, an information *ex officio* was laid against him, wherein he was charged with publishing a false, wicked, seditious, and malicious libel. A suit had already been brought against Woodfall, the publisher of the *Public Advertiser*, in which the letter originally appeared, but the prosecution had not turned out to the satisfaction of the government, nor had the great question been definitely settled. So this action was brought against Mr. Miller, who reprinted the original letter the day of its first appearance.[2]

Solicitor-General Thurlow, — whom you have met before, Gentlemen, — opened the case for the Crown, and said: —

"I have not of myself been able to imagine . . . that there is a serious man of the profession in the kingdom who has the smallest doubt whether this ought to be deemed a libel or not;" "for I neither do, nor ever will, attempt to lay before a jury, a cause, in which I was under the necessity of stating a single principle that went to intrench, in the smallest degree, upon the avowed and acknowledged liberty of the subjects of this country, even with regard to the press. The complaint I have to lay before you is that that liberty has been so abused, so turned to licentiousness, . . . that under the notion of arrogating liberty to one man, that is the writer, printer, and publisher of

[1] 18 St. Tr. 1203; 14 Parl. Hist. 888, 1063; 3 Hallam, 200; 2 Campbell, Justices, 198.

[2] 20 St. Tr. 803, 895, 869; Woodfall's Junius (Bohn, 1850), Preface, p. 94, Appendix, p. 471; 2 Campbell, Justices, 363; 5 Mahon.

this paper, they do . . . annihilate and destroy the liberty of all men, more or less. Undoubtedly the man that has indulged the *liberty of robbing upon the highway*, has a very considerable portion of it allotted to him." The defendant "has published a paper, in which, concerning the King, concerning the House of Commons, and concerning the great officers of State, concerning the public affairs of the realm, there are uttered things of such tendency and application as ought to be punished." "When we are come to that situation, when it shall be lawful for any men in this country to speak of the sovereign [George III.] in terms attempting to fix upon him such contempt, abhorrence, and hatred, there is an end of all government whatsoever, and then liberty is indeed to shift for itself." He quotes from the paper: "'He [the king] has taken a decisive personal part against the subjects of America, and those subjects know how to distinguish the sovereign and a venal Parliament, upon one side, from the real sentiments of the English nation upon the other.' For God's sake is that no libel? To *talk of the king as taking a part of an hostile sort against one branch of his subjects*, and at the same time to *connect him . . . with the parliament which he calls a venal parliament*; is that no libel?"

Lord Mansfield,—the bitterest enemy of the citizens' right of speech and of the trial by jury,—charged upon the jury, "The question for you to try . . . is, whether the *defendant did print*, or publish, or both, a *paper of the tenor*, and of the meaning, so *charged by the information*." "If it is of the tenor and meaning set out in the information, the next consideration is, whether he *did print and publish it*." "If you . . . find the defendant not guilty, the fact established by that verdict is, he *did not publish a paper of that meaning*;" "the fact finally established by your verdict, if you find him guilty, is, that *he printed* and published *a paper*, *of the tenor* and of the meaning set *forth in the information*;" "but you do *not give an opinion . . . whether it is or not lawful to print a paper* . . . of the tenor and meaning in the information;" "if in point of fact it is innocent, it would be an innocent thing."

Thus practically the judge left the jury only one thing to determine, Did Mr. Miller print Junius's letter to the king? That was a fact as notorious as it now is in Boston that the *Daily Advertiser* supported the fugitive slave bill, and helped its execution, for the letter to the king was there in Mr. Miller's journal as plainly as those defences of the fugitive slave bill were in the *Advertiser*. If the jury said "guilty," the court had the defendant in their claws,—and all the wrath of the most malignant tories would fall on him and rend him in pieces. But the jury fell back on their legitimate function to determine the Fact, the Law, and the Application of the law to the fact, and returned a verdict, Not Guilty, which a great multitude repeated with loud acclaim!

7. Next, Gentlemen, I will relate a few cases in which the government set all justice at defiance and clove down the right of speech,

commonly packing submissive juries. In 1790 and following years, while the French Revolution was in progress, the thoughtful eyes of England fell on the evils of her own country. America was already a Republic, just recovering from the shock of violent separation from her mother, — young, poor, but not unprosperous, and full of future promise too obvious to escape the sagacious politicians who there saw a cause —

"——— with fear of change,
Perplexing Kings."

The people of France, by a few spasmodic efforts, broke the threefold chain of Priest, King, and Noble, and began to lift up their head. But Saxon England is sober, and so went to work more solemnly than her mercurial neighbor. And besides, the British people had already a firm, broad basis of personal freedom to stand on. Much was thought, written, and spoken about reform in England, then most desperately needing it. The American Revolution had English admirers whom no courts could silence. Nay, at first the French Revolution delighted some of the ablest and best men in Britain, who therein beheld the carrying out of the great Principles which Aristotle and Machiavelli had laid down as the law of the historical development and social evolution of mankind. They wished some improvement in England itself. But of course there was a strong opposition made to all change. Parliament refused to relieve the evils which were made obvious. The upper House of Nobles was composed of the Elder Sons of the families which had a social and pecuniary interest in oppressing the people, and the lower House "consisted mainly of the Younger Sons of the same families, or still worse the purchased dependents" of their families. Societies were organized for Reform, such as the "London Corresponding Society," "the Friends of the People," etc., etc. The last mentioned contained many literary, scientific, and political men, and about thirty members of Parliament. Great complaints were made in public at the inequality of Representation in Parliament. Stormy debates took place in Parliament itself — such as we have not yet heard in America, but which wicked and abandoned men are fast bringing upon us. Pitt and Fox were on opposite sides.

"——— and such a frown
Each cast at the other, as when two black clouds,
With Heaven's artillery fraught, come rattling on
Over the Caspian, then stand front to front,
Hovering a space, till winds the signal blow
To join their dark encounter in mid air."

At that time the House of Commons was mainly filled with creatures of a few powerful men; thus 91 commoners elected 139 members of the commons, and 71 peers also elected 163; so 302 British members of Parliament, besides 45 more from Scotland,— 347 in all, — were returned by 162 persons. This was called "Representation of the People." From the party who feared to lose their power of tyranny, there went out the decree, "Discussion on the subject of national grievances must be suppressed, in Parliament and out of Parliament." Violent attempts were made to suppress discussion. In short, the same efforts were made in England which were attempted in New York and Boston in 1850 and the two following years, till they were ended by a little sprinkling of dust. But in Britain the public mind is harsher than ever in America, and the weapons which broke in the hand of Old England were much more formidable than that which here so suddenly snapped, and with such damage to the assassinating hand.

(1.) In 1792, John Lambert and two others published an advertisement in the London Morning Chronicle, with which they were connected as printers or proprietors, addressed "to the friends of free inquiry and the general good," inviting them in a peaceful, calm, and unbiased manner to endeavor to improve the public morals in respect to law, taxation, representation, and political administration. They were prosecuted, on *ex officio* information, for a "false, wicked, scandalous, and seditious libel." The government made every effort to secure their conviction. But it failed.[1]

(2.) The same year, Duffin and Lloyd, two debtors in the Fleet Prison, one an American citizen, wrote on the door of the prison chapel "this house to let; peaceable possession will be given by the present tenants on or before the first day of January, 1793, being the commencement of liberty in Great Britain. The republic of France having rooted out despotism, their glorious example and success against tyrants renders infamous Bastiles no longer necessary in Europe." They also were indicted for a "wicked, infamous, and seditious libel," and found guilty. Lloyd was put in the pillory![2]

(3.) In 1793, Rev. William Frend, of the University of Cambridge, published a harmless pamphlet entitled "Peace and Union recommended to the associated bodies of Republicans and anti-Republicans." He was brought to trial, represented as a "heretic, deist, infidel, and atheist," and by sentence of the court banished from the university.[3]

[1] 22 St. Tr. 923. [2] 2 St. Tr. 1793.

[3] 22 St. Tr. 523.— So late as 1820, the chief justice punished an editor with a fine of £500, for publishing an account of a trial for high treason. See 33 St. Tr. 1564, also 22 St. Tr. 298; 2 Campbell, Justices, 363, 371 *et al.*

(4.) The same year, John Frost, Esq., "a gentleman" and attorney, when slightly intoxicated after dinner, and provoked by others, said, "I am for equality. I see no reason why any man should not be upon a footing with another; it is every man's birthright." And when asked if he would have no king, he answered, "Yes, no king; the constitution of this country is a bad one." This took place in a random talk at a tavern in London. He was indicted as a person of a "depraved, impious, and disquiet mind, and of a seditious disposition, and contriving, practising, and maliciously, turbulently, and seditiously intending the peace and common tranquillity of our lord the king and his laws to disturb," "to the evil example of all others in like case offending." He was sentenced to six months in Newgate, and one hour in the pillory! He must find sureties for good behavior for five years, himself in £500, two others in £100 each, be imprisoned until the sureties were found, and be struck from the list of attornies![1]

(5.) Rev. William Winterbotham, the same year, in two sermons, exposed some of the evils in the constitution and administration of England, and for that was fined £200, and sentenced to jail for four years, — a good deal more than $300 and twelve months' imprisonment.[2]

(6.) The same year, Thomas Briellat, a London pump-maker, in a private conversation said, "A reformation cannot be effected without a revolution; we have no occasion for kings; there never will be any good time until all kings are abolished from the face of the earth; it is my wish that there were no kings at all." "I wish the French would land 500,000 men to fight the government party." He was tried, found guilty, and sentenced to a fine of £100, and sent to jail for a year.[3]

(7.) Richard Phillips, afterwards Sheriff of London, was sent to jail for eighteen months for selling Paine's Rights of Man; for the same offence two other booksellers were fined and sent to Newgate *for four years!* A surgeon and a physician were sent to Newgate for two years for having "*seditious libels in their possession.*" Thirteen persons were indicted at once.[4]

(8.) In 1793 a charge was brought against the Rev. Thomas Fyshe Palmer, formerly a Senior Fellow of Queen's College, Cambridge, and then a Unitarian minister at Dundee. Mr. Palmer wrote an Address which was adopted at a meeting of the Friends of Liberty and published by them, which, in moderate language, called on the People "to join us in our exertions for the preservation of our perishing liberty, and the recovery of our long lost rights." He distributed

[1] 22 St. Tr. 471. [2] Ibid. 823. [3] Ib. 909.
[4] Ibid. 471. Wade, Brit. Hist. (1847), 582, *et seq.*

copies of this address. He was prosecuted for "Leasing-making," for publishing a "seditious and inflammatory writing." The (Scotch) jury found him guilty, and the judges sentenced him to *transportation for seven years*. The sentence was executed with rigorous harshness.[1]

(9.) The same year Thomas Muir, Esq., was brought to trial for Leasing-making or public Libel at Edinburgh. He was a promising young lawyer, with liberal tendencies in politics, desiring the education of the great mass of the people and a reform in Parliament. He was a member of various Reform societies, and sometimes spoke at their meetings in a moderate tone recommending only legal efforts — by discussion and petition — to remedy the public grievances. His Honor (Mr. Curtis) who belongs to a family so notoriously "democratic" in the beginning of this century, and so eager in its denunciations of the Federalists of that period, knows that the law even of England — which they so much hated — allows all that. It appeared that Mr. Muir also lent a copy of Thomas Paine's "Rights of Man" to a mechanic who asked the loan as a favor. For these offences he was indicted for sedition, charged with instituting "a Society for Reform," and with an endeavor "to represent the government of this country as oppressive and tyrannical, and the legislative body as venal and corrupt." It was alleged in the indictment that he complained of the government of England as "costly," the monarchy as "useless, cumbersome, and expensive," that he advised persons to read Paine's Rights of Man, and circulated copies of a periodical called "the *Patriot*," which complained of the grievances of the people. On trial he was treated with great insolence and harshness, reprimanded, interrupted, and insulted by the agents of the government — the court. An association of men had offered a reward of five guineas for the discovery of any person who circulated the writings of Thomas Paine. Five of the fifteen jurors were members of that association, — and in Scotland a bare majority of the jurors convicts. Mr. Muir defended himself, and that ably. Lord Justice Clark charged his packed jury: —

"There are two things which you should attend to, which require no proof. The first is that the British Constitution is the *best in the world!*" "Is not every man *secure in his life, liberty, and property? Is not happiness in the power of every man?* 'Does not every man sit safely under his own vine and fig-tree' and none shall make him afraid?" "The other circumstance . . . is the state of the country during last winter. *There was a spirit of sedition and revolt going abroad.*" "I leave it for you to judge whether it was perfectly innocent or not in Mr. Muir . . . to go about . . . among *the lower classes of the people . . . inducing them to believe that a reform was absolutely necessary, to preserve their safety and their liberty*, which, had it not been for

[1] 23 St. Tr. 237; Belsham's History of George III.

him, they never would have suspected to have been in danger." "He ran a parallel between the French and English Constitutions, and *talked of their respective taxes . . .* and gave a preference to the French." "He has brought many witnesses to prove his general good behavior, and his recommending peaceable measures, and petitioning to Parliament." "Mr. Muir might have known that *no attention could be paid to such a rabble, what right had they to representation?* He could have told them the *Parliament would never listen to their petition!* How could they think of it? A government in any country should be just like a corporation; and in this country it is *made up of the landed interest, which alone has a right to be represented.*"

Gentlemen, you might think this speech was made by the "Castle Garden Committee," or at the Boston "Union Meeting" in 1850, but it comes from the year 1793.

Of course the jury found him guilty: the judges sentenced him to *transportation for fourteen years!* Lord Swinton quoted from the Roman law, that the punishment for sedition was *crucifixion*, or exposure *to be torn to pieces by wild beasts*, or transportation. "We have chosen the *mildest of these punishments.*" This sentence was executed with great cruelty. But Mr. Pitt, then in the high places of power, declared these punishments were dictated by a "sound discretion." [1]

For like offences several others underwent the same or similar punishment. But these enormities were perpetrated by the government in Scotland — where the Roman Law had early been introduced and had accustomed the Semi-Saxons to forms of injustice foreign to the ethnologic instinct and historic customs of the parent tribe. But begun is half done. Emboldened by their success in punishing the friends of Humanity in Scotland, the ministry proceeded to attempt the same thing in England itself. Then began that British Reign of Terror, which lasted longer than the French, and brought the liberties of the People into such peril as they had not known since William of Orange hurled the last of the Stuarts from his throne. Dreadful laws were passed, atrocious almost as our own fugitive slave bill. First came "the Traitorous Correspondence Bill;" next the "Habeas Corpus Suspension Act;" and then the "Seditious Practices Act," with the "Treasonable Attempts Bill" by legislative exposition establishing constructive treason! All these iniquitous measures were brought forward in Parliament by Sir John Scott — then Attorney-General, one of those North Britons who find the pleasantest prospect in Scotland is the road to London. He also was vehemently active in defending the tyranny of the Scotch judges just referred to, as indeed all judicial insolence and legal wrong.[2] He opposed all attempts to reform the law which punished with death a

[1] 23 St. Tr. 117; 30 Parl. Hist. 1486, for Adams' Speech in Commons.

[2] 30 Parl. Hist. 581; 31 Parl. Hist. 520, 929, 1153, *et al.;* 32 Parl. Hist. 370.

theft of five shillings. In two years there were more prosecutions for seditious libel than in twenty before. But Scott had his reward, and was made Lord Chancellor in 1801, and elevated to the peerage as Lord Eldon.[1]

8. Then came that series of trials for high treason which disgraced the British nation and glutted the sanguinary vengeance of the court. The government suborned spies to feign themselves "radicals," join the various Reform Societies, worm themselves into the confidence of patriotic and philanthropic or rash men, possess themselves of their secrets, catch at their words, and then repeat in court what they were paid for fabricating in their secret haunts. A ridiculous fable was got up that there was a plot to assassinate the King! Many were arrested, charged with treason — "constructive treason." On the evidence of spies of the government, hired informers — such men, Gentlemen of Jury, as Commissioner Loring and Marshal Freeman jointly made use of last year to kidnap Mr. Burns — estimable men were seized and locked up in the most loathsome dungeons of the kingdom, with intentional malignity confined amongst the vilest of notorious criminals. The judges wrested the law, constructing libels, seditions, "misdemeanors," treasons — any crime which it served their purpose to forge out of acts innocent, or only rash or indiscreet. Juries were packed by bribed sheriffs, and purchased spies were brought in evidence to swear away the liberty or the life of noble men. One of the government witnesses was subsequently convicted of ten perjuries! No man was safe who dared utter a serious word against George III. or Mr. Pitt.

Here, Gentlemen, I shall mention two cases of great importance in which the jury did their duty and turned the stream of ministerial and judicial tyranny.

(1.) In 1794 in a bill suspending the Habeas Corpus, Parliament declared "that a treacherous and detestable conspiracy had been formed for subverting the existing laws and constitution, and for introducing the system of anarchy and violence which had lately prevailed in France." Soon after the grand-jury for Middlesex indicted twelve men for high treason; they were members of some of the Societies mentioned just now. "The overt act charged against them was, that they had engaged *in a conspiracy to call a convention*, the object of which was to bring about a revolution in the country," but it was not alleged that there was any plot against the King's life, or any preparation for force.[2] Thomas Hardy, a shoemaker, was first brought to trial. The trial began October 28, 1794, just sixty years

[1] 7 Campbell, 119; 1 Townsend's Judges; Life of Vic. Gibbs.
[2] 6 Campbell, 366.

before Mr. Curtis's grand-jury found a bill against me. Sir John Scott, the attorney-general, in opening the Prosecution, made a *speech nine hours' long*, attempting to construct treason out of belonging to a society. All who belonged to it were to be considered guilty of "compassing the death of our Lord the King." Chief Justice Eyre, in addressing the grand-jury, referred to the act of Parliament as *proof of a conspiracy.*[1] Mr. Erskine defended Hardy in a speech which "will live forever." Seldom had English Liberty been in such peril; never did English lawyers more manfully defend it. The jury, a London jury, returned "NOT GUILTY."[2] Gentlemen, the report of the trial occupies more than twelve hundred pages in this volume,[3] and it shook the nation. The British juries for a long time had slept on their post, and allowed the enemy to enter the camp and murder its inmates. But the trial of Hardy woke up those heedless sentinels, and Liberty was safe — in England, I mean.

(2.) Still the infatuated government went on, not conscious of the spirit of Anglo-Saxon liberty it had at last roused from long, heavy and deathlike sleep, and eleven days after brought Mr. John Horne Tooke to trial. You remember, Gentlemen, that on the first anniversary of the Declaration of Independence, he was tried for publishing a notice of a meeting which raised £100 for the widows and orphan children of our citizens who fell at Lexington on the 19th of April, 1775, and for that offence was punished with fine and imprisonment.[4] After the acquittal of Hardy, the government brought Mr. Tooke to trial, relying on the same evidence to convict him which had so signally failed a fortnight before. The overt act relied on to convict him of "levying war" and "compassing the death of our Lord the King," was membership of a Reform society! Mr. Erskine defended him: "I *will* assert the freedom of an Englishman; I will maintain the dignity of man, I will vindicate and glory in the principles which raised this country to her preëminence among the nations of the earth; and as she shone the bright star of the morning to shed the light of liberty upon nations which now enjoy it, so may she continue in her radiant sphere to revive the ancient privileges of the world which have been lost, and still to bring them forward to tongues and people who have never known them yet, in the mysterious progression of things."[5]

Gentlemen, Horne Tooke was acquitted — the government routed and overwhelmed with disgrace, gave up the other prosecutions, and the treason trials ended. Even George III. had wit enough left to

[1] 34 George III. c. 54.
[2] 24 St. Tr. 199; Annual Register, 1794, p. 274; 31 Parl. Hist. 1062, *et al.*
[3] 24 St. Tr. [4] See above, p. 35. [5] 25 St. Tr. 1.

see the blunder which his ministers — the Slave Power of England in 1794 — had committed, and stammered forth, "You have got us into the wrong box my Lord [Loughborough]; you have got us into the wrong box. Constructive treason won't do my Lord; constructive treason won't do." By and by, Gentlemen, other men, wiser than poor feeble-minded George III., will find out that "constructive *misdemeanors* won't do."

Of these trials, Mr. Campbell, himself a Judge, declares, "This [the conduct of the government] was more exceptionable in principle than any thing done during the reign of Charles II.; for then the fabricators of the Popish Plot did not think of corroborating the testimony of Oates and Bedloe by a public statute; and then, if the facts alleged had been true, they would have amounted to a plain case of actual treason; whereas here, admitting the truth of all the facts alleged, there was no pretence for saying that any treason contemplated by the legislature had been committed. If this scheme had succeeded, not only would there have been a sacrifice of life contrary to law, but all political 'agitation' must have been extinguished in England, as there would have been a precedent for holding that the effort to carry a measure by influencing public opinion through the means openly resorted to in our days, is a 'compassing the death of the sovereign.' The only chance of escaping such servitude would have been civil war. It is frightful to think of the perils to which the nation was exposed. . . . . But Erskine and the crisis were framed for each other. . . . . His contemporaries, who without him might have seen the extinction of freedom among us, saw it, by his peculiar genius, placed on an imperishable basis."[1] But Erskine without a Jury, Gentlemen, what could he have done? He could only wail, O Jerusalem, Jerusalem — when she would not!

Now, Gentlemen, let us come over to this side of the water. I shall mention some cases in which the Jury have manfully done their duty, some others in which they have allowed themselves to be browbeaten and bullied by a judge, and so have done the greatest wrong.

1. First look at the famous case of John Peter Zenger.[2] Here are the facts. In 1733, Mr. Zenger established a newspaper in New York — there was only one there before — called the "New York Weekly Journal," "containing the freshest Advices foreign and domestic." In some numbers of this he complained, modestly enough, of various grievances in the administration of the Province, then ruled by Governor Cosby. He said, "as matters now stand their [the People's] liberties and properties are precarious, and that Slavery is

[1] 5 Campbell, 367.

[2] 3 Doc. Hist. N. Y. p. 340, 341.

likely to be entailed on them and their posterity, if some past things be not amended." He published the remarks of some one who said he "should be glad to hear that the Assembly would exert themselves, as became them, by showing that they have the interest of their country more at heart than the gratification of any private view of any of their members, or being at all affected by the smiles or frowns of a Governor, both which ought equally to be despised when the interest of the country is at stake." "We see men's deeds destroyed, judges arbitrarily displaced, new courts erected without consent of the legislature, by which, it seems to me, trials by juries are taken away when a Governor pleases." "Who, then, in that province can call any thing his own, or enjoy any liberty longer than those in the administration will condescend to let him do it?"

In October, 1734, Chief Justice de Lancey gave a charge to the Grand-Jury, urging them to indict Mr. Zenger for a libel. He says, "It is a very high aggravation of a libel that it tends to scandalize the government by *reflecting on those who are intrusted with the administration of public affairs*, which . . . has a direct tendency to breed in the public a dislike of their Governors." "If he who hath either read a libel himself, or hath heard it read by another, *do afterwards* maliciously *read or report any part of it in the presence of others*, or *lend or show it to another, he is guilty of an unlawful publication of it.*"

But the Judge had not packed the Grand-Jury with sufficient care, and so no bill was found. Thereupon the Governor's Council sent a message to the General Assembly of New York, complaining of Mr. Zenger's Journal as tending "to alienate the affections of the people of this province from his majesty's government," and asking them to inquire into the said papers and the authors thereof; the Council required that the obnoxious numbers might "be *burned by the hands of the common hangman or whipper, near the pillory.*" The Assembly let them lie on the table. The Court of Quarter-sessions was applied to to burn the papers; but as that body refused, the sheriff "delivered them unto the hands *of his own negro*, and ordered him to put them into the fire, which he did."

Mr. Zenger was imprisoned by a warrant from the Governor, a *lettre de cachet*, and "for several days denied the use of pen, ink, and paper, and the liberty of speech with any person." An *ex officio* information was brought against him, charging him with "malicious and seditious libel." His counsel, Messrs. Alexander and Smith, took exceptions to the proceedings. The Chief Justice would neither hear nor allow the exceptions, "for" said he, "you thought to have gained a great deal of applause and popularity by opposing this court . . . . but you have brought it to that point, that either we must go from the bench or you from the bar, therefore we exclude you. So "for contempt of court" their names were struck from the list of attorneys. The case came on for trial. The clerk of the Court sought to pack his jury, and instead of producing the "Freeholders' book" to select the Jury from, presented a list of forty-eight persons which he said he had taken from that book. This Honorable Court knows how easy it is to violate the law in summoning jurors; none knew it better a hundred and twenty years ago. Of the 48 some were not freeholders at all; others held commissions and offices at the Governor's pleasure; others were of the late displaced magistrates who had a grudge against Mr. Zenger for exposing their official conduct; besides, there were the governor's baker, tailor, shoemaker, candle-maker, and joiner. But it does not appear that this Judge had any Brother-in-law on the list; corruption had not yet reached that height. But that wicked list was set aside after much ado, and a Jury summoned in the legal manner. It may astonish the Court but it was really done — and a Jury summoned according to law. The trial went on. Andrew Hamilton of Philadelphia defended Mr. Zenger with law, wit, learning, and eloquence. He admitted the fact of printing and publishing the documents, and rested the defence on the truth of their assertions. The Attorney-General, Mr. Bradley, said, "supposing they were true, the law says that they are not the less libellous for that: nay, indeed, the law says, *their being true is an aggravation of the crime*." He "did not know what could be said in defence of a man that had so notoriously scandalized the governor and principal magistrates . . . . by *charging them with depriving the people of their rights and liberties, and taking away trials by juries, and in short putting an end to the law itself*. If this was not a libel, he did not know what was one. Such persons as did take these liberties . . . . ought to suffer for stirring up sedition and discontent among the people."

The Chief Justice declared, "It is far from being a justification of a libel that the contents thereof are true . . . . since the *greater appearance there is of truth, so much the more provoking is it!*" "The jury may find that Mr. Zenger printed and published these papers, and *leave it to the court to judge whether they are libellous!*"

That would be to put the dove's neck in the mouth of the fox, and allow him to decide whether he would bite it off. Mr. Hamilton replied: —

"This of leaving it to the judgment of the court whether the words are libellous or not, in effect renders Juries useless (to say no worse), in many cases." "If the faults, mistakes, nay even the vices of such a person be private and personal, and don't affect the peace of the public, or the liberty or property of our neighbor, it is unmanly and unmannerly to expose them, either by word or writing. But, when a ruler of the people brings his personal failings, but much more his vices, into his administration, and the people find themselves affected by them, either in their liberties or properties, that will alter the case mightily; and all the high things that are said in favor of rulers and of deputies, and upon the side of power, will not be able to stop people's mouths when they feel themselves oppressed, I mean in a free government. It is true *in times past it was a crime to speak truth;* and in that terrible court of Star-Chamber many worthy and brave men suffered for so doing; and yet even in that court, and in those bad times, a great and good man durst say, what I hope will not be taken amiss of me to say in this place, namely, 'The practice of informations for libels is a sword in the hands of a wicked king, and an arrant coward, to cut down and destroy the innocent; the one cannot because of his high station, and the other dares not, because of his want of courage, redress himself in another manner.'

"It is a right which all persons claim and are entitled to, to complain when they are hurt; they have a right publicly to remonstrate against the abuses of power, in the strongest terms; to put their neighbors upon their guard against the craft or open violence of men in authority; and to assert with courage the sense they have of the blessings of liberty, the value they put upon it, and their resolution at all hazards to preserve it as one of the greatest blessings Heaven can bestow." "It is a duty which all good men owe to their country, to guard against the unhappy influence of ill men when intrusted with power, and especially against their creatures and dependants, who as they are generally more necessitous, are surely more covetous and cruel."

According to the Judge the Jury had only one question before them, "Did Zenger publish the words charged in the information?" That fact was clear; nay, he did not himself deny it. He confessed it in court. But the jury fell back on their rights and duties to decide the Question of Fact, of Law, and of the Application of the Law to the Fact, and returned "NOT GUILTY," "upon which there were three huzzas in the Hall." Had this Honorable Court been then in existence I suppose it would have talked of indicting the jurors for "perjury," and would doubtless have had its labor for its pains. For the Common Council of New York presented Mr. Hamilton with a costly gold box and the freedom of the city. Gentlemen, this took place one hundred and twenty years ago. Forty years before the Revolution, Andrew Hamilton helped lay the "brilliant foundation of liberty," whereon another Hamilton was also to raise up noble walls of freedom. Gentlemen of the Jury, by Wisdom is a house builded, but the foolish plucketh it down with her own hands. Will you allow that to be done? What if the jury in 1735 had been faithless? The axe which smote down Zenger in New York, bloody and cruel, would have shorn off the heads of Otis and Quincy, and Adams and Hancock at Boston; the family of Scroggs alone would be held in honor in New England.[1]

Gentlemen, it once happened in New York that Governor Nicholson was offended with one of the clergymen of the Province. He

[1] 17 St. Tr. 675.

met him on the road one day, and "as it was usual with him (under the protection of his commission) used the poor minister with the worst of language, threatened to cut off his ears, slit his nose, and at last to shoot him through the head." The minister, "being a reverend man, continued all this time uncovered in the heat of the sun, until he found an opportunity to fly for it, and coming to a neighbor's house fell ill of a fever and wrote for a doctor," relating the facts and concluding that the governor was crazy, for no man in his right mind would behave so ill. The doctor showed the letter; the governor brought a prosecution against the minister for publishing a "scandalous, wicked, and seditious libel." No doubt he could have found a judge even then who would twist the law so as to make the letter "sedition" and "libel;" nay, perhaps he could construct a jury so as to secure a conviction, but before it reached trial the prosecution was stopped by the order of Queen Anne.

2. In 1816, in Massachusetts, there occurred the celebrated case of Commonwealth *vs.* Bowen, to which I shall again refer in a subsequent part of this defence. These are the facts. In September, 1815, Jonathan Jewett was convicted of murder in Hampshire county, Massachusetts, and sentenced to be hanged on the 9th of the following November. He was confined at Northampton, and hung himself in his cell on the night preceding the morning appointed for his public execution. George Bowen was confined in the same jail, in an apartment adjacent to Jewett's, and in such a situation that they could freely converse together. Bowen repeatedly and frequently advised and urged Jewett to destroy himself and thus disappoint the sheriff and the expectant people. He did so, and the coroner's jury returned that he committed suicide. But nevertheless, Bowen was indicted for the wilful murder of Jewett. It was charged that he "feloniously, wilfully, and of his malice aforethought, did counsel, hire, persuade, and procure the said Jewett the said felony and murder of himself to do and commit;" or that he himself murdered the said Jewett by hanging him.

At the trial Attorney-General Perez Morton contended that Bowen "was guilty of *murder as principal;*" and he cited and relied chiefly on the following authority from the Reports of our old friend Kelyng.

"Memorandum, that my brother *Twisden* showed me a report which he had of a charge given by Justice *Jones* to the grand-jury, at the King's Bench barre, *Michaelmas Term*, 9 *Car.* 1, in which he said, that poisoning another was murder at common law. And the statute of 1 *Ed.* 6, was but declaratory of the common law, and an affirmation of it. If one drinks poison by the provocation of another, and dieth of it, this is murder in the person that persuaded it. And he took this difference. If A. give poison to J. S. to give to J. D., and J. S. knowing it to be poison, give it to J. D. who taketh it in the absence of J. S., and dieth of it; in this case J. S., who gave it to

J. D., is principal; and A. who gave the poison to J. S., and was absent when it was taken, is but accessory before the fact. But if A. buyeth poison for J. S., and J. S., in the absence of A., taketh it and dieth of it, in this case A., though he be absent, yet he is principal. So it is if A. giveth poison to B. to give unto C.; and B., not knowing it to be poison, but believing it to be a good medicine, giveth it to C., who dieth of it; in this case A., who is absent, is principal, or else a man should be murdered, and there should be no principal. For B., who knoweth nothing of the poison, is in no fault, though he gave it to C. So if A. puts a sword into the hands of a madman, and bids him kill B. with it, and then A. goeth away, and the madman kills B. with the sword, as A. commanded him, this is murder in A., though absent, and he is principal; for it is no crime in the madman, who did the fact by reason of his madness."[1]

Mr. Morton also laid down this as law, "*the adviser of one who commits a felony of himself is a murderer.*" He might have added, "the adviser of one who breaks into his own house is a burglar."

Chief Justice Parker — who once declared that the jury had nothing to do with the harshness of a law — charged the jury that the important question for them was, Did Bowen's advice induce Jewett to kill himself? if so, they were to find him guilty of wilful murder! "The community has an interest *in the public execution* of criminals [the crowd having an *interest in the spectacle*] and to take such an one out of the reach of the law [by advising him to self-destruction] is no trivial offence." "*You are not to consider the atrocity of this offence in the least degree diminished by the consideration that justice was thirsting for its sacrifice;* and that but a small portion of Jewett's earthly existence could, in any event, remain to him."[2]

There was no doubt that Bowen advised Jewett to commit suicide; but the jury, in defiance of the judge's charge and Mr. Kelyng's law, nevertheless returned "NOT GUILTY."

Here, Gentlemen, is a remarkable instance of a judge, in private a benevolent man, perverting his official power, and constructing the crime of murder out of advice given to a man to anticipate a public execution by privately hanging himself! The law relied on was the Memorandum of the charge to a grand-jury made by a judge who notoriously broke the fundamental laws of England, by declaring that the king had a constitutional right to imprison, at will and as long as he liked, any of his subjects without trial, even members of Parliament for words uttered in public debate; and also the right to levy ship-money contrary to the Acts of Parliament. This charge was made in the tyrannical reign of Charles I. in 1634, by a tyrannical judge. There was no report, only *a memorandum* of it, and that not printed till seventy-four years after! It had not the force of law

[1] See the case in Kelyng's Reports (London, 1708), p. 52. The opinion of Justice *Jones* was only the charge of an inferior judge given to the grand-jury in 1634.

[2] 13 Mass. Rep. 356.

even then: it was only the memorandum of the "opinion" of a single judge, not even the "opinion" of the full court. The memorandum is contained in Kelyng's Book, which Lord Campbell calls "a folio volume of decisions in criminal cases, which are of no value whatever, except to make us laugh at some of the silly egotisms with which they abound."[1] On such authority in 1816 would even a Massachusetts court, with a judge who was a kindly man in private, dash away the life of a fellow-creature, — with such mockery of law! But, Gentlemen, the jury at that time did not slumber; they set the matter right, and did justice spite of Judge Kelyng and his "law." They made nothing of the judge's charge!

Gentlemen of the Jury, I will now mention some cases of gross injustice perpetrated by the Federal Courts of the United States.

The tenth article of amendments to the Constitution provides that "powers not delegated to the United States by the Constitution, nor prohibited by it to the States, are reserved to the States respectively, or to the People." The Constitution itself confers no Common Law Jurisdiction on the Government. Neither the People nor their Representatives had ever decreed the Common Law of England to be a part of the law of the United States. Yet, spite of the absence of positive enactment and the express words of the above amendment to the Constitution, the Supreme Court at once assumed this jurisdiction. In 1799, Chief Justice Ellsworth said, "the Common Law of this country remains the same as it was before the Revolution;"[2] and proceeded on that supposition to exercise the powers of English Judges of Common Law, undertaking to punish men for offences which no Act of Congress forbid. You see at once what monstrous tyranny would follow from that usurpation. Had the English Common Law power of punishing for "seditious libel," for example, been allowed to the Federal court, Gentlemen, you know too well what would follow. But this monstrous assumption was presently brought to an ignominious end; and strange as it may appear, by one of the judges of the court itself. Samuel Chase of Maryland, one of the signers of the Declaration of Independence, had been an Anti-Federalist and a strong State-Right's man, as such insisting on a strict construction of the Constitution. Singular as it may appear he was made a Judge in 1796, and what is yet more surprising, in 1798, declared "the United States as a Federal govern-

[1] 2 Campbell, Judges, 406.

[2] Wharton, State Trials, 653. See too Virginia Resolutions (Richmond, 1850), Preface, xiii. *et seq.*; Virginia Resolutions by Madison, and his Report thereon; Kentucky Resolutions by Jefferson, in 4 Eliot's Debates (1836).

ment, had no Common Law," and thus ended this claim.[1] But tyranny did not end; nay, he himself, a man of uncommon powers and legal attainments, became a most atrocious example of Judicial despotism.

1. In 1791 a direct tax was levied by Act of Congress on all lands and houses; excise officers were to ascertain their value. The "Alien and Sedition Laws" were also passed the same year. The execution of the law relative to the direct tax was resisted in Northampton county, Penn., and some prisoners rescued from an officer of the United States. The President, Mr. Adams, issued his proclamation. In 1799 John Fries was arrested on the charge of treason. The overt act alleged was resistance to that one special law of Congress. Judge Iredell charged the Grand-Jury, "You have heard the government as grossly abused as if it had been guilty of the vilest tyranny." Had he read the private correspondence of the Cabinet, he might have found other specimens of "abuse." He defended both the Alien and Sedition Laws.— They were "constitutional" and "proper."[2]

Mr. Fries was indicted for treason. The Judiciary Act of Congress of 1789 provides that "in cases punishable with death the trial shall be had in the county where the offence was committed; or when that cannot be done without great inconvenience, twelve petit jurors at least shall be summoned from thence." The offence was committed in Northampton county, and he was indicted and brought to trial in Philadelphia county, nor could the court be induced to comply with the statute!

The government laid down the law and constructed treason with the usual ingenuity of officials working by the job. Judge Kelyng's loose opinion that an attack on a brothel was high treason, was cited by Mr. Rawle, the District Attorney, as good law.[3] What "in England is called constructive levying of war, in this country must be called direct levying of war." Judge Peters charged that though force was necessary to constitute the crime of treason, yet "the quantum of force is immaterial," of course it may be wielding a wheat straw, or a word, I suppose. "The doctrine of constructive treason has produced much real mischief in another country" [England]. "The *greater part of the objections to it are irrelevant here.*"

Fries was found guilty. His counsel moved for a new trial, on the ground that before the trial one of the jurors had declared, "Fries ought to be hung;" "I myself shall be in danger unless we hang

[1] Wharton, 197; 3 Dallas, 384; see 5 Hildreth, 230.

[2] See a defence of them in 2 Gibbs's Administration, 74, 78; also 162.

[3] Wharton, 539; Kelyng, R. 70, 75.

them all;" that the jurors were irregularly drawn, and the trial was not held in the county where the offence was committed. Judge Iredell ruled that it was "*a high contempt* at this time *to call for a renewal of an argument whereon a solemn, decisive opinion was delivered*." Judge Peters declared the juror had "said no more than all friends to the laws and the government were warranted in thinking and saying." Yet a new trial was granted.

The new trial was held before Judge Chase, who had, as Mr. Wharton says, a "singular instinct for tumults which scents it at a distance . . . and irresistibly impels a participation in it," "moving perpetually with a mob at his heels." Yet "apart from his criminal jurisdiction he was reckoned a wise and impartial judge, a master of the Common Law, and a thorough and indefatigable administrator of public functions." "It was this despotic ardor of temperament . . . which made him, when a young man, employ with resolute audacity the engine of popular revolt, and which led him when older, and when in possession of that power against which he had so steadily warred, to wield with the same vigor the sword of constituted authority."[1] Gentlemen, he was like many that this Honorable Court perhaps have known, who were privateering Democrats in 1812, and Kidnapping Whigs in 1850. To him we are indebted for the invaluable decision that the United States courts have no Common Law jurisdiction.

At this new trial he treated the defendants' counsel in such a manner that they abandoned the case, and left the Prisoner without defence. The District Attorney, taking his law from Kelyng and similar servants of British despots, laid it down that treason "may consist in *assembling together in numbers*, and by actual force, or by terror, *opposing any particular law;*" "*Force need not be used* to manifest this spirit of rebellion." "Even *if the matter made a grievance of was illegal, the demolition of it* in this way *was*, nevertheless, *treason*," "a rising with intent by force to prevent the execution of a law . . . . preventing the marshal executing his warrants, and preventing the other officers . . . . amounted to levying war." "In short an opposition to the acts of Congress in whole or in part [that is to *any one law*] . . . . either by collecting numbers, or by a display of force . . . . which should operate . . . . either throughout the United States, or in *any part thereof to procure a repeal or a suspension* of the law . . . . this offence he considered to be *strictly* treason."

Judge Chase laid it down as law not to be questioned in his court, "that any . . . rising of any body of the people . . . to attain by force . . . any object of a great public nature . . . is a levying of war:"

[1] 4 Hildreth, 571; 1 Gibbs, 300; 2 Gibbs, 419.

"any such . . . rising to resist . . . the execution of any statutes of United States . . . or for any other object of a general nature or national concern, under any pretence as that the statute was unjust . . . or unconstitutional is a levying war;" "*any force . . . will constitute the crime* of levying war."

If that be law, then an old negro woman who, with a dishcloth, frightens officer Butman away from kidnapping her granddaughter in Southac street, does thereby levy war against the United States and commits the crime of treason.

The jury, overborne by the assumptions of the judge, or ignorant of their duties and their rights, allowed this tyrannical court to have its way, surrendered the necks of the people, and brought in a verdict of guilty. Judge Chase made an insolent address to the prisoner and sentenced him to death. But Mr. Adams, with a remarkable degree of justice, gave him a full pardon, and drew down upon himself thereby the wrath of his cabinet.[1]

2. In 1788 Mathew Lyon, a native of Ireland, a Revolutionary soldier, a member of congress, and editor of a newspaper in Vermont, was brought to trial under the Sedition Law, for a false, malicious, and seditious libel. He had published in his newspaper a somewhat severe attack on the Federalists then in power. The article, alleged to be "seditious," was a letter written and mailed at the seat of government seven days before, and published nine days after, the passage of the Sedition Law itself. It was as much a political trial, Gentlemen, as this — purely political. Judge Patterson — United States Circuit Judge of Vermont — charged that the jury had nothing whatever to do with the constitutionality of the Sedition Law. "Congress has said that the author and publisher of seditious libels is to be punished." "The only question you are to determine is . . . Did Mr. Lyon publish the writing? . . . Did he do so seditiously, with the intent of making odious or contemptible the President and government, and bringing them both into disrepute?"

Mr. Lyon was found guilty, and punished by a fine of $1,000 and imprisonment for four months. The "Seditious Libel" would now be thought a quite moderate Editorial or "Letter from our Correspondent." His imprisonment was enforced with such rigor that his constituents threatened to tear down the jail, which he prevented.[2]

3. In 1799 Thomas Cooper, a native of England, residing at Northumberland, Pennsylvania, published a handbill reflecting severely on the conduct of President Adams. He was prosecuted by an In-

[1] Wheaton, 458; 9 Adams's Works, 57; 2 Gibbs, 360; 5 Hildreth, 366; Chase's Trial, 18.

[2] Wharton, 333; 4 Jefferson's Works (1853), 262.

formation *ex officio*, in the Circuit Court for Pennsylvania, and brought to trial before Judge Chase, already referred to, charged with a "false, scandalous, and malicious attack" on the President. Mr. Chase charged the jury, " A Republican government can only be destroyed in two ways: the introduction of luxury, or the licentiousness of the press. This latter is the more slow, but most sure and certain means of bringing about the destruction of the government." He made a fierce and violent harangue, arguing the case against the defendant with the spirit which has since become so notorious in the United States courts in that State. The pliant jury found Mr. Cooper guilty, and he was fined $400 and sent to jail for six months. He subsequently became a judge in Pennsylvania, as conspicuous for judicial tyranny as Mr. Chase himself, and was removed by Address of the Legislature from his seat, but afterwards went to South Carolina where he became Professor at her college, and a famous nullifier in 1830.[1]

4. In 1799, or 1800, Mr. Callender, a native of England, then residing at Richmond, in Virginia — a base and mean fellow, as his whole history proved, depraved in morals and malignant in temper — published a pamphlet called " The Prospect before us," full of the common abuse of Mr. Adams and his administration. He was indicted for a false, malicious, and seditious libel, and brought to trial before Judge Chase who pressed the Sedition Law with inquisitorial energy and executed it with intolerant rigor.[2] As he started for Richmond to hold the trial, he declared " he would teach the lawyers in Virginia the difference between the liberty and the licentiousness of the press." He told the marshal " not to put any of those creatures called Democrats on the jury," — it does not appear that he had his own Brother-in-Law on it however; — " he likened himself to a schoolmaster who was to turn the unruly boys of the Virginia courts over his knee and give them a little wholesome chastisement."

Some of the ablest lawyers in Virginia were engaged for the defence. But they could not secure any decent regard to the common forms of law, or to the claims of justice. He would not grant the delay always usual in such cases, and indispensable to the defence. He refused to allow the defendants' counsel to examine their most important witness, and allowed them to put none but written questions approved of by him! The defendant was not allowed to prove the truth of any statements, alleged to be libellous, by establishing the truth of one part through one witness and of another through a different one. He would not allow him to argue to the jury that the law was unconstitutional. " We all know that juries have the right to decide the law as well as the fact, and the Constitution is the

[1] Wharton, 659. [2] Wharton, 45, 688; Chase's Trial, 33; 4 Jefferson, 445, 447.

Supreme law of the land." "Then," said Mr. Wirt, "since the jury have a right to consider the law, and since the Constitution is law, it is certainly syllogistic that the jury have a right to consider the Constitution;" and the judge exclaimed, "a *non sequitur*, Sir!" "Sit down, Sir!" Mr. Wirt sat down. The judge declared "a right is given to the jury to determine what the law is in the case before them, and not to decide whether a statute is a law or not, or whether it is void, under an opinion that it is unconstitutional." "It appears to me the right now claimed has a direct tendency to dissolve the Union." "No citizen of knowledge and information . . . will believe, without very strong and indubitable proof, that Congress will, intentionally, make any law in violation of the Federal Constitution." "If such a case should happen, the mode of redress is pointed out in the Constitution." It was obvious that Congress had made laws in violation of the Constitution, and he insisted that the jury should enforce those laws against their own conscience. After all his violent injustice he of course declared "the decisions of courts of justice will not be influenced by political and *local* principles and prejudices." The packed jury found the prisoner guilty. He was fined $200 and sent to jail for nine months.

But Virginia was too high-spirited to bear this. Nay, Gentlemen of the Jury, the whole Nation then was too fond of justice and liberty to allow such wickedness to proceed in the name of law. "Virginia was in a flame;" the lawyers "throughout the country were stung to the quick." They had not been so long under the slave-power then as now. At this day, Gentlemen, such conduct, such insolence, yet more oppressive, rouses no general indignation in the lawyers. But then the Alien and Sedition Laws ruined the Administration, and sent Mr. Adams — who yet never favored them — from his seat; his successor, Mr. Jefferson, says, "*I discharged every person under punishment*, or prosecution, *under the Sedition Law, because I considered and now consider, that law to be a nullity as absolute and as palpable as if Congress had ordered us to fall down and worship a golden image*."[1] Judge Chase was impeached by the House of Representatives, tried by the Senate, and only escaped condemnation by the prejudice of the political partisans. As it was, a majority were in favor of his condemnation. But the Constitution, properly, requires two thirds. Judge Chase escaped by this provision. But his influence was gone.

The Alien and Sedition Laws, which sought to gag the People, and make a Speech a "misdemeanor," soon went to their own place; and on the 4th of July, 1840, Congress passed a law to pay Mr. Lyon

[1] 4 Jefferson, Correspondence in Wharton, 721.

and others the full amount of the fine and costs levied upon them, with interest to the date of payment: a Committee of the House had made a report on Lyon's case, stating that "the law was unconstitutional, null, and void, passed under a mistaken exercise of undelegated power, and that the mistake ought to be remedied by returning the fine so obtained, with interest thereon."[1] Just now, Gentlemen, Judge Chase and the principles of the Sedition Law appear to be in high favor with the Federal Courts: but one day the fugitive slave bill will follow the Alien and Sedition Bill, and Congress will refund all the money it has wrenched unjustly from victims of the Court. There is a To-morrow after to-day, and a Higher Law which crushes all fugitive slave bills into their kindred dust.

Gentlemen, allow me to vary this narrative of British and American despotism by an example from a different nation. I will refresh you with a case more nearly resembling that before you; it is an instance of German tyranny. In 1853, Dr. Gervinus, Professor of History in the University of Heidelberg in Germany, published this little volume of about 200 pages,[2] "An Introduction to the History of the 19th Century." Mr. Gervinus is one of the most enlightened men in the world, a man of great genius for the philosophical investigation of human history, and enriched with such culture and learning as is not common even in that home of learned men. His book, designed only for scholars, and hardly intelligible to the majority of readers even in America, sets forth this great fact,— The democratic tendency of mankind shown in all history.

Gervinus was seized and brought to trial on the 24th of February, 1853, at Mannheim, charged with publishing a work against constitutional monarchy, intending thereby to depose the lawful head of the State, the Grand Duke Charles Leopold, and with changing and endangering the constitution, "disturbing the public tranquillity and order, and incurring the guilt of High Treason." In short he was charged with "obstructing an officer" and attempting to dissolve the Union," with "levying war." For his trial the judge purposely selected a small room, though four times larger than what now circumscribes the dignity of this Honorable Court; he did not wish the people to hear Gervinus's defence. But I will read you some extracts from the preface to the English translation of his book:—

"I offer nothing purely theoretical or speculative, and as few opinions and conclusions as can possibly be given in a historical narrative. The work finally reaches a

[1] 2 Sess. 26th, Cong. Doc. 86, Ho. Rep.; Wharton, 344, 679. See also Virginia Resolutions (1850), and the remarks in the Debates. Then Virginia was faithful to State Rights, and did a service to the cause of Liberty which no subsequent misconduct should make us forget.

[2] 2 Einleitung in die Geschichte des neunzehnten Jahrhunderts; Leipzig, 1853. 8vo. pp. 181.

period when the Present and the Future become its subject, and when therefore it can no longer relate any events of history which have been completed; and is confined to the simple statement of *the Fact* that opposite opinions exist, and may yet be advanced, concerning the problem of the Future. These opinions are themselves weighed against one another, but their value is not determined by dogmas, or phrases, or declamations, but simply by facts. If the balance incline towards a more liberal form of government, towards democratic institutions, and therefore towards self-government, and the participation of the many rather than of the few in the affairs of the State, I am not to blame, nor is it my ordinance, but that of History and of Providence. My work is only (what all historical narrative should be) a vindication of the decrees of Providence; and to revolt against them appears to me neither pious in a moral point of view, nor wise in a political. That which is proved by the most remarkable facts of History, will not be altered in the smallest degree, by the suppression of my work, or by my condemnation. The charge on this head is an absurdity, since no rational end can be attained by it. It aims at the suppression of a truth which, should *I* not tell it, will be ever louder and louder proclaimed by the *Facts of History*.

"To believe such a thing possible is a proof how limited an idea exists of the eager inquiry going on after knowledge — and truth, the source and origin of all knowledge. There will always be so eager a demand for a history of the Present time, that, even should *I* be prevented, ten others would arise, only to proclaim the louder, and to repeat the oftener, the truth which is here suppressed. To believe that the philosophy of History can be silenced by persecution, argues an entire ignorance even of the external mechanism of philosophy. A political pamphlet, intended to serve a particular purpose at a particular period, may be suppressed. The author of such a pamphlet, bent on agitation, can easily console himself for its suppression. It has cost him little time and trouble; it is only a means to an end, one means out of many means, any of which, when this is lost, will serve the author as well. But it is not thus with philosophical works, it is not thus with the work before me. This book is deeply rooted in the vocation of my whole life, and is the end of my philosophical research; I have prepared myself for it by the labor of years, and the labor of years will be necessary for its completion. I have reached a time of life when I can neither change my vocation, nor even cease to labor in this vocation. I am also so imbued with my philosophy, that even if I could change I would not. I may be hindered in the prosecution of this work for four months, but in the fifth I shall return to it. For a judicial sentence cannot arrest (like a mere pamphlet) the philosophical scheme interwoven into a whole existence."

"If it is possible that this 'Introduction' can be condemned in Germany, that it can be prohibited, that by these means the work should be strangled in its birth, then the philosophy of history has no longer a place in Germany. The tribunal of Baden will have given the first blow, in pronouncing judgment on a matter which is purely philosophical, and Germany, whose freedom of philosophical research has been her pride and her boast, of which even the various administrations of the nation have never been jealous, will receive a shock such as she never before sustained."

"My book is on so strictly a philosophical plan, and treats of such comprehensive historical questions, that, properly, no judgment of any value could be pronounced upon it but by the professed historian, of whom there are not two dozen in all Germany. Among them there has not, to this hour, been found one competent to give an opinion in a few weeks on a book which is the fruit of half a life. On the other hand, there was soon a whole set of fanatical partisans and obstreperous bunglers in a neighboring press, who in eight days had condemned this work, in some instances, by calling it an historical commonplace, and in others, a political pamphlet with '*destructive tendencies*.' At the same time, and in a manner easily accounted for, under the influence of such an expression of public opinion, and almost before any other could make itself heard, accusations were made against the book, and it was confiscated. Let no one take it amiss if, in the urgency of my defence, *I* for a moment lay aside modesty, as far as such modesty might prove injurious to my cause. My work demonstrates a law of historical development, which I do not claim as my property, or as originating in me, but which has been demonstrated more than two thousand years ago by the greatest thinker of all ages, derived from observations on the history of the Grecian State. To repeat a law which has been already demonstrated, ought to appear but a trifling circumstance, and indeed might merit the term of an historical commonplace; we could even suppose that it might be mentioned in a popular as well as in a philosophical book. Nevertheless this law has scarcely been twice repeated in the course of two thousand years, and then only by two imitators, who scarcely understood its whole purport, though they were the most thinking heads of the most thinking nations — Machiavelli in Italy, and Hegel in Germany. I solemnly ask of the whole philosophical world if my words can be gainsaid, and to name for me the third, by whom the Aristotelian law, of which I speak, has been repeated and understood. I have ventured to consider the thought of Aristotle, and to apply it to the history of modern European States, and I found it confirmed by a series of developments which have occupied two thousand years. I also found that the whole series of events confirmatory of this law (itself deduced from experience) are not yet entirely fulfilled. Like the astronomer, who, from a known fraction of the path of a newly discovered planet, calculates its whole course, I ventured to divine that which is still wanting, and which may yet take centuries to complete. I turned silently to those whose profession was the study of history, to prove the justice of my calculations; I handed my book over to coming generations and coming centuries, with the silent demand, when the required series of events shall be fulfilled, then to pronounce the final sentence, whether this law, and its purport as now explained, be just or not. This is the philosophical character, and these the contents of my book — no more than was indispensably necessary to make this calculation. And now comes the charge, and pronounces that in the character of a pamphleteer, I have endeavored to excite a revolution in the Grand Duchy of Baden, or in the German Confederation."

On the 8th of March — it should have been the *fifth* — the thing came to a close. On account of "his hostility to constitutional monarchy, and his declaration of its weakness, his denial of its goodwill [towards the people], and his representing that the American Democracy was a universal necessity and a desirable fact," sentence was pronounced against him, condemning him to an imprisonment of four months, and ordering his book to be destroyed." There was no Jury of the People to try him! Here our own Court has an admirable precedent for punishing me for a word.[1]

But even in Massachusetts, within twenty years, an attempt was made to punish a man for his opinions on a matter of history which had no connection with politics, or even with American Slavery. In July, 1834, Rev. George R. Noyes, a Unitarian Minister at Petersham, a retired scholar, a blameless man of fine abilities and very

[1] See Preface to English Translation of Gervinus (London, 1853); and Allg. Lit. Zeitung für 1853, pp. 867, 883, 931, 946, 994, 1131.

large attainments in theological learning, wrote an elaborate article in the Christian Examiner, the organ of the "Liberal Christians" in America, in which he maintained that Jesus of Nazareth is not the Messiah predicted in the Old Testament. "It is difficult," said this accomplished Theologian, "to point out any predictions which have been properly fulfilled in Jesus." Peter and Paul found the death and resurrection of Jesus in the 16th Psalm, but they "were in an error," which should not surprise us, for "the Evangelists and Apostles never claimed to be *inspired reasoners and interpreters;*" "they partook of the errors and prejudices of their age in things in which Christ had not instructed them." "The commonly received doctrine of the inspiration of all the writings included in the Bible, is a millstone hung round its neck [the neck of Christianity], sufficient to sink it."

The article was written with remarkable candor and moderation, and indicated a devout and holy purpose in the author. The doctrines were by no means new. But Hon. James T. Austin, was then Attorney-General of the State; his attention being called to it by an anonymous writer in a newspaper, he attacked Mr. Noyes's article, thus giving vent to his opinion thereon: "He considers its learning very ill bestowed, its researches worse than useless, and that its tendency is to strike down one of the pillars on which the fabric of Christianity is supported." "Its tendency is to shock the pious,—confound the unlearned,—overwhelm those who are but moderately versed in the recondite investigations of theology, and above all to open an arsenal whence all the small wits of the infidel army may supply themselves with arms. Its greater evil is to disarm the power of public opinion." "It certainly disarms to a great degree the power of the law."[1]

Gentlemen, suppose it had not been necessary to submit the matter to a Jury, what would the right of freedom of conscience be worth in the hands of such a man, "dressed in a little brief authority?" It was said at the time that the author was actually presented to the Grand-Jury, and an attempt made to procure an indictment for Blasphemy, or Misdemeanor. I know not how true the rumor was. The threat of prosecution came to nought, and Dr. Noyes, one of the most scholarly men in America, is now Professor of Theology in the Divinity School at Cambridge, and an honor to the liberal sect which maintains him there.

Gentlemen, when laws are unjustly severe, denouncing a punishment highly excessive, the juries refuse to convict. Examples of this

[1] 16 Examiner, 321; 17 ibid. 127; Boston Atlas, July 8th and 9th, 1834.

are very common in trials for capital offences, now that the conscience of moral men has become so justly hostile to the judicial shedding of blood. There is no doubt with the Jurors as to the Fact, none as to the Law; but they say it is unjust to apply such a law to such a fact and hang a man. The Jury exercising their moral discretion, spite of the judge, and spite of the special statute or custom, are yet faithful to their official obligation and manly duty, and serve Justice, the ultimate End and Purpose of Law, whereto the statutes and customs are only provisional means. Foolish judges accuse such juries of "Perjury;" but it is clear enough, Gentlemen, where the falseness is.

"Do you take notice of that juryman dressed in blue?" said one of the judges at the old Bailey to Judge Nares. "Yes." "Well, then, take my word for it, there will not be a single conviction to-day for any capital offence." So it turned out. The "gentleman in blue" thought it unjust and wicked, contrary to the ultimate Purpose of law, to hang men, and he was faithful to his juror's oath in refusing to convict. Of course he did not doubt of the Fact, or the Law, only of the Justice of its Application. One day there will be a good many "gentlemen in blue."

To prevent this moral independence of the jury from defeating the immoral aim of the government, or of the judges, or the legislature — the court questions the jurors beforehand, and drives off from the panel all who think the statute unfit for such application. Gentlemen, that is a piece of wicked tyranny. It would be as unfair to exclude such men from the legislature, or from the polls, as from the jury box. In such cases the defendant is not tried by his "country," but by a jury packed for the purpose of convicting him, spite of the moral feelings of the people.

Sometimes the statute is so framed that the jurors must by their verdict tell an apparent falsehood, or commit a great injustice. When it was a capital offence in England to steal forty shillings, and evidence made it plain that the accused had actually stolen eight or ten times that value, you all know how often the jurors brought in a verdict of "*stealing thirty-nine shillings*."[1] They preferred to tell what seemed to be a lie, rather than kill a man for stealing fifteen or twenty dollars. The verdict of NOT GUILTY would have been perfectly just in form as in substance, and conformable to their official oath.

Gentlemen, tyrannical rulers, and their servants, despotic and corrupt judges, have sought to frighten the juries from the exercise of all discretion — either moral or intellectual. To that end they threaten

[1] See several cases of this kind in Sullivan on Abolition of Punishment of Death, (N. Y. 1841), 73. Rantoul's Works, 459.

them before the verdict, and punish them when they decide contrary to the wish of the tyrant. To make the jurors agree in a unanimous verdict, they were kept without "fire or water or food or bed" until they came to a conclusion; if eleven were of one mind and the twelfth not convinced, the refractory juror was fined or put in jail.[1] If the verdict, when unanimously given, did not satisfy the judge or his master, the jurors were often punished.[2] I have already shown you how the juries were treated — with fine and imprisonment — who acquitted Throckmorton and Penn.[3] When John Lilburne was tried for his life in 1653, he censured the authorities which prosecuted him and appealed to the "honorable Jury, the Keepers of the Liberties of England:" they found him Not Guilty, and were themselves brought before the council of State for punishment. "Thomas Greene of Snow-hill, tallow chandler, Foreman of the Jury, being asked what the grounds and reasons were that moved him to find . . . Lilburne not guilty, . . . saith '*that he did discharge his conscience in what he then did, and that he will give no further answer to any questions which shall be asked him upon that matter.*'"[4] This was in the time of Cromwell; but as the People were indignant at his tyrannical conduct in that matter, and his insolent attempt to punish the jurors, they escaped without fine or imprisonment. Indeed more than a hundred and twenty-five years before, Thomas Smith had declared "such doings to be very violent, tyrannical, and contrary to the liberty and customs of the realm of England." Sir Matthew Hale said at a later day, "It would be a most unhappy case for the judge himself, if the prisoner's fate depended upon his directions; unhappy also for the prisoner; for if the judge's opinion must rule the verdict, the trial by jury would be useless."[5] Judge Kelyng was particularly hostile to the jury, throwing aside "all regard to moderation and decency." He compelled the grand-jury of Somersetshire to find an indictment against their consciences, reproaching Sir Hugh Wyndham, the foreman, as the "Head of a Faction." He told the jury, "You are all my servants, and I will make the best in England stoop!" He said it was a "misdemeanor" for them to discriminate between murder and manslaughter; that was for the court to determine. But, Gentlemen, it does not appear that he had his brother-in-law on that grand-jury. Several persons were indicted for "attending a conven-

[1] Forsyth, 241, 243.

[2] Thomas Smith, Commonwealth, (London, 1589,) b. iii. c. 1. Hargrave, in 6 St. Tr. 1019.

[3] See above, p. 95. 1 St. Tr. 901; 6 St. Tr. 967, 969, 999; 21 St. Tr. 925.

[4] 1 St. Tr. 445.

[5] 6 St. Tr. 967, note; Bushell's Case, Ibid. 999, and Hargrave's note, 1013.

ticle;" the jury acquitted them contrary to his wish, and he fined them $334 apiece, and put them in jail till it was paid. On another occasion, this servile creature of Charles II. fined and imprisoned all the jurors because they convicted of *manslaughter* a man whom he wanted to hang. But for this conduct he was accused in the House of Commons, and brought to answer for it at their bar.[1]

In 1680 Chief Justice Scroggs was brought up before the House of Commons for discharging "a refractory grand-jury"—such an one as was discharged in Boston last July: Sir Francis Winnington said, "If the judges instead of acting by law shall be acted by their own ambition, and endeavor to get promotion rather by worshipping the rising sun than doing justice, this nation will soon be reduced to a miserable condition." "As faults committed by judges are of more dangerous consequence than others to the public, so there do not want precedents of severer chastisements for them than for others."[2]

But spite of the continual attempt to destroy the value of the trial by jury, and take from the People their ancient, sevenfold shield, the progress of liberty is perpetual. Now and then there arose lawyers and judges like Sir Matthew Hale, Holt, Vaughan, Somers, Camden, and Erskine, who reached out a helping hand. Nay, politicians came up to its defence. But the great power which has sustained and developed it is the sturdy and unconquerable Love of individual Liberty which is one of the most marked characteristics of the Anglo-Saxon, whether Briton or American. The Common People of England sent Juries, as well as regiments of Ironsides, to do battle for the Right. Gentlemen, let us devoutly thank God for this Safeguard of Freedom, and take heed that it suffers no detriment in our day, but serves always the Higher Law of the Infinite God.

Now, Gentlemen of the Jury, I come to the end.

IV. Of the Circumstances of this Special Case, United States versus Theodore Parker.

Here, Gentlemen, I shall speak of three things.

(I.) Of the Fugitive Slave Bill.

At the close of the Revolution there was a contradiction in the national consciousness: the People were divided between the Idea of Freedom and the Idea of Slavery. There consequently ensued a

[1] 2 Campbell, Justices, 405; 6 St. Tr. 910; Kelyng, 50; 3 Hallam, 6, note; Commons Journals, 16 Oct. 1667.

[2] 4 Parl. Hist. 1224.

struggle between the two elements. This has continued ever since the Treaty of Peace in 1783.

Twice the Idea of Freedom has won an important victory: in 1787 Slavery was prohibited in the North-West Territory; in 1808 the African Slave Trade was abolished. Gentlemen, this is all that has been done for seventy-two years; the last triumph of American Freedom over American Slavery was forty-seven years ago!

But the victories of Slavery have been manifold: in 1787 Slavery came into the Constitution, — it was left in the individual States as a part of their "Republican form of government;" the slaves were counted fractions of men, without the personal rights of integral humanity, and so to be represented by their masters; and the rendition of fugitive slaves was provided for. In 1792 out of old territory a new Slave State was made and Kentucky came into the Union. Tennessee followed in 1796, Mississippi in 1817, Alabama in 1819, and thus four Slave States were newly made out of soil which the Declaration of Independence covered with ideal freedom. In 1793 the Federal government took Slavery under its special patronage and passed the first fugitive slave bill for the capture of such as should escape from bondage in one State, and flee to another. In 1803 Louisiana was purchased and Slavery left in that vast territory; thus the first expansion of our borders was an extension of bondage, — out of that soil three great States, Louisiana, Missouri, Arkansas, have since been made, all despotic, with more than half a million of Americans fettered there to-day. Florida was purchased as slave soil, and in 1845 made a State with perpetual Slavery written in its Constitution. In 1845 Texas was annexed and Slavery extended over nearly four hundred thousand square miles of once free soil; in 1848 Slavery was spread over California, Utah, and New Mexico. Here were seven great victories of Slavery over Freedom.

At first it seemed doubtful which was master in the federal councils; but in 1820, in a great battle — the Missouri Compromise — Slavery triumphed, and has ever since been master. In 1845 Texas was annexed, and Slavery became the open, acknowledged, and most insolent master. The rich, intelligent, and submissive North only registers the decrees of the poor, the ignorant, but the controlling South; accepts for Officers such as the master appoints, for laws what the Slave-driver commands. The Slave-Power became predominant in American politics, business, literature, and "Religion."

Gentlemen of the Jury, do you doubt what I say? Look at this Honorable Court, — at its Judges, its Attorney, at its Marshal, and its Marshal's Guard: they all hold their offices by petty serjeantry of menial service rendered to the Slave-Power. It would be an insult to any one of this august fraternity to hint that he had the faintest respect for the great Principles of American Liberty, or any love of justice for all men. I shall not be guilty of that "contempt of court." Gentlemen, I had expected that this Court would be solemnly opened with prayer. I knew whom the Slave-Power would select as its priest to "intercede with Heaven." I expected to hear the Rev. Nehemiah Adams, D.D., ask the God he worships and serves to take "a South-side view of American Slavery" in general, and in special of this prosecution of a minister of the Christian Religion for attempting to keep the Golden Rule. Should the Court hereafter indulge its public proclivity to prayer, that eminent divine will doubtless be its advocate — fit mediator for a Court which knows no Higher Law.

Well, Gentlemen, that sevenfold triumph was not enough. Slavery will never be contented so long as there is an inch of free soil in the United States! New victories must be attempted. Mr. Toombs has declared to this noble Advocate of Justice and Defender of Humanity, [John P. Hale] who renews the virtuous glories of his illustrious namesake, Sir Matthew Hale, that, "Before long the master will sit down with his slaves at the foot of Bunker Hill Monument." But one thing disturbed our masters at the South — the concubine runs away from her lusty lord, the mulatto slave child from her white father; I have had the "best blood of Virginia," fugitive children of her "first families" in my own house, and have given many a dollar to help the sons and daughters of "Southern Democrats" enjoy a taste of Northern Democracy. The slaves would run away. The law of 1793 was not adequate to keep or catch these African Christians who heeded not the Southern command, "Slaves, obey your masters." The Decision of the Supreme Court in the Prigg case,[1] showed the disposition of the Federal Government, and took out of the hands of the individual States the defence of their own citizens. Still the slaves would run away. In 1849 there were more than five hundred fugitives from Southern Democracy in Boston — and their masters could not catch them. What a misfortune! Boston retained $200,000 of human Property of the Christian and chivalric South! Surely the Union was "in danger."

In 1850 came the fugitive slave bill. When first concocted, its author, — a restless politician, a man of small mind and mean character, with "Plantation manners," — thought it was "too bad to pass." He designed it not for an actual law, but an insult to the North so aggravating that she must resist the outrage, and then there would be an opportunity for some excitement and agitation at the South — and perhaps some "nullification" in South Carolina and Virginia; and in that general fermentation who knows what scum would be thrown

[1] 16 Peters, 616.

up! Even Mr. Clay "never expected the law would be enforced." "No Northern *gentleman*," said he, "will ever help return a fugitive slave." It seemed impossible for the bill to pass.

But at that time Massachusetts had in the Senate of the nation a disappointed politician, a man of great understanding, of most mighty powers of speech, —

> "Created hugest that swim the ocean stream," —

and what more than all else contributed to his success in life, the most magnificent and commanding personal appearance. At that time — his ambition nothing abated by the many years which make men venerable, — he was a bankrupt in money, a bankrupt in reputation, and a bankrupt in morals — I speak only of his public morals, not his private, — a bankrupt in political character, pensioned by the Money Power of the North. Thrice disappointed, he was at that time gaming for the Presidency. When the South laid down the fugitive slave bill, on the national Faro-table, Mr. Webster bet his all upon that card. He staked his mind — and it was one of vast compass; his eloquence, which could shake the continent; his position, the senatorial influence of Massachusetts; his wide reputation, which rung with many a noble word for justice and the Rights of man; he staked his conscience and his life. Gentlemen, you know the rest, — the card won, the South took the *trick*, and Webster lost all he could lose, — his conscience, his position, his reputation; not his wide-compassing mind, not his earth-shaking eloquence. Finally he lost his — life. Peace to his mighty shade. God be merciful to him that showed no mercy. The warning of his fall is worth more than the guidance of his success. Let us forgive; it were wicked to forget. For fifty years no American has had such opportunity to serve his country in an hour of need. Never has an American so signally betrayed the trust — not once since Benedict Arnold turned a less ignoble traitor!

Gentlemen, you know the speech of the 7th of March. You know it too well. He proposed to support the fugitive slave bill "with all its provisions, to the fullest extent." At that time this bill of abominations was worse than even now; for then it left the liberty of a man to the discretion not only of any judge or commissioner of any Federal court, but to any clerk or marshal thereof, nay, to any collector of the customs and every one of the seventeen thousand postmasters in the United States! It provided that an affidavit made before any officer empowered, by the United States or any State, to administer oaths, should be taken as conclusive evidence to prove a man a slave! So John Smith of some unknown town in Texas, might make affidavit before John Jones, a justice of peace in the same place, that Lewis Hayden, or Wendell Phillips, or his Honor Judge Curtis, was his (Smith's) slave, and had escaped to Boston: might bring hither John Brown, a Postmaster from Texas, or find some collector of the customs or minion of the court in Massachusetts, seize his victim, and swear away his liberty; and any man might be at once consigned to eternal bondage! All that the bill provided for, — and authorized the kidnapper to employ as many persons as he might think proper to accomplish his purpose by force, at the expense of the United States! All this Mr. Webster volunteered to support "to the fullest extent."

The bill was amended, here bettered, there worsened, and came to the final vote. Gentlemen, the Money Power of the North joined the Slave Power of the South to kidnap men in America after 1850, as it had kidnapped them in Africa before 1808. Out of fifty Senators only twelve said, No; while in the House 109 voted Yea. The Hon. Samuel A. Eliot gave the vote of Beacon and State Streets for kidnapping men on the soil of Boston. The one Massachusetts vote for manstealing must come from the town which once bore a Franklin and an Adams in her bosom; yes, from under the eaves of John Hancock's house! That one vote was not disgrace enough; his successor [Hon. William Appleton] must take a needless delight in reaffirming the infamy. When the bill passed, Gentlemen, you remember how Mr. Webster rejoiced: —

> "Now is the winter of our discontent
> Made glorious summer,"

was his public outcry on the housetop! And Boston fired a hundred guns of joy! Do you know *who* fired them? Ask Mr. Attorney Hallett; ask Mr. Justice Curtis. They can "instruct the jury."

Gentlemen, you know the operation of the fugitive slave bill. It subverts the Purposes of the Constitution, it destroys Justice, disturbs domestic Tranquillity, hinders the common Defence and the general Welfare, and annihilates the Blessings of Liberty. It defies the first Principles of the Declaration of Independence, — think of the fugitive slave bill as an appendix to that document! It violates the Idea of Democracy. It contradicts the very substance of the Christian Religion — the two great commandments of Love to God, and Love to man, whereon "hang all the Law and the Prophets." It makes natural humanity a crime; it subjects all the Christian virtues to fine and imprisonment. It is a *lettre de cachet* against Philanthropy.

Gentlemen of the Jury, you know the fugitive slave bill is unconstitutional. I need not argue the matter; it is too plain to need proof.

See how it opposes Justice, the ultimate purpose of human law; nay, the declared objects of the Constitution itself! But yet its unconstitutionality has been most abundantly shown by our own fellow-citizens. I need not go out of Massachusetts for defenders of Justice and Law. You remember the Speeches of Mr. Phillips, Mr. Sewall, Mr. Rantoul, Mr. Sumner, Mr. Mann, the arguments of Mr. Hildreth. The judges before you by nature are able-minded men, both of them; both also learned as lawyers and otherwise well educated, — I love to honor their natural powers, and their acquired learning; would I could offer higher praise. Now, I will not insult their manly understanding with the supposition that either of them ever thought the fugitive slave bill constitutional. No, Gentlemen, it is not possible that in the *personal* opinion of Mr. Sprague, or even Mr. Curtis, this bill can be held for a constitutional law. But the Court has its official dress: part of it is of silk — or supposed to be, — the gown which decorates the outward figure of the man who wears its ample folds; it is made after a prescribed pattern. But part of it also is made of *opinion* which hides the ability and learning of the honorable Court. The constitutionality of the fugitive slave bill is a part of the judge's official dress: accordingly, as no federal judge sits without his "silk gown," so none appears without his "opinion" that the fugitive slave bill is constitutional. But if the court should solemnly declare that such was its *personal opinion* — Gentlemen of the Jury, I, — I — should not believe it — any more than if they declared the gown of silk was the natural judicial covering, the actual "true skin" of the judges. No, Gentlemen, these judges are not monsters, not naturally idiotic in their Conscience. This opinion is their official robe, a supplementary cuticle, an artificial epidermis, woven from without, to be thrown off one day, when it shall serve their turn, by political desquamation. Let them wear it; "they have their reward." But you and I, Gentlemen, let us thank God we are not officially barked about with such a leprous elephantiasis as that. You are to judge of its constitutionality for yourselves, not to take the *purchased, official opinion* of the judge as veil for your Conscience; let it hide the judges' if they like.

Gentlemen, I lack words to describe the fugitive slave bill; its sins outrun my power of speech. But you know the consequences which follow if it be accepted by the People, submitted to, and enforced: the State of Massachusetts is nothing; her courts nothing; her juries nothing; her laws nothing; her Constitution nothing — the Rights of the State are whistled away by the "opinion" of a fugitive slave bill judge, the rights of the citizen — all gone; his right to life, liberty, and the pursuit of happiness lies at the mercy of the meanest man whom this Court shall ever make a Commissioner to kidnap men.

Yes, Gentlemen of the Jury, you hold your liberty at the mercy of George T. Curtis and Seth J. Thomas! You are the People, "the Country" to determine whether it shall come to this.

You know the motive which led the South to desire this bill, — it was partly pecuniary, the desire to get the work of men and not pay for it; partly political, the desire to establish Slavery at the North. Mr. Toombs is not the only man who wishes the master to sit down with his slaves at the foot of Bunker Hill Monument! You know the motive of the Northern men who supported the bill; — words are idle here!

Gentlemen, I said that Boston fired a hundred jubilant cannon when the fugitive slave bill became a law. It was only a *part of Boston* that fired them. The bill was odious here to all just and honorable men. Massachusetts hated the bill, and was in no haste to "conquer her prejudices" in favor of Justice, Humanity, and the Christian Religion; she did not like the "disagreeable duty" of making a public profession of practical Atheism. At first the yellow fever of the slave-hunters did not extend much beyond the pavements of Boston and Salem; so pains must be taken to spread the malady. The greatest efforts were made to induce the People to renounce their Christianity, to accept and enforce the wicked measure. The cry was raised, "The Union is in danger:" nobody believed it; they least of all who raised the cry. Some clergymen in the Churches of Commerce were coaxed, wheedled, or bought over, and they declared kidnapping would be imputed unto men for "righteousness." The actual manstealer in Boston was likened to "faithful Abraham" in the Hebrew mythic tale, — "the rendition of a slave was like the sacrifice of Isaac." One Trinitarian minister, a son of Massachusetts, laid Conscience down before the Juggernaut of the fugitive slave bill, another would send his own mother into Slavery; both had their reward. Editors were brought over to the true faith of kidnapping. Alas, there were some in Boston who needed no conversion; who were always on the side of inhumanity. There were "Union meetings" called to save the Nation; and the meanest men in the great towns came to serve as Redeemers in this Salvation unto kidnapping. Mr. Webster outdid himself in giant efforts — and though old and sick, he wrought with mighty strength. So in the great poem the fallen angel, his Paradise of Virtue lost, —

——— "with bold words
Breaking the horrid silence thus began."
"To do aught good never will be our task,
But ever to do ill our sole delight,
As being the contrary to His high will
Whom we resist . . . .

Let us not slip the occasion . . . .
But reassembling our afflicted powers
Consult how we may henceforth most offend
Our enemy; our own loss how repair,
How overcome this dire calamity;
What reinforcement we may gain from hope,
If not what resolution from despair.'"

One class of men needed no change, no stimulation. They were ready to execute this unjust, this unconstitutional Act; their lamps were trimmed and burning, their loins girt about, their feet swift to shed blood. Who were they? Ask Philadelphia, ask New York, ask Boston. Look at this bench. The Federal Courts were as ready to betray justice in 1850 as Kelyng and Jeffreys and Scroggs and the other pliant judges of Charles II. or James II. to support his iniquities. I must speak of this.

(II.) Of the conduct of the Federal Courts.

Gentlemen of the Jury, that you may understand the enormity of the conduct of the federal courts and the peril they bring upon their victims, I must refresh your memory with a few facts.

1. I shall begin with the cases in Pennsylvania. In that State four officials of government have acquired great distinction by their zeal in enslaving men, McAllister, Ingraham, Grier, and Kane; the two first are "Commissioners," the latter two "Judges." In one year they had the glory of kidnapping twenty-six Americans and delivering them over to Slavery. Look at a few cases.

(1.) On the 10th of March, 1851, Hannah Dellam was brought before Judge Kane charged with being a fugitive slave. She was far advanced in pregnancy, hourly expecting to give birth to a child. If a convicted murderess is in that condition, the law delays the execution of its ghastly sentence till the baby is born, whom the gallows orphans soon. The poor negro woman's counsel begged for delay that the child might be born in Pennsylvania and so be free,—a poor boon, but too great for a fugitive slave bill judge to grant. The judge who inherits the name of the first murderer, disgraced the family of Cain; he prolonged his court late into night, that he might send the child into Slavery while in the bowels of its mother! Judge Kane held his "court" and gave his decision in the very building where the Declaration of Independence was signed and published to the world. The memorable bell which summons his court, has for motto on its brazen lips, "Proclaim Liberty throughout the Land, to all the inhabitants thereof."

(2.) The same year Rachel Parker, a free colored girl, was seized

12

in the house of Joseph C. Miller of West-Nottingham, Chester County, by Thomas McCreary of Elkton, Maryland. Mr. Miller pursued the kidnapper and found the girl at Baltimore, and brought a charge of kidnapping against McCreary. But before the matter was decided Mr. Miller was decoyed away and murdered! The man-hunter was set free and the girl kept as a slave, but after long confinement in jail was at last pronounced free — not by the Pennsylvania "judge" but by a Baltimore Jury![1]

(3.) The same year occurred the Christiana Tragedy. Here are the facts.

In Virginia a general law confers a reward of $100 on any man who shall bring back to Virginia a slave that has escaped into another State, and gives him also ten cents for each mile of travel in the chase after a man. Accordingly, beside the officers of the fugitive slave bill courts commissioned for that purpose, there is a body of professional Slave-hunters, who prowl about the borders of Pennsylvania and entrap their prey. In September, 1850, "a colored man, known in the neighborhood around Christiana to be free, was seized and carried away by professional kidnappers, and never afterwards seen by his family." In March, 1851, in the same neighborhood, under the roof of his employer, during the night, another colored man was tied, gagged, and carried away, "marking the road along which he was dragged by his own blood." He was never afterwards heard from. "These and many other acts of a similar kind had so alarmed the neighborhood, that the very name of Kidnapper was sufficient to create a panic."[2]

"On the 11th of September, Edward Gorsuch, of Maryland, his son, Dickerson Gorsuch, with a party of friends, and a United States officer named Kline, who bore the warrant of Commissioner Ingraham, made their appearance in a neighborhood near Christiana, Lancaster County, Pennsylvania, in pursuit of a Slave. They lay in wait for their prey near the house of William Parker, a colored man. When discovered and challenged, they approached the house, and Gorsuch demanded his Slave. It was denied that he was there. High words ensued, and two shots were fired by the assailants at the house. The alarm was then given by blowing a horn, and the neighborhood roused. A party of colored men, from thirty to fifty strong, most of them armed in some way, were before long on the ground. Castner Hanway and Elijah Lewis, both white men and Friends, rode up before the engagement began and endeavored to prevent bloodshed by persuading both parties to disperse peaceably. Kline, the Deputy Marshal, ordered them to join the *posse*, which they, of course, refused to do, but urged upon him the necessity of withdrawing his men for their own safety. This he finally did, as far as he personally was concerned, when satisfied that there was actual danger of bloody resistance. Gorsuch, however, and his party persisted in their attempt, and he and two of his party fired on the colored men, who returned the fire with deadly

1 20 Anti-Slavery Report, 28 and 21; Ibid. 34.

2 History of the Trial of Castner Hanway and others for Treason (Philadelphia, 1852), 35.

effect. Gorsuch was killed on the spot, his son severely, though not mortally, wounded, and the rest of the party put to flight. The dead and wounded were cared for by the neighbors, mostly Friends and Abolitionists. The Slave, for the capture of whom this enterprise was undertaken, made his escape and reached a land of safety.

"Judge Grier denounced the act from the Bench as one of Treason. A party of marines were ordered to the ground to keep the peace after the battle had been fought and won. United States Marshal Roberts, Commissioner Ingraham, United States District Attorney Ashmead, with a strong body of police, accompanied them, and kept the seat of war under a kind of martial law for several days. The country was scoured, houses ransacked, and about thirty arrests made. Among those arrested were Castner Hanway and Elijah Lewis, whose only crime had been endeavoring to prevent the effusion of blood. The prisoners were brought to Philadelphia, examined before a Commissioner, and committed on a charge of High Treason. At the next term of the District Court, under a charge from Judge Kane, the Grand-Jury found indictments against all of them for this crime."[1]

Mr. Hanway was brought to trial — for his life, charged with "treason." It appears that this was his overt act. — He was a Quaker, an anti-slavery Quaker, and a "non-resistant;" when he heard of the attack on the colored people, he rode on a sorrel horse to the spot, in his shirt-sleeves, with a broad felt hat on; he advised the colored men not to fire, "For God's sake don't fire;" but when Deputy Marshal Kline ordered him to assist in the kidnapping, he refused and would have nothing to do with it. Some of the colored people fired, and with such effect on the Kidnappers as I have just now shown. It appeared also that Mr. Hanway had said the fugitive slave bill was unconstitutional, and that he would never aid in kidnapping a man — words which I suppose this Honorable Court will consider as a constructive "misdemeanor;" "obstructing an officer."

For this "offence" his case was presented to the grand-jury of the Circuit Court the 29th of September, 1851. Judge Kane charged the jury — laying down the law of treason. Mr. Hanway was indicted for "wickedly devising and intending the peace and tranquillity of the . . . United States to disturb;" and that he "wickedly and traitorously did intend to levy war against the said United States." And also that he "with force and arms, maliciously and traitorously did prepare and compose and . . . and cause and procure to be prepared and composed, divers books, pamphlets, letters, and declarations, resolutions, addresses, papers, and writings, and did . . . maliciously and traitorously publish and disperse . . . divers other books . . . containing . . . incitement, encouragement, and exhortations, to move, induce, and persuade persons held to service in any of the United States . . . who had escaped . . . to resist, oppose, and prevent, by

[1] 20 Anti-Slavery Report, pp. 30, 31.

violence and intimidation, the execution of the said laws, [that is the law for kidnapping their own persons]."

He was brought to trial at Philadelphia, November 24th 1851, before Honorable Judges Kane and Grier, then and subsequently so eminent for their zeal in perverting law and doing judicial iniquity. Gentlemen of the Jury — it is no slander to say this. It is their great glory that in the cause of Slavery they have struck at the first principles of American Democracy, and set at nought the Christian Religion. It is only their panegyric which I pronounce.

On behalf of the government there appeared six persons as prosecuting officers. One United States Senator from Pennsylvania (Mr. Cooper), the Attorney-General of Maryland, the District Attorney of Pennsylvania, the Recorder of the City of Philadelphia, and two members of her bar.[1] For Mr. Webster, then Secretary of State, was highly desirous that Maryland should send her Attorney-General, Hon. Mr. Brent, to help the government of the United States prosecute a Quaker miller, a Non-resistant, for the crime of treason. Hon. James Cooper, the Pennsylvania Senator, also appeared on behalf of Maryland, seeking to convict one of his own constituents! Gentlemen, such conduct carries us back to the time of the Stuarts; but despotism is always the same. It was very proper that the United States government should thus outrage the common decencies of judicial process.

This question amongst others was put to each juror: —

> "Have you formed an opinion that the law of the United States, known as the Fugitive Slave Law of 1850, is unconstitutional, so that you cannot for that reason convict a person indicted for a forcible resistance thereto, if the facts alleged in the indictment are proved and the court hold the statute to be constitutional?"

Thus all persons were excluded from the jury who believed this wicked bill a violation of the constitution; and one most important means of the prisoner's legitimate defence was purposely swept away by the court.

Now look at the law as laid down by the government.

Mr. Ashmead, the government's Attorney, said when the Constitution was adopted "Men had not then become wiser than the laws [the laws of England and colonial laws which they were born under and broke away from]; nor had they learned to measure the plain and unambiguous letter of the Constitution by an artificial standard of their own creation [that is the Self-evident Truth that all men have a natural and unalienable Right to Life, Liberty, and the Pur-

[1] History, 55, 57; Report, 19; 2 Wallace.

suit of Happiness]; to obey or disregard it acccording as it came up to or fell beneath it [as the law was just or unjust]."

"*You will receive the law from the court.*" "You *are bound by the instructions which the court may give* in respect to it;" "*it is in no sense true that you are judges of the law.*" "*You must take the interpretation which the court puts upon it.* You have a right to apply the law to the facts, but you have no right to go further."

"The crime charged against this defendant is . . . that of *levying war against the United States.* The phrase *levying war* was long before the adoption of the Constitution, a phrase . . . *embracing such a forcible resistance to the laws as that charged against this defendant* [that is, speaking against the fugitive slave bill and refusing to kidnap a man is "levying war against the United States]!"

It is treason "if the intention is by force to prevent the execution of *any one . . . of the general laws of the United States*, or *to resist* the exercise of *any legitimate authority of the government.*"

"Levying war embraces . . . any combination forcibly to prevent or oppose the execution . . . of a public statute, if accompanied or followed by an act of forcible opposition." Of course the court is to determine the meaning of *force;* and using the same latitude of construction as in interpreting *levying war*, it would mean, a *word*, a *look*, a *thought*, a *wish*, a *fancy* even.

Mr. Ludlow enforced the same opinions, relying in part on the old tyrannical decisions of the British courts in the ages of despotism, and on the opinion of Judge Chase — who had derived his law of treason from that source, and was impeached before the American Senate for his oppressive conduct while judge in the very trials whence these iniquitous doctrines were derived! But Mr. Ludlow says "if a *spurious doctrine have been introduced into the common law . . . it would require great hardihood in a judge to reject it.*" So the jury must accept "a spurious doctrine" as genuine law!

"In treason, all the *participes criminis* are principals; there are no accessaries to this crime. Every act which . . . would render a man an *accessary* will . . . make him a *principal.*" "If any man joins and acts with an assembly of people, *his intent is always to be considered . . . the same as theirs; the law . . . judgeth of the intent by the Fact.*" *This was Judge Kelyng's "law."*

"It may be . . . advanced that because Hanway was not armed, he was not guilty. It is perfectly well settled that *arms are not necessary.*" "Military weapons . . . are not necessary . . . to a levying war." "This is the opinion of Judge Chase," and "it may be alleged that Judge Chase was impeached, and that [therefore] his opinions are of little weight. Whatever may have been the grounds of that impeachment, *it is not for us to discuss.*"

"If a body of men be assembled for the purpose of effecting a treasonable object [that is, 'to oppose the execution of a public statute,' no matter what or how] *all those who perform any part, however minute, or however remote from the scene of action . . . are equally traitors.*"

Mr. Brent, the Maryland State Attorney, whom Mr. Webster had sent there, declared that "*any combination* like this, of colored and white persons, *to prevent the execution of the Fugitive Slave Law, is treason.*"

Mr. Cooper, the Pennsylvania Senator, adds, "Castner Hanway . . . having been present . . . at the time the overt act was committed, he is a principal . . . provided he was there aiding and abetting the objects of the confederated parties." "*Persons* procuring, contriving, or *consenting*, come within the words aid and abet." So "*if he* encourages, *assists, or consents to the act*, it is enough; *he becomes at once an aider and abettor*, and *obnoxious to all the pains and penalties denounced against it.*" "If persons *do assemble themselves* and act with *some* force in opposition to *some* law . . . and *hope thereby to get it repealed, this is a levying war and high treason.*" That is, an assembly of men acting against any law, with any force of argument, in order to procure its repeal, levies war and is guilty of treason!

To connect Mr. Hanway with this constructive treason, the government relied on the evidence of Mr. Kline, the Deputy Marshal of the court, a man like Mr. Butman and Mr. Patrick Riley, so well known in this court, and so conspicuous for courage and general elevation of character. Witnesses testified that Kline was so much addicted to falsehood that they would not believe him on oath, — but what of that? He had "conquered his prejudices." It appeared that Mr. Hanway went to the scene of action on a sorrel horse, in his shirt-sleeves, with a felt hat on, and did not join the Deputy in attempting to kidnap when commanded. Hear how Mr. Ludlow constructs levying war out of the disobedience of a non-resistant Quaker in a felt hat and shirt-sleeves, mounted on a sorrel horse! Hearken to this voice of the government: —

> "Suddenly he sees the assembled band of infuriated men . . . Does he leave the spot? No, Sir! Does he restrain the negroes? Take the evidence for the defence in its fullest latitude, and you will perceive he raised the feeble cry, 'Don't shoot! for God's sake don't shoot!' and there it ended. Is that consistent with innocence? . . . according to their own evidence the conclusion is irresistible that he was not innocent."

"But he does more than this." When summoned by the Deputy to steal a man "he is thrown off his guard, and exclaims, 'I will not assist you;' 'he allowed the colored people had a right to defend themselves.' 'He did not care for that Act of Congress or any other Act of Congress.'"

And so with his unsaddled sorrel nag this non-resistant miller levies war upon the United States by crying "Don't fire," and commits treason by the force and arms of a broad-brimmed Quaker hat. "The smallest amount of force is sufficient," "military weapons are not necessary to levy war!"

Mr. Brent thought if Mr. Hanway was not hanged it would appear that a "small and miserable and traitorous faction can resist and annul the laws of the United States." "Put down these factions [the Free-Soil Party, the Liberty Party, the Anti-Slavery Societies], overwhelm them with shame, disgrace, and ruin, or you are not good citizens fulfilling the bonds that bind you to us of the South."

The government Attorney declared that Mr. Hanway and others

> "Had no right to refuse to assist because it was repugnant to their consciences. Conscience! Conscience . . . is the pretended justification for an American citizen to refuse to execute a law of his country." "*Damnable, treasonable doctrine.*" "He has become a conspirator, he has connected himself with them, and all their acts are his acts, and all their intentions are his intentions."
>
> "The whole neighborhood was not only disloyal, but wanting in common humanity:" "the whole region is infected," "in *that horde of traitors;*" "a whole county, a whole township, a whole neighborhood are involved in plotting treason." "When you see these things *can you not infer . . . that he went there by pre-arrangement!*" "When you see a man . . . not saying one word to save his dear colored friends from the guilt of murder, I say it is passing human credulity to say that you cannot *infer* in all that *a feeling of hostility to the law, and an intention to resist it.*"
>
> "The consequences [of the verdict] are not with the jury:" the responsibility will not be with you — you are not responsible for those just consequences."
>
> "When you allege that a master has come into Pennsylvania and illegally seized and possessed himself of his slave without process, you are to inquire, 'Has he done that which he had authority to do in his own State?' You are to look to the *laws of his own State;* for the Supreme Court says,[1] 'He *has the same right to repossess his slave here as in his own State.*'" "He who employs a man said to have come from Maryland without being satisfied of his freedom, is himself guilty of the first wrong."

Senator Cooper closed for the government. Law was not enough for him; he would have the sanction of "Religion" also. So he read extract from a Sermon. Gentlemen of the Jury, you have not had the benefit of Rev. Dr. Adams's prayers in this court; it is a pity you should not be blessed with the theology of despotism; listen therefore to the "Thanksgiving Sermon" of Rev. Dr. Wadsworth, which Hon. Mr. Cooper read to the Jury in Independence Hall.

> "For passing by all other causes of irritation as just now secondary and subordinate, look for a moment, at the influence which the Gospel of Christ would have in this great sectional controversy about slavery.

[1] 16 Peters, Prigg *v.* Penn.

"First, It would say to the Northern fanatic, who *vapors about man-stealing* as if there were no other evil under the sun but this one evil of Slavery — it would say to him, Emulate the spirit of your blessed Master and his apostles, *who, against this very evil* [man-stealing] in their own times, *brought no railing accusation;* but in one instance at least, *sent back a fugitive* from the household of Philemon.

"In treating Southern Christian slaveholders with Christian courtesy, and sending *back their fugitives when apprehended among you, you neither indorse the system nor* partake of its evil; you are only performing in good faith the agreement, and redeeming the pledges of your forefathers, and leaving to each man for himself to answer for his own acts at the judgment-seat of Jesus. It would tear away from the man, as the foulest cloak of hypocrisy, that pretence of a religious principle in this whole matter of political abolitionism.

"Religious principle! Oh my God! That religious principle, that for the sake of *an abstract right* whose very exercise were disastrous to the unprepared bondmen who inherit it, would tear this blest confederacy in pieces, and deluge these smiling plains in fraternal blood, and barter the loftiest freedom that the world ever saw, for the armed despotism of a great civil warfare! That religious principle which, in disaster to man's last great experiment, would fling the whole race back into the gloom of an older barbarism — rearing out of the ruin of these free homes, the thrones of a more adamantine despotism — freedom's beacons all extinguished, and the whole race slaves. That religious principle through which, losing sight of God's great purpose of evangelizing the nations, [by American Slavery,] would shatter the mightiest wheel in the mechanism of salvation, and palsy the wing of God's preaching angel in its flight through the skies.

"Alas — alas! ye that count as little this bond of blessed brotherhood, wrought by our fathers' mighty hands and bleeding hearts — we tell you, sorrowing and in tears, that your pretence is foul hypocrisy. Ye have reversed the first precept of the gospel, for your wisdom is a dove's, and your harmlessness a serpent's. *Ye have not the first principle within you either of religion or philanthropy, or common human benevolence.* Your principle is the principle of Judas Iscariot, and with the doom of the traitor ye shall go to your own place."

"No, Sir — no, Sir," concludes the Senator thirsting for his constituent's blood, "'There is no gospel in all this treasonable fanaticism — for treason to my country is rebellion to my God.'"

Judge Grier charged the Jury; — but as *he struck out from the phonographer's report* — of which the proof-sheets were sent to him — *the most offensive portion*, Gentlemen of the Jury, I shall not be able to enlighten you with all the legal words of this "consummate judge." So be content with the following Elegant Extracts.

"With the exception of a few individuals of perverted intellect in some small districts or neighborhoods whose moral atmosphere has been tainted and poisoned by male and female vagrant lecturers and conventions, no party in politics, no sect of religion, or any respectable numbers or character can be found within our borders, who have viewed with approbation or have looked with any other than feelings of abhorrence upon this disgraceful tragedy."

"It is not in this Hall of Independence that meetings of infuriated fanatics and unprincipled demagogues have been held to counsel a bloody resistance to the laws of the land. It is not in *this* city that conventions are held denouncing the Constitution, the

Laws, and the Bible. It is not *here* that the pulpit has been desecrated by seditious exhortations, teaching that theft [a man stealing his own limbs and person from his 'lawful owner'] is meritorious, murder [in self-defence killing a man-stealer] excusable, and treason [opposition to the fugitive slave bill] a virtue!"

"The guilt of this foul murder [the shooting of a kidnapper by the men whom he intended for his victims, and whose premises he invaded without due process of law, and with armed force], rests not alone on the deluded individuals who were its immediate perpetrators, but the blood taints with even deeper dye the skirts of those who promulgated doctrines subversive of all morality and all government, [that is, of Slavery and the fugitive slave bill]."

"This murderous tragedy is but the necessary development of principles and the natural fruit from seed sown by others whom the arm of the law cannot reach," [such as the Authors of the Declaration of Independence, and still more the Author of the "Sermon on the Mount]."

"This [the slave clause of the Constitution] is the Supreme law of the land, *binding . . . on the conscience* and conduct of every individual citizen of the United States." "The shout of disapprobation with which this [the fugitive slave bill] has been received by some, has been caused . . . because it is an act which can be executed. . . . the real objection . . . is to the Constitution itself, which is supposed to be void in this particular, from the effect of some 'higher law.' It is true that the number of persons whose consciences affect to be governed by such a law [that is the law of Natural Morality and Religion], is very small. But there is a much larger number who take up opinions on trust, — and have concluded this must be a very pernicious and unjust enactment, for no other reason than because the others shout their disapprobation with such violence and vituperation."

"This law is Constitutional." "The question of its Constitutionality is to be settled by the Courts, [fugitive slave bill courts,] and not by conventions either of laymen or ecclesiastics." "*We are as much bound to support this law as any other.*" "The jury should regard the construction of the Constitution as given them by the court as to what is the true meaning of the words *levying war.*" "In treason all are principals, and a man may be guilty of aiding and abetting, though not present."

He spoke of those "associations, or conventions, which occasionally or annually infest the neighboring village of West-Chester, for the purpose of railing at and resisting the Constitution and laws of the land [that is the fugitive slave bill and other laws which annihilate a man's unalienable right to his liberty], and denouncing those who execute them as no better than a Scroggs or a Jeffries; — who stimulate and exhort poor negroes to the perpetration of offences which they know must bring them to the penitentiary or the gallows."

But he thought refusing to aid the deputy marshal in kidnapping was not an act of levying war, or treason against the United States. "In so doing he is not acting the part of an honest, loyal citizen [who ought to do any wickedness which a bum-bailiff commands]; he may be *liable to be punished for a misdemeanor for his refusal to interfere.*"

But he thought the government was right "in procuring an indictment for Treason." For "meetings had been held in many places in the North, denouncing the law, and advising a traitorous resistance to its execution: conventions of infuriated fanatics had invited to acts of rebellion; and even the pulpit had been defiled with furious denunciations of the law, and exhortations to a rebellious resistance to it.

"The government was perfectly justified in supposing that this transaction was but the first overt act of a treasonable conspiracy, extending over many of the Northern States, to resist by force of arms the execution of this article of the Constitution and the laws framed in pursuance of it. In making these arrests, and having this investigation, the officers of government have done no more than their strict duty.

The activity, zeal, and ability, which have been exhibited by the learned Attorney of the United States, in endeavoring to bring to condign punishment the perpetrators of this gross offence, are deserving of all praise. *It has given great satisfaction to the Court also, that the learned Attorney-General of Maryland, and the very able counsel associated with him* [Senator Cooper of Pennsylvania] *have taken part in this prosecution.*"

In about fifteen minutes the Jury returned a verdict of NOT GUILTY."[1]

(4.) On the 29th of April, 1852, a man named William Smith was arrested by Commissioner McAllister of Columbia, Pennsylvania, on complaint of one Ridgeley of Baltimore. While in the custody of the officers, Smith endeavored to escape, and Ridgeley drew a pistol and shot him dead. The murderer escaped. No serious efforts were made by the State authorities to bring that offender to justice. "He has the same right to repossess his slave here as in his own State;" the same right to kill him if he attempts to escape! Mr. Toombs is modest — but we shall soon see the slaveholder not only sit down with his slaves at the foot of Bunker Hill Monument, but *shoot them if they attempt to run away!* Nay, Gentlemen, we shall see this Court defending the slave-hunter's "privilege."

(5.) Here is another case, Gentlemen of the Jury, in which this same Judge Grier appears, and with his usual humanity. This is a brief account of the case of Daniel Kauffman. In 1852 he allowed a party of fugitive slaves to pass the night in his barn, and gave them food in the morning. For this he was brought before Judge Grier's court and fined $2,800! It was more than his entire property. Gentlemen, there are persons in this room who gave money to Mr. Kauffman, to indemnify him for his losses; were not they also guilty of treason, at least of a "misdemeanor?" They "evinced an express liking" for Freedom and Humanity, not Slavery and bloodshed.

(6.) But here is yet one more, — which you shall have in the language of another: —

[1] See Report of Trial of Castner Hanway, Phil. 1852.

"In a case of attempted Slave-catching at Wilkesbarre, in Pennsylvania, the Deputy Marshal, Wyncoop and his assistants, had behaved with such atrocious and abominable cruelty, that the citizens felt that justice demanded their punishment for the outrage. They were, accordingly, arrested on a warrant issued by a most respectable magistrate, on the oath of one of the principal inhabitants of the place. A writ of habeas corpus was forthwith sued out, returnable before Judge Grier. When the District Attorney, Ashmead, moved the discharge of the relators, (which, it is needless to say, was ordered,) Judge Grier delivered himself to the following effect. "If *habeas corpuses* are to be taken out after that manner, *I will have an indictment sent to the United States Grand-Jury against the person who applies for the writ, or assists in getting it, the lawyer who defends it, and the sheriff who serves the writ*, to see whether the United States officers are to be arrested and harassed whenever they attempt to serve a process of the United States."

2. Gentlemen of the Jury, you might suppose that love of liberty had altogether vanished from the "Free" States, else how could such men ride over the local law as well as natural justice? But I am happy to find one case where the wickedness of the fugitive slave bill courts was resisted by the people and the local judges — it is a solitary case, and occurred in Wisconsin: —

"About the middle of March, 1854, a man named Joshua Glover, was seized near Racine, in Wisconsin, as a Fugitive Slave. His arrest was marked by the circumstances of cruelty and cowardice which seem to be essential to the execution of this Law above all others. He was brought, chained and bleeding, to Milwaukee, where he was lodged in jail. As soon as the news spread, an indignation, as general as it was righteous, prevailed throughout the city. A public meeting was forthwith called, and held in the open air, at which several of the principal citizens assisted. Stirring speeches were made, and strong resolutions passed, to the effect that the rights of the man should be asserted and defended to the utmost. Counsel learned in the law volunteered, and all necessary process was issued, as well against the claimant for the assault and battery, as in behalf of the man restrained of his liberty. A vigilance committee was appointed to see that Glover was not secretly hurried off, and the bells were ordered to be rung in case any such attempt should be made. But the people were not disposed to trust to the operation of the Slave Law, administered by United States Judges or Commissioners, and they stepped in and settled the question for themselves in a summary manner. A hundred men arrived, in the afternoon, from Racine, the town from which the man had been kidnapped, who marched in order to the jail. They were soon reinforced by multitudes more, and a formal demand was made for the slave. This being denied, an attack was made upon the door, which was soon broken in, the man released, and carried back in triumph to Racine, whence he was afterwards conveyed beyond the jurisdiction of the star-spangled banner. A mass convention of the citizens of Wisconsin was afterwards held to provide for similar cases, should they occur, and a most sound and healthy tone of feeling appears to have pervaded that youthful commonwealth.

"After the rescue had been effected, the United States Marshal arrested several persons for the offence of resisting an officer in the discharge of his duties. Among these was Mr. Sherman M. Booth, the editor of the Free Democrat. When brought before a Commissioner, in the custody of the Marshal, a writ of habeas corpus was sued out on his behalf, and he was brought before Judge A. D. Smith, of the Supreme Court. After a full hearing, Judge Smith granted him his discharge, on the ground that the fugitive slave law was unconstitutional. The Marshal then had the proceedings removed by a writ of certiorari before a full bench of the Supreme Court, when the decision of Judge Smith was confirmed, and Mr. Booth discharged from custody. Immediately afterwards, Judge Miller, of the United States District Court, issued another warrant for the arrest of Mr. Booth, making no mention of the fugitive slave act, but directing his arrest to answer to a charge for abetting the escape of a prisoner from the custody of the United States Marshal. Another writ of habeas corpus was sued out, but it was denied by the Supreme Court, on the ground that there was nothing on the face of the record to bring it within range of their former decision."

"In the mean time the United States Judge and Marshal were busy in their vocation. It is affirmed that the Grand-Jury was packed in the most unblushing manner, until an inquest was made up that would answer the purpose of the Government. However this may have been, indictments were found in the District Court, against Mr. Booth and several other persons. A petty Jury selected with the same care that had been bestowed on the composition of the Grand-Jury, convicted Mr. Booth and Mr. Ryecraft. All the weight of the government was thrown against the defendants. Special counsel were retained to assist the District Attorney, the intructions of the Court were precise and definite against them; all motions in their behalf resting on the irregularities and injustices of the proceedings were overruled. So were all motions subsequent to the conviction for an arrest of judgment. They were sentenced to fine and imprisonment — Mr. Booth to pay one thousand dollars and costs, and to be imprisoned one month, and Mr. Ryecraft to pay two hundred dollars, and to be imprisoned for ten days. On these sentences they were committed to jail. The public excitement in Milwaukee, and throughout the State, was intense. It was with difficulty that the people could be restrained from forcibly liberating the prisoners. Fortunately there was no occasion for any such extreme measures. They found protection, where it ought to be found, in the constituted authorities of their State. A writ of habeas corpus was issued in their behalf by the Supreme Court, then sitting at Madison, the Capital of the State, returnable before them there. Escorted by two thousand of their fellow-citizens, thither, in charge of the High Sheriff, they had a hearing at once. After full deliberation, the Court unanimously ordered them to be discharged. The majority of the Court made this decision on the ground of the unconstitutionality of the fugitive slave law, one Judge (Crawford) sustaining the law, but concurring in the order on the ground that no offence, under that Act, was charged in the indictment. So the prisoners were discharged, and brought home in triumph."

Gentlemen, that matter will be carried up to the Supreme Court of the United States, and you may yet hear the opinion of the Hon. Associate Justice Curtis, for which let us wait with becoming reverence.

3. Here is the case of Mr. Sloane, which happened in the State of Ohio.

In October, 1852, several colored persons were about leaving Sandusky in a steamer for Detroit, when they were seized and taken before Mr. Follet, mayor of the city, and claimed as fugitive slaves. This seizure was made by the city marshal and three persons claiming to act for the owners of the slaves.

After the colored persons were brought before the mayor, their friends engaged Mr. Rush R. Sloane to act as counsel in their defence.

He demanded of the mayor and the claimants by what authority the prisoners were detained. There was no reply. He then asked, whether they were in the custody of a United States Marshal or Commissioner. Again there was no reply. He next called for any writs, papers, or evidences by which they were detained. Still there was no answer. He then said to his clients, "*I see no authority to detain your colored friends.*"

At that time some one near the door cried out, "Hustle them out," and soon the crowd and the alleged fugitives were in the street. Then one of the claimants said to Mr. Sloane, "I own these slaves; they are my property, and I shall hold you individually liable for their escape." *These were the first and only words he spoke to Mr. Sloane, and then not until the black men were in the street.*

In due time Mr. Sloane was arrested for resisting the execution of the fugitive slave bill, though he had *only acted as legal counsel for the alleged slaves and had offered no resistance to the law, by deed, or word, or sign.*

He was brought to trial at Columbus. Before the jurors were sworn they were all asked "whether they had any conscientious scruples against the fugitive slave law, and would hesitate to convict under it." If they said "Yes," they were rejected. Thus a jury was packed for the purpose, and the trial went on. Thirteen unimpeached witnesses deposed to the facts stated before, while the slave claimant had no evidence but the *city marshal* of Sandusky — the Tukey of that place — and *two of the three slave-catchers* — who swore that they had with them *powers of attorney for the seizure of twenty-four slaves.*

Gentlemen, such was the action of the court, and such the complexion of the packed jury, that Mr. Sloane was found "guilty." The Judge, Hon. Mr. Leavitt, refused to sign a bill of exceptions, enabling him to bring the matter before the Supreme Court. Mr. Sloane was sentenced to pay a fine of $3,000, and $930 *as costs of court!* Such was the penalty for a lawyer telling his clients that he saw no authority to detain them, — after having three times demanded the authority, and none had been shown!

4. Gentlemen of the Jury, I now come to cases which have happened in our own State, — in this city. Some alarm was felt as soon as Mr. Mason's fugitive slave bill was proposed in the Senate. But men said, "No northern man will support it. There is much smoke and no fire." But when on the 7th of March, 1850, Mr. Webster adopted the bill, and promised to defend it and the amendments to it, "with all its provisions to the fullest extent;" when he declared that Massachusetts would execute the infamous measure

"with alacrity" — then not only alarm but indignation took possession of northern breasts. The friends of Slavery at Boston must do all in their power to secure the passage of the bill, the prosperity of its adoptive father, and its ultimate enforcement — the kidnapping of men in Massachusetts. Here are the measures resorted to for attaining this end.

i. A meeting was called at the Revere House, that Mr. Webster might defend his scheme for stealing his constituents and putting himself into the Presidency.

ii. A public letter was written to him approving of his attempts to restore man-stealing, and other accompaniments of slavery, to the free States. This letter declared the "deep obligations" of the signers "for what this speech has done and is doing;" "we wish to thank you," they say, "for recalling us to our duties under the constitution;" "you have pointed out to a whole people the path of duty, have convinced the understanding, and touched the conscience of the nation;" "we desire, therefore, to express to you our entire concurrence in the sentiments of your speech." This letter was dated at Boston, March 25th, 1850, and received 987 signatures, it is said.

iii. When the bill became an Act of government, a hundred cannons, as I have before stated, were fired on Boston Common in token of joy at the restoration of slavery to our New England soil.

iv. Articles were written in the newspapers in defence of kidnapping, in justification of the fugitive slave bill. The *Boston Courier* and *Boston Daily Advertiser* gave what influence they had in support of that crime against America.

v. Several ministers of Boston came out and publicly, in sermons in their own pulpits, defended the fugitive slave bill, and called on their parishioners to enforce the law!

Gentlemen of the Jury, need I tell you of the feelings of the Philanthropists of Boston, — of the colored citizens who were to be the victims of this new abomination! Within twenty-four hours of its passage more than thirty citizens of Boston, colored citizens, fled in their peril to a man whose delight it is to undo the heavy burthens and let the oppressed go free. While others were firing their joyful cannon at the prospect of kidnapping their brothers and sisters, Francis Jackson helped his fellow Christians into the ark of Deliverance which he set afloat on that flood of Sin. Gentlemen, he is here to day — he is one of my bondsmen. There are the others — this venerable gentleman [Samuel May], this steadfast friend [John R. Manley.]

vi. It was not long before the kidnappers came here for their prey.

(1.) I must dwell a moment on the first attempt. Gentlemen

of the Jury, you know the story of William and Ellen Craft. They were slaves in Georgia; their master was said to be a "very pious man," "an excellent Christian." Ellen had a little baby, — it was sick and ready to die. But one day her "owner" — for this wife and mother was only a piece of property — had a dinner party at his house. Ellen must leave her dying child and wait upon the table. She was not permitted to catch the last sighing of her only child with her own lips; other and ruder hands must attend to the mother's sad privilege. But the groans and moanings of the dying child came to her ear and mingled with the joy and merriment of the guests whom the mother must wait upon. At length the moanings all were still — for Death took a North-side view of the little boy, and the born-slave had gone where the servant is free from his master and the weary is at rest — for *there* the wicked cease from troubling. Ellen and William resolved to flee to the North. They cherished the plan for years; he was a joiner, and hired himself of his owner for about two hundred dollars a year. They saved a little money, and stealthily, piece by piece, they bought a suit of gentleman's clothes to fit the wife; no two garments were obtained of the same dealer. Ellen disguised herself as a man, William attending as her servant, and so they fled off and came to Boston. No doubt these Hon. Judges think it was a very "immoral" thing. Mr. Curtis knows no morality here but "legality." Nay, it was a wicked thing — for Mr. Everett, a most accomplished scholar, and once a Unitarian minister, makes St. Paul command "SLAVES, obey your masters!" Nay, Hon. Judge Sprague says it is a "precept" of our "Divine Master!"

Ellen and William lived here in Boston, intelligent, respected, happy. The first blow of the fugitive slave bill must fall on them. In October, 1850, one Hughes, a jailer from Macon, Georgia, a public negro-whipper, who had once beaten Ellen's uncle "almost to death," came here with one Knight, his attendant, to kidnap William and Ellen Craft. They applied to Hon. Mr. Hallett for a writ. Perhaps they had heard (false) rumors that the Hon. Commissioner was "a little slippery in his character;" that he was "not overscrupulous in his conduct;" that he "would do any dirty work for political preferment." Gentlemen, you know that such rumors will get abroad, and will be whispered of the best of men. Of course you would never believe them in this case: but a kidnapper from Georgia might; "distance lends" illusion, as well as "enchantment, to the view." But be that as it may, Mr. Hallett (in 1850) appeared to have too much manhood to kidnap a man. He was better than his reputation; I mean his reputation with Knight and Hughes, and would not (then) steal Mr. and Mrs. Craft. This is small praise; it is large in comparison with the conduct of his official brethren. But for the salvation of the Union another Commissioner was found who had no such scruples. This Honorable Court — Mr. Woodbury was then in the chief place, and Mr. Sprague in his present position — issued the writ of man-stealing. Two gentlemen of this city were eminently, but secretly, active in their attempt to kidnap their victim. I shall speak of them by and by. Somebody took care of Ellen Craft. William less needed help; he armed himself with pistols and a poignard, and walked in the streets in the face of the sun. He was a tall, brave man, and was quite as cool then as this Honorable Court is now, while I relate their "glorious first essay" in man-stealing. Public opinion at length drove the (southern) kidnappers from Boston. Then the Crafts also left the town and the country, and found in the Monarchical Aristocracy of Old England what the New England Democracy refused to allow them — protection of their unalienable right to Life, Liberty, and the pursuit of Happiness.

Gentlemen, the Evangelists of slavery could not allow a Southern kidnapper to come to Boston and not steal his man: they were in great wrath at the defeat of Hughes and Knights. So they procured a meeting at Fanueil Hall to make ready for effectual kidnapping and restoring Slavery to Boston. "The great Union meeting" was held at Fanueil Hall November 26th, 1850, — two days before the annual Thanksgiving; it was "a preparatory meeting" to make ready the hearts of the People for that dear New England festival when we thank God for the Harvest of the Land, and the Harvest of the Sea, and still more for the State whose laws are Righteousness, and the Church that offers us "the Liberty wherewith Christ hath made us free," "the glorious Liberty of the Sons of God." Here are the Resolutions which were passed.

"Resolved, That the preservation of the Constitution and the Union is the paramount duty of all citizens; — that the blessings which have flowed from them in times past, which the whole country is now enjoying under them, and which we firmly believe posterity will derive from them hereafter, are incalculable; and that they vastly transcend in importance all other political objects and considerations whatever.

"Resolved, That it would be folly to deny that there has been and still is danger to the existence of the Union, where there is prevalent so much of a spirit of disunion, constantly weakening its strength and alienating the minds of one part of the people of the United States from another; and that if this spirit be not checked and restrained, and do not give way to a spirit of conciliation and of patriotic devotion to the general good of the whole country, we cannot expect a long continuance of the political tie which has hitherto made us one people; but must rather look to see groups of rival neighboring republics, whose existence will be a state of perpetual conflict and open war.

"Resolved, That all the provisions of the Constitution of the United States — the supreme law of the land — are equally binding upon every citizen, and upon every State in the Union; — that ALL laws passed by Congress, in pursuance of the Constitution, are equally binding on all the citizens, and no man is at liberty to resist or disobey any one constitutional act of Congress any more than another; and that we do not desire or intend to claim the benefit of any one of the powers or advantages of the Constitution, and to refuse, or seem to refuse, to perform any part of its duties, or to submit to any part of its obligations.

"Resolved, That the adjustment of the measures which disturbed the action of Congress for nearly ten months of its last session, ought to be carried out by the people of the United States in good faith, in all the substantial provisions; *because*, although we may differ with each other about the details of those measures, yet, in our judgment, a renewed popular agitation of any of the main questions then settled, would be fraught with new and extreme dangers to the peace and harmony of the country, which this adjustment has happily restored.

"Resolved, That every species and form of resistance to the execution of a regularly enacted law, except by peaceable appeal to the regular action of the judicial tribunals upon the question of its constitutionality — an appeal which ought never to be opposed or impeded — is mischievous, and subversive of the first principles of social order, and tends to anarchy and bloodshed.

"Resolved, That men, who directly or indirectly instigate or encourage those who are or may be the subjects of legal process, to offer violent resistance to the officers of the law, deserve the reprehension of an indignant community, and the severest punishment which its laws have provided for their offence; and that we have entire confidence that any combination or attempt to fix such a blot upon the fair fame of our State or city, will be promptly rebuked and punished, by an independent and impartial judiciary, and by firm and enlightened juries.

"Resolved, That we will at all times, in all places, and under all circumstances, so far as our acts or influence may extend, sustain the Federal Union, uphold its Constitution, and enforce the duty of obedience to the laws."

A singular preparation for a Thanksgiving day in Boston! But on that festival, Gentlemen, three Unitarian ministers thanked God that the fugitive slave bill would be kept in all the land!

Several speeches were made at the meeting, some by Whigs, some by Democrats, for it was a "Union meeting," where Herod and Pilate were made friends. Gentlemen, I must depart a little from the severity of this defence and indulge you with some of the remarks of my distinguished opponent, Hon. Attorney Hallett: then he was merely a lawyer, and fugitive slave bill Commissioner, appointed "to take bail, affidavits," and colored men, — he was only an expectant Attorney. His speech was a forerunner of the "Indictment" which has brought us together. Hearken to the words of Mr. Hallett in his "preparatory lecture:" —

"We can now say that there is no law of the United States which cannot be executed in Massachusetts. If there was any doubt before, *there can be no doubt now;* and if there be any wild enough hereafter to resort to a fancied 'Higher Law' to put down law [that is, the fugitive slave bill], they will find in your determined will a stronger law to sustain *all the laws of the United States.*" "The threatened nullification comes from Massachusetts upon a law [the fugitive slave bill] which the whole South insist is *vital to the protection of their property and industry* [much of their "property" and "industry" being addicted to running away]. *And shall Massachusetts nullify that law?*" "The question for us to-day is whether we will in good faith abide by, and carry out these *Peace Measures* [for the rendition of fugitive slaves, the new establishment of Slavery in Utah and New Mexico, and the restoration of it to all the North] or whether we shall rush into renewed agitation," etc. "Resort is had to a new form of *moral treason* which assumes by the mysterious power of a '*Higher Law*' to trample down all law [that is, the fugitive slave bill]. Some of our fellow-citizens have avowed that the fugitive slave bill is to be treated like the *Stamp Act*, and never to be enforced in Massachusetts. If that means any thing, it means that which our fathers meant when they resisted the Stamp Act and threw the tea overboard — Revolution.[1] *It* [opposition to the fugitive slave bill] *is revolution, or it is treason. If it only resists law, and obstructs its officers, it is treason; and he who risks it, must risk hanging for it.*"[2]

Gentlemen, that meeting determined to execute the fugitive slave bill "with all its provisions, to the fullest extent." It is dreadful to remember the articles in the Daily Advertiser and the Courier at that period. Some of the sermons in the Churches of Commerce on the following Thursday, Thanksgiving day, were filled with the most odious doctrines of practical atheism. The "preparatory meeting" had its effect. Soon the seed bore fruit after its kind. But some ministers were faithful to their Brother and their Lord.

(2.) February 15th, 1851, a colored man named "Shadrach" was arrested under a warrant from that Commissioner who had been so active in the attempt to kidnap Mr. and Mrs. Craft. But a "miracle" was wrought: "where sin abounded Grace did much more abound," and "the Lord delivered him out of their hands." Shadrach went free to Canada, where he is now a useful citizen. He was rescued by a small number of colored persons at noonday. The kidnapping Commissioner telegraphed to Mr. Webster, "It is levying war — it is treason." Another asked, "What is to be done?" The answer from Washington was, "Mr. Webster was very much mortified."

On the 18th, President Fillmore, at Mr. Webster's instigation, issued his proclamation calling on all well disposed citizens, and *commanding all officers*, "civil and military, to aid and assist in quelling this, and all other such combinations, *and to assist in recapturing the above-named person*" Shadrach. General orders came down from the Secretaries of War and the Navy, commanding the *military and naval officers to yield all practicable assistance* in the event of such another "*insurrection*." The City Government of Boston passed Resolutions regretting that a man had been saved from the shackles of slavery; cordially approving of the President's proclamation, and

[1] The learned counsel for the fugitive slave bill confounds two events. The Stamp Act was passed March 22d, 1765, and repealed the 28th of the next March. The tea was destroyed December 16th, 1773.

[2] Report in Boston Courier of November 27th, 1850.

promising their earnest efforts to carry out his recommendations. At that time Hon. Mr. Tukey was Marshal; Hon. John P. Bigelow was Mayor; Hon. Henry J. Gardner, a man equally remarkable for his temperance, truthfulness, and general integrity, was President of the Common Council.

It was not long, Gentlemen, before the City Government had an opportunity to keep its word.

(3.) On the night of the 3d of April, 1851, Thomas Sims was kidnapped by two police officers of Boston, pretending to arrest him for theft! Gentlemen of the Jury, you know the rest. He was on trial nine days. He never saw the face of a jury, a judge only once — who refused the *Habeas Corpus*, the great "Writ of Right." That judge — I wish his successors may better serve mankind — has gone to his own place; where, may God Almighty have mercy on his soul! You remember, Gentlemen, the chains round the Court House; the Judges of your own Supreme Court crawling under the southern chain. You do not forget the "Sims Brigade" — citizen soldiers called out and billeted in Faneuil Hall. You recollect the Cradle of Liberty shut to a Free Soil Convention, but open to those hirelings of the Slave Master. You will never forget the Pro-Slavery Sermons that stained so many Boston pulpits on the "Fast-day" which intervened during the mock trial!

Mr. Sims had able defenders, — I speak now only of such as appeared on his behalf, others not less noble and powerful, aided by their unrecorded service — Mr. Sewall, Mr. Rantoul, men always on the side of Liberty, and one more from whose subsequent conduct, Gentlemen of the Jury, I grieve to say it, you would not expect such magnanimity then, Mr. Charles G. Loring. But of what avail was all this before such a Commissioner? Thomas Sims was declared "a chattel personal to all intents, uses, and purposes whatsoever." After it became plain that he would be decreed a slave, the poor victim of Boston kidnappers asked one boon of his counsel, "I cannot go back to Slavery," said he, "give me a knife, and when the Commissioner declares me a slave I will stab myself to the heart, and die before his eyes! I will not be a slave." The knife was withheld! At the darkest hour of the night Mayor Bigelow and Marshal Tukey, suitable companions, admirably joined by nature as by vocation, with two or three hundred police-men armed, some with bludgeons, some with drawn swords and horse pistols, took the poor boy out of his cell, chained, weeping, and bore him over the spot where, on the 5th of March, 1770, the British tyrant first shed New England blood; by another spot where your fathers and mine threw to the ocean the taxed tea of the oppressor. They put him on board a vessel, the "*Acorn*," and carried him off to eternal bondage. "And this is Massachusetts liberty!" said he, as he stepped on board. Boston sent her Delegates to escort him back, and on the 19th of April, 1851, she delivered him up to his tormentors in the jail at Savannah, where he was scourged till human nature could bear no more, while his captors were feasted at the public cost. Seventy-six years before there was another 19th of April, also famous!

(4.) Then came the examination and "trial" of the Shadrach Rescuers in February and the following months. Some of these trials took place before his Honor Judge Peleg Sprague. Therefore, you will allow me, Gentlemen, to refresh your memories with a word or two respecting the antecedents of this Judge — his previous history.

In 1835 the abolition of Slavery in the British West Indies and the efforts of the friends of Freedom in the Northern States, excited great alarm at the South, lest the "peculiar institution" should itself be brought into peril. Fear of a "general insurrection of the slaves" was talked about and perhaps felt. The mails were opened in search of "incendiary publications;" a piano-forte sent from Boston to Virginia, was returned because the purchaser found an old copy of the "Emancipator" in the case which contained it. Public meetings for the promotion of American Slavery were held. There was one at Boston in Faneuil Hall, August 21, 1835, at which a remarkable speech was made by a lawyer who had graduated at Harvard College in 1812, a man no longer young, of large talents and great attainments in the law. He spoke against discussion, and in behalf of Slavery and Slaveholders: he could see no good, but only unmixed evil "consequent upon agitating this subject here." He said: —

"When did fear ever induce a man to relax his power over the object that excited it? No, he will hold him down with a stronger grasp, he will draw the cords tighter, he will make the chains heavier and sink his victim to a still deeper dungeon."

"The language and measures of the abolitionists clearly tend to insurrection and violence." "They [the slaves] hear that their masters have no legal or moral authority over them. That every moment's exercise of such dominion is sin, and that the laws that sanction it are morally void: that they are entitled to immediate emancipation, and that their masters are to be regarded as kidnappers and robbers for refusing it." "It is deluding these unfortunate beings to their own destruction, we should not aid them. The Constitution provides for the suppressing of insurrections . . . we should respond to its call [if the slaves attempted to recover their liberty]; nay, we should not wait for such a requisition, but on the instant should rush forward with fraternal emotions to defend our brethren from desolation and massacre."

"The South will not tolerate our interference with their slaves, [by our discussing the matter in the newspapers and elsewhere]." "The Union then, if used to disturb this institution of Slavery, will be then as the 'spider's web; a breath will agitate, a blast will sweep it away forever.'"

"If, then, these abolitionists shall go on . . . the fate of our government is sealed. . . . And who will attempt to fathom the immeasurable abyss of a dissolution of the Union?"

"Tell the abolitionists this; present to them in full array the consequences of their attempts at immediate emancipation, and they meet all by a cold abstraction. They answer, '*We must do right regardless of consequences.*'" "They assume that such a course [undoing the heavy burthens and letting the oppressed go free, and loving your neighbor as yourself] *is* right. When that is the very point in controversy, and when inevitable consequences demonstrate that it must be wrong."

"They [the abolitionists] insist upon immediate, instantaneous emancipation. . . . . No man, say they, can be rightfully restrained of his liberty except for crime." "They come to the conclusion that no laws that sanction or uphold it [Slavery] can have any moral obligation. The Constitution is the Supreme law of the land. It does sanction, it does uphold Slavery; and if this doctrine be true, that sacred compact has always been [so far] morally null and void." "He [Washington] THAT SLAVEHOLDER . . . came with other Slaveholders to drive the British myrmidons from this city and this Hall. Our fathers did not refuse to hold communion with him or with them. With Slaveholders they formed the Confederation . . . with them they made the Declaration of Independence." "And in the original draft of the Declaration was contained a most *eloquent passage upon this very topic of negro Slavery, which was stricken out in deference to the wishes of members from the South.*" "Slavery existed then as now." "Our fathers were not less devoted friends of liberty, not less pure as philanthropists or pious as Christians than any of their children of the present day." [Therefore *we* must not attempt to emancipate a slave!]

Here is the passage which the speaker thought it so praiseworthy in the Revolutionary Congress to strike out from the Declaration of Independence:—

"He [the king] has waged cruel war against human nature itself, violating its most sacred rights of life and liberty in the persons of a distant people who never offended him, captivating and carrying them into slavery in another hemisphere, or to incur miserable death in their transportation thither. This piratical warfare, the opprobrium of INFIDEL nations, is the warfare of the CHRISTIAN King of Great Britain. Determined to keep open a market where MEN should be bought and sold, he has prostituted his negative for suppressing every legislative attempt to prohibit or to restrain this execrable commerce. And that this assemblage of horrors might want no fact of distinguished dye, he is now exciting those very people to rise in arms among us, and to purchase that liberty of which he has deprived them, by murdering the people on whom he also obtruded them: thus paying off former crimes committed against the LIBERTIES of one people with crimes which he urges them to commit against the LIVES of another."

Mr. Jefferson says, "It was struck out in *compliance to South Carolina and Georgia,* who had never attempted to restrain the importation of slaves, and who, on the contrary, still wished to continue it. Our Northern brethren also, I believe, felt a little tender under it, for though their people have very few slaves themselves, yet they have been pretty considerable carriers of them to others."

But the orator went on protesting against righteousness:—

"I would beseech them [the Abolitionists] to discard their dangerous abstractions [that men are endowed by their Creator with certain natural, equal, and unalienable

Rights — to Life, Liberty, and the Pursuit of Happiness] which they [in common with the Declaration of Independence] adopt as universal rules of human conduct — without regard to time, condition, or circumstances; which *darken the understanding and mislead the judgment*, and urge them forward to consequences from which they will shrink back with horror. I would ask them to reflect that . . . the religion they profess is not to be advanced by forgetting the precepts and the example of their Divine Master. Upon that example I would ask them to pause. He found Slavery, Roman Slavery, an institution of the country in which he lived. Did he denounce it? Did he attempt its immediate abolition? Did he do any thing, or say any thing which could in its remotest tendency encourage resistance and violence? No, his precept was, 'Servants (Slaves) obey your Masters.'"[1] "It was because *he would not interfere with the administration of the laws, or abrogate their authority*."

Gentlemen of the Jury, this alleged precept of the "Divine Master" does not occur in any one of the four canonical Evangelists of the New Testament; nor have I found it in any of those Spurious and Apocryphal Records of old time. It appears originally in the Gospel according to the Hon. Peleg Sprague. "Slaves, obey your masters," "a comfortable Scripture" truly; a beatitude for the stealers of men!

Gentlemen of the Jury, that was the language of Mr. Peleg Sprague at the time when the State of Georgia offered $5,000 for the head of Mr. Garrison; when the Governors of Virginia and other Slave States, sent letters to the Governor of Massachusetts asking for "penal statutes" to prohibit our discussion in Boston; it was the very year that a mob of "Gentlemen of Property and Standing" in Boston broke up a meeting of women assembled to endeavor to abolish Slavery. Gentlemen of the Jury, Mr. Sprague had his reward — he sits on the bench to try me for a "misdemeanor" — "obstructing, resisting, and opposing an officer of the United States," "while in the discharge of his duty" to steal a man in Boston, that his "owner" might sell him in Richmond. The "chief commandment" of the New Testament is, "Slaves, obey your masters;" on that commandment he would now hang all the law, and the Abolitionists.

It would take a long time to tell the dark, sad tale of the trial of the Shadrach Rescuers; how the Judge constructed and charged the Jury; how he constructed his "law." It was the old story of the Stuart despotism, wickedness in the name of the law and with its forms. Gentlemen, in that trial you saw the value of the jury. The Judges of Massachusetts went under the chain which the kidnappers placed about the Court House in 1851. The Federal Judges sought to kidnap the citizens of Boston and to punish all such as opposed man-stealing. The Massachusetts Judges allowed the law, which they had sworn to execute, to be struck down to the ground; nay, themselves

[1] The learned counsel for the slaveholders probably referred to Eph. vi. 5; or Coloss. iii. 22; or Tit. ii. 9; or 1 Pet. ii. 18.

sought to strike it down. The Federal Judges perverted the law to make it an instrument of torture against all such as love mankind. But the jury held up the Shield of Justice, and the poisoned weapons of the court fell blunted to the ground. The government took nothing by that motion — nothing but defeat. There was no conviction. One of the jurors said, "You may get one Hunker on any panel; it is not easy to get twelve. There was no danger of a conviction." But still it is painful to think in what peril our lives and our liberties then were.

(5.) At length came the "Burns case." You know it too well. On the night of Wednesday, May 26, 1854, in virtue of Commissioner Loring's warrant, Anthony Burns was arrested on the charge of burglary, and thrust into jail. The next morning he was brought up for condemnation. Two noble men, Mr. Dana and my friend Mr. Ellis, defended Mr. Burns. There was to be no regular trial before Commissioner Loring.

On the evening of Friday, May 28th, there was a meeting at Faneuil Hall, and an attack on the Court House where Mr. Burns was illegally held in duress. In the attack a Mr. Batchelder was killed, — a man hired to aid in this kidnapping, as he had been in the stealing of Mr. Sims. To judge from the evidence offered before the Grand-Jury of the Massachusetts Court, and especially from the testimony of Marshal Freeman, it appears he was accidentally killed by some of his own confederates in that wickedness, and before the door of the Court House was broken through. But that is of no consequence: as Mr. Dana has said, "He went went in for his pay, and has got his *corn*." On Friday, June 4th, Mr. Burns was declared a slave by Commissioner Loring and delivered up to eternal bondage.

It seems to be in consequence of my connection with this case that I am indicted; so you now approach the end of this long defence. I come to the last part of it.

(III.) Of the Indictment against Theodore Parker.

I am indicted, gentlemen, for "resisting an officer" who was engaged in kidnapping Mr. Burns; and it is charged that I, at Boston, May 26th, "with force and arms did knowingly and wilfully, obstruct, resist, and oppose, . . . Watson Freeman, then and there being an officer of the United States, to the great damage of the said Watson Freeman; to the great hinderance and obstruction of justice, [to wit, of the kidnapping of Anthony Burns,] to the evil example of all others in like case offending, against the peace and dignity of the said United States and contrary to the form of the statute made and provided."

It is also charged that "one Theodore Parker of Boston, . . . with force and arms in and upon the said Watson Freeman, then and there, in the peace of the said United States being, an assault did make, he the said Freeman also then and there being an officer of the said United States, to wit, Marshal of the United States, . . . and then and there also being in the due and lawful discharge of his duties as such officer" [to wit, stealing and kidnapping one Anthony Burns]. These and various other pleasant charges, Mr. Hallett, in the jocose manner of indictments, alleges against me; wherefrom I must defend myself, as best I may.

Now, Gentlemen, that you may completely understand the accusation brought against me, I must go back a little, and bring up several other matters of fact that have straggled away from this long column of argument which I have led into the field thus far; — and also rally some new forces not before drawn into the line of defence. I must speak of the Hon. Justice Curtis; of his conduct in relation to Slavery in general, to this particular prosecution, and to this special case, *United States* vs. *Theodore Parker.*

First, Gentlemen, let me speak of some events which preceded Mr. Curtis's elevation to his present distinguished post. To make the whole case perfectly clear, I must make mention of some others intimately connected with him.

There is a family in Boston which may be called the Curtis family. So far as it relates to the matter in hand, it may be said to consist of six persons, namely, Charles P. Curtis, lawyer, and Thomas B. Curtis, merchant, sons of the late Thomas Curtis; Benjamin R. Curtis, by birth a kinsman, and by marriage a son-in-law of Charles P. Curtis, late a practising lawyer, now this Honorable Judge of the Supreme Court of the United States, and his brother, George T. Curtis, lawyer, and United States Commissioner for the District of Massachusetts; Edward G. Loring, a step-son of the late Thomas Curtis, and accordingly step-brother of Charles P. and Thomas B. Curtis, lawyer, Judge of Probate for Boston, United States Commissioner, and, until recently, Lecturer at the Cambridge Law School; and also William W. Greenough, son-in-law of Charles P. Curtis, merchant.

This family, though possessing many good qualities, has had a remarkably close and intimate connection with all, or most, of the recent cases of kidnapping in Boston. Here are some of the facts, so painful for me to relate, but so indispensable to a full understanding of this case.

1. In 1836 Charles P. Curtis and Benjamin R. Curtis appeared as counsel for the slave-hunters in the famous case of the girl Med, originally a slave in the West Indies, and brought to Boston by her mistress. Med claimed her freedom on the ground that slavery was not

recognized by the laws of Massachusetts, and could not exist here unless it were in the special case, under the Federal Constitution, of fugitives from the slave States of this Union. The Messrs. Curtis contended with all their skill — *totis viribus*, as lawyers say — that slavery might, by legal comity, exist in Massachusetts — that slaves were property by the law of nations; and that an ownership which is legal in the West Indies continued in Boston, at least so far as to leave the right to seize and carry away.

Mr. Charles P. Curtis had already appeared as counsel for a slave-hunter in 1832, and had succeeded in restoring a slave child, only twelve or fourteen years of age, to his claimant who took him to Cuba with the valuable promise that he should be free in the Spanish West Indies.[1]

In the Med case Mr. Benjamin R. Curtis made a long and elaborate argument to show that "a citizen of a slaveholding State, who comes to Massachusetts for a temporary purpose of business or pleasure and brings his slave as a personal attendant, may restrain that slave for the purpose of carrying him out of the State and returning him to the domicil of his owner." To support this proposition, he made two points: —

"1. That this child by the law of Louisiana is *now* a slave."

"2. That the law of Massachusetts will so far recognize and give effect to the law of Louisiana, as to allow the master to exercise this restricted power over his slave." That is, the power to keep her here as a slave, to remove her to Louisiana, and so make her a slave for ever and her children after her.

To prove this last point he says by quotation, "we always *import*, together with their persons, *the existing relations of foreigners between themselves*." So as we "import" the natural relation of husband and wife, or parent and child, in the Irish immigrants, and respect the same, we ought equally to import and respect the unnatural and forcible relation of master and slave in our visitors from Cuba or Louisiana.

"It will be urged," he said, "that though we claim to exercise only a qualified and limited right over the slave, namely the right to remove him from the State, yet if this is allowed, all the rights of the master must be allowed, . . . and thus Slavery will be introduced into the Commonwealth. To this I answer,

"(1.) There is no practical difficulty in giving this qualified effect to the law of Louisiana, [allowing the master to bring and keep his slaves here and remove them when he

[1] Daily Advertiser, Dec. 7th, 1832. Mr. Sewall, the early and indefatigable friend of the slave, asked the Court to appoint a guardian *ad litem* for the child, who was not 14, who should see that he was not enslaved. But the slaveholder's counsel objected, and the Judge (Shaw) refused; yet to his honor be it said in a similar case in 1841, when Mr. Sewall was counsel for a slave child under the same circumstances, he delivered him to a guardian appointed by the Probate Court. 3 Metcalf, 72.

will]. The Constitution of the United States has settled this question. That provides for and secures to the master, the exercise of his right to the very extent claimed in this case."

"(2.) Neither is there any theoretical difficulty."

To do this, he thinks, will "promote harmony and good feeling, where it is extremely desirable to promote it, encourage frequent intercourse, and soften prejudices by increasing acquaintance, and tend to peace and union and good-will." "It will work no injury to the State [Massachusetts], by violating any public law of the State. The only law in the statute-book applicable to the subject of Slavery is the law against kidnapping." "It will work no direct injury to the citizens of this State for, . . . it respects only strangers." "It is consistent with the public policy of Massachusetts, to permit this . . . right of the master." "*It may be perfectly consistent with our policy not only to recognize the validity and propriety of those institutions* [of Slavery] *in the States where they exist*, but *even to interfere actively to enable the citizens of those States to enjoy those institutions at home.*" That is, it may be the duty of Massachusetts, "to interfere actively" in Louisiana for the establishment and support of Slavery there!

Pennsylvania, New York, New Jersey, and Rhode Island, he adds, have made laws allowing the slaveholder this right: "The legislatures of those States are the legitimate and highest authority in regard to their public policy; what they have declared on this subject, must be deemed to be true. . . . We are not at liberty to suppose that it is contrary to their public policy, that the master should exercise this right within their territory. I respectfully ask what difference there is between the policy of Pennsylvania, New York, Rhode Island, and New Jersey, and the policy of Massachusetts, on the subject of Slavery."

"I shall now attempt," he adds, "to prove that *Slavery is not immoral.*" How do you think he proved that? Did he cite the Bible? No, he left that to lower law divines. Did he manufacture Bible? No, the Hon. Peleg Sprague had sufficiently done that a year before. He took a shorter cut—he denied there was any morality but Legality. "I take it to be perfectly clear," said this young man in all the moral enthusiasm of his youth, "that the Standard of Morality by which Courts of Justice are to be guided is that which the law prescribes. Your Honors' Opinion as Men or as Moralists has no bearing on the question. Your Honors are to declare what the Law deems moral or immoral."

Gentlemen, that needs no comment; this trial is comment enough. But according to that rule no law is immoral. It was "not immoral" in 1410 to hang and burn thirty-nine men in one day for reading the

Bible in English; the Catholic Inquisition in Spain was "not immoral;" the butchery of Martyrs was all right soon as lawful! There is no Higher Law!

It was "not immoral" for the servants of King Pharaoh to drown all the new-born Hebrew boys; nor for Herod's butchers to murder the Innocents at Bethlehem. Nay, all the atrocities of the Saint Bartholomew Massacres, Gentlemen, they were "not immoral," for "the Standard of Morality" is "that which the law prescribes." So any legislature that can frame an act, any tyrant who can issue a decree, any court which can deliver an "opinion," can at once nullify the legislation of the Universe and "dissolve the union" of Man and God: "Religion has nothing to do with politics; there it makes men mad." Is that the doctrine of Young Massachusetts? Hearken then to the Old. In 1765 her House of Representatives unanimously resolved that "there are certain essential Rights . . . which are founded on the Law of God and Nature, and are the Common Rights of Mankind, and that the inhabitants of this Province are unalienably entitled to these essential Rights in common with all men, and *that no law of Society . . . can divest them of these Rights.*" No "Standard of Morality" but Law! A thousand years before Jesus of Nazareth taught his Beatitudes of Humanity, the old Hebrews knew better. Hearken to a Psalm nearly three thousand years old.

Among the assemblies of the great,
A Greater Ruler takes his seat;
The God of Heaven, as Judge, surveys
Those Gods on earth, and all their ways.
Why will ye, then, frame wicked laws?
Or why support the unrighteous cause?
When will ye once defend the poor,
That sinners vex the Saints no more?
Arise, oh Lord, and let thy Son
Possess his universal Throne,
And rule the nations with his rod;
He is our Judge, and he our God.

"By the *law of this Commonwealth,*" added Mr. Curtis, "*Slavery is not immoral.* By the Supreme law of this Commonwealth Slavery is not only recognized as a valid institution, but to a certain extent is incorporated into our own law. Before you [the court] rise from your seats, you may be called upon by the master of a fugitive slave, to grant a certificate . . . which *will put the whole force of the Commonwealth at his disposal, to remove his slave from our Territory.*"

Gentlemen of the Jury, that was conquering his prejudices "with alacrity;" it was obeying the fugitive slave bill fourteen years before it was heard of.

He adds still further, by quotation, "I have no doubt but the citizen of a Slave State has a right to pass, upon business or pleasure, through any of the States attended by his slaves—and his right to reclaim his slave would be unquestioned. An escape from the attendance upon the person of his master, while on a journey through a free State, should be considered as an escape from the State where the master had a right of citizenship."

Mr. Charles P. Curtis thus sustained his kinsman:—

> "Is that to be considered immoral which the Court is bound to assist in doing? *It is not for us to denounce as* legally *immoral a practice which is permitted* and sanctioned *by the supreme law of the land!*" "It is said the practice of Slavery is corrupting in its influence on public morals. But the practice of bringing slaves here was much more common thirty years ago than now. If this practice be so corrupting, why is it tolerated in other States?" . . . "The law of New York allows even foreigners to go there with their slaves; and have the morals of that State suffered in consequence? In Pennsylvania the law is similar, but where is the evidence of its pernicious influence?" "As to the *right to using them,* [the slaves voluntarily brought here by their masters,] *notwithstanding the supposed horror at such an admission,* the legislatures of New York and Pennsylvania, Rhode Island and New Jersey, have actually enacted statutes allowing precisely that privilege."[1]

But the Supreme Court of Massachusetts held otherwise. Med was declared free. Chief Justice Shaw covered himself with honor by his decision. And soon after, (Aug. 29,) the Daily Advertiser, the "organ" of the opinions of this family, said:—

> "In some of the States there is . . . legislative provision for cases of this sort, [allowing masters to bring and hold slaves therein,] and it would seem that *some such provision is necessary in this State,* unless we would prohibit citizens of the Slave States from travelling in this State with their families, and unless we would permit such of them as wish to emancipate their slaves, to throw them, at their pleasure, upon the people of this State."

Gentlemen, Mr. Curtis in 1836 contended for all which Mr. Toombs boasts he shall get—the right of the slaveholder to sit down at the foot of Bunker Hill monument with his slaves! Nay, Mr. Curtis granted more: it may be the duty of Massachusetts "to interfere actively," and establish slavery in Louisiana, or in Kansas. It may be said, this was only a lawyer pleading for his client. It was—a lawyer asking the Supreme Court of Massachusetts to establish slavery in this Commonwealth. Is it innocent in a lawyer to ask the court to do a wicked thing, to urge the court to do it? Then is it equally innocent to ask the Treasurer of a Railroad to forge stock, or an editor to publish lies, or a counterfeiter to make and utter base coin, or an assassin to murder men. Surely it is as innocent to urge men to kidnap blacks in Africa as in Boston.

[1] Med. Case, 1836.

Gentlemen, That declaration — that the Statute supersedes natural Justice, and that the only "Standard of Morality" by which the courts are to be guided is "that which the law prescribes" — deserves your careful consideration. "He that squares his conscience by the law is a scoundrel" — say the proverbs of many nations. What do you think of a man who knows no lawgiver but the General Court of Massachusetts, or the American Congress: no Justice but the Statutes? If Mr. Curtis's doctrine is correct, then Franklin, Hancock, Adams, Washington, were only Rebels and Traitors! They refused that "Standard of Morality." Nay, our Puritan Fathers were all "criminals;" the twelve Apostles committed not only "misdemeanors" but sins; and Jesus of Nazareth was only a malefactor, a wanton disturber of the public peace of the world!

The slave child Med, poor, fatherless, and unprotected, comes before the Supreme Court of Massachusetts, claiming her natural and unalienable Right to Liberty and the Pursuit of Happiness, — if not granted she is a slave for ever. In behalf of her wealthy "owner" Mr. Curtis resists the girl's claim; tells the court she "is now a slave;" there is "no practical difficulty" in allowing the master to keep her in that condition, no "theoretical difficulty;" "slavery is not immoral;" it may be the duty of Massachusetts not only to recognize slavery at home, but also "even to interfere actively" to support slavery abroad; the law is the only "Standard of Morality" for the courts; that establishes slavery in Massachusetts! Gentlemen, what do mankind say to such sophistry? Hearken to this Hebrew Bible: "Wo unto them that decree unrighteous decrees, and that write grievousness which they have prescribed, to turn aside the needy from judgment, and to take away the Right from the poor of my people, that widows may be their prey, and *that they may rob the fatherless.*" Let the stern Psalm of the Puritans still further answer from the manly bosom of the Bible.

"Judges who rule the world by laws,
Will ye despise the righteous cause,
When the injured poor before you stands?
Dare ye condemn the righteous poor
And let rich sinners 'scape secure,
While Gold and Greatness bribe your hands?

"Have ye forgot, or never knew,
That God will judge the judges too?
High in the Heavens his Justice reigns;
Yet you invade the rights of God,
And send your bold decrees abroad,
To bind the Conscience in your chains.

"Break out their teeth, eternal God,
Those teeth of lions dy'd in blood;

And crush the serpents in the dust;
As empty chaff, when whirlwinds rise,
Before the sweeping tempest flies,
So let their hopes and names be lost.

"Thus shall the Justice of the Lord
Freedom and peace to men afford;
And all that hear shall join and say,
Sure there's a God that rules on high,
A God that hears his children cry,
And all their sufferings will repay."

2. After Mr. Webster had made his speech of March 7, 1850, pledging himself and his State to the support of the fugitive slave bill, then before Congress, "to the fullest extent," Thomas B. Curtis, with the help of others, got up a letter to Mr. Webster, dated March 25, 1850, signed, it is said, by 987 persons, who say: "We desire to express to you our deep obligations for what this speech has done and is doing." "You have pointed out to a whole people the path of duty, have convinced the understanding and touched the conscience of the nation." "We desire, therefore, to express to you our entire concurrence in the sentiments of your speech."

3. A little later, Mr. Webster returned to Boston, and was "rapturously received" at the Revere House, April 29, 1850, by a "great multitude," when Benjamin R. Curtis made a public address, and expressed his "abounding gratitude for the ability and fidelity" which Mr. Webster had "brought to the defence of the Constitution and of the Union," and commended him as "*eminently vigilant, wise, and faithful to his country, without a shadow of turning.*"

4. Presently, after the passage of the fugitive slave bill, at a dinner party, at the house of a distinguished counsellor of Boston, Charles P. Curtis declared that he hoped the first fugitive slave who should come to Boston would be seized and sent back!

5. Charles P. Curtis and his step-brother Edward G. Loring, and George T. Curtis, defended the fugitive slave bill by writing articles in the *Boston Daily Advertiser.*

6. In November, 1850, the slave-hunters, thus invited and encouraged, came to Boston, seeking to kidnap William and Ellen Craft: but they in vain applied to Commissioner Benj. F. Hallett, and to Judges Woodbury and Sprague, for a warrant to arrest their prey. Finally, they betook themselves to Commissioner George T. Curtis, who at once agreed to grant a warrant; but, according to his own statement, in a letter to Mr. Webster, Nov. 23, 1850, as he anticipated resistance, and considered it very important that the Marshal should have more support than it was in his power as a Commissioner to afford, he procured a meeting of the Commissioners, four in num-

ber, and with their aid succeeded in persuading the Circuit Court, then in session, to issue the warrant.

Gentlemen, as that letter of Mr. George T. Curtis contains some matters which are of great importance, you will thank me for refreshing your memory with such pieces of history.

"An application [for a warrant to arrest Mr. Craft] had already been made to the judges [Messrs. Woodbury and Sprague] privately . . . they could not grant a warrant on account of the pendency of an important Patent Cause then on trial before a jury." "To this I replied, that . . . the ordinary business of the Court ought to give way for a sufficient length of time, to enable the judges to receive this application and to hear the case." "On a private intimation to the presiding judge of our desire to confer with him [the desire of the kidnapping commissioners, Mr. B. F. Hallett, Mr. Edward G. Loring, Mr. C. L. Woodbury, and Mr. G. T. Curtis] the jury were dismissed at *an earlier hour than usual*, . . . *and every person present except the Marshal's deputies left the room, and the doors were closed.*" "The learned Judge said . . . that he would attend at half past eight the next morning, to grant the warrant." "A process was placed in the hands of the Marshal . . . in the execution of which he might be called upon to *break open dwelling-houses, and perhaps take life*, by quelling resistance, actual or *threatened.*" "I devoted at once a good deal of time to the necessary investigations of the subject." "There is a great deal of legislation needed to make the general government independent of State control," says this "Expounder of the Constitution," "and independent of the power of mobs, whenever and wherever its measures chance to be unpopular." "The office of United States Marshal is by no means organized and fortified by legislation as it should be to encounter popular disturbance."

7. The warrant having been issued for the seizure of Mr. Craft, Marshal Devens applied to Benjamin R. Curtis for legal advice as to the degree of force he might use in serving it, and whether it ought to be regarded as a civil or a criminal process. George T. Curtis was employed by his brother to search for authorities on these points. They two, together, as appears from the letter of George T. Curtis to Mr. Webster, induced Marshal Devens to ask a further question, which gave Benjamin R. Curtis an opportunity to come out with an elaborate opinion in favor of the constitutionality of the fugitive slave bill, dated November 9, 1850. This was published in the newspapers. In order to maintain the constitutionality of this act, Benjamin R. Curtis was driven to assume, as all its defenders must, that the Commissioner, in returning the fugitive, performs none of the duties of a Judge; that the hearing before him is not "a case arising under the laws of the United States;" that he acts not as a judicial, but merely as an executive and "ministerial" officer — not deciding him to be a slave, but merely giving him up, to enable that point to be tried elsewhere.[1] But, spite of this opinion, public justice and the

[1] On this see Hildreth's Despotism, 262, 280. Commissioner Loring considers that the fugitive slave bill commissioners have "*judicial* duties." Remonstrance to General Court, 2.

Vigilance Committee forced the (Southern) slave-hunters to flee from Boston, after which, Mr. and Mrs. Craft left America to find safety in England, the evident rage and fierce threats of the disappointed Boston slave-hunters making it unsafe for them to remain.

8. After the failure of this attempt to arrest Mr. Craft, Thomas B. Curtis got up a "Union Meeting" at Faneuil Hall, November 26, 1850.[1] The call was addressed to such as "regard with disfavor all further popular agitation" of the subject of Slavery. Thomas B. Curtis called the meeting to order: William W. Greenough, from the "Committee of Arrangements," presented the resolutions, which you have already heard.[2] It was said at the time that they were written, wholly or in part, by Mr. Benjamin R. Curtis, who moved their adoption and made a long and elaborate speech thereon.

Gentlemen of the Jury, as I just now gave you some passages from Mr. Hallett's speech on that occasion, allow me now to read you some extracts from Mr. Curtis's address. The general aim of the speech was to reconcile the People to kidnapping; the rhetorical means to this end were an attempt to show that kidnapping was expedient; that it was indispensable; that it had been long since agreed to; that the Slaves were foreigners and had no right in *Massachusetts.* He said: —

"We have come here not to consider particular measures of government but to assert that we have a government, not to determine whether this or that law be wise or just, but to declare that there is law, and its duties and power."

"Every sovereign State has and must have the right to judge *what persons from abroad* shall be admitted."

"Are not these persons [fugitive slaves] foreigners as to us — and what right have they to come here at all, *against the will of the legislative power of the State.* [Massachusetts had no legislation forbidding them!] And if their coming here or remaining here, is not consistent with the safety of the State and the welfare of the citizens *may we not* prohibit their coming, or *send them back* if they come?" "*To deny this* is to deny the right of self-preservation to a State. . . . It . . . *throws us back at once into a condition below the most degraded savages who have a semblance of government.*" "You know that the great duty of justice could not otherwise be performed, [that is without the fugitive-from-labor clause in the Constitution]; that our peace at home and our safety from foreign aggression could not otherwise be insured; and that only by this means could we obtain 'the Blessings of Liberty' to the people of Massachusetts and their posterity." "In no other way could we become an example of, and security for, the capacity of man, safely and peacefully and wisely to govern himself under free and popular institutions."

So the fugitive slave bill is an argument against human depravity, showing the capacity of man to govern himself "safely and peacefully and wisely."

[1] See Mr. Curtis's letter in Daily Advertiser of February 7, 1855.

[2] See above, p. 148, 149.

He adds, as early as 1643 the New England colonies found it necessary "to insert an article substantially like this one," for the rendition of fugitive servants, and in 1789 the Federal government demanded that the Spaniards should surrender the fugitive slaves of Georgia. Injustice, Gentlemen, has never lacked a precedent since Cain killed Abel. Mr. Curtis continues: —

> "When I look abroad over 100,000 happy homes in Massachusetts and see a people, such as the blessed sun has rarely shone upon, so intelligent and educated, moral, religious, progressive, and free to do every thing but wrong — I fear to say that I should not be in the wrong to put all this at risk, because our *passionate will* impels us to break a promise our wise and good fathers made, not to allow a *class of foreigners* to come here, or to *send them back if they came.*"

So the refusal to kidnap Ellen and William Craft came of the "*passionate will*" of the people, and is likely to ruin the happy homes of a moral and religious people!

> "*With the rights of these persons* I firmly believe *Massachusetts has nothing to do.* It is enough for us that they have no right to be *here.* Whatever natural rights they have — and I admit these natural rights to their fullest extent — this is not the *soil* on which to vindicate them. This is *our* soil, sacred to *our* peace, on which we intend to perform *our* promises, and work out for the benefit of ourselves and our posterity and the world, the destiny which our Creator has assigned to *us.*"

Gentlemen of the Jury, it is written of that Creator that He is "no Respecter of Persons;" and "hath made of one blood all nations of men for to dwell on all the face of the earth." The "Our Creator" of Mr. Curtis is also the Father of William and Ellen Craft; and that great Soul who has ploughed his moral truths deep into the history of mankind, represents the final Judge of us all as saying to such as scorned his natural Law of Justice and Humanity, "INASMUCH AS YE DID IT NOT TO ONE OF THE LEAST OF THESE YE DID IT NOT TO ME."

Massachusetts is "our soil," is it; "sacred to *our* peace," which is to be made sure of by stealing our brother men, and giving to Commissioners George T. Curtis and Edward G. Loring ten dollars for making a slave, and only five for setting free a man! Peace and the fugitive slave bill! No, Gentlemen of the Jury, it is vain to cry Peace, Peace — when there is no peace! Ay, there *is* no peace to the wicked; and though the counsel of the ungodly be carried, it is carried headlong!

In that speech, Gentlemen, Mr. Curtis made a special attack upon me: —

> "There has been made within these walls," said he, "the declaration that an article

of the Constitution [the rendition clause] of the United States 'shall not be executed, *law or no law.*' A gentleman offered a resolve . . . . that 'constitution or no constitution, law or no law, we will not allow a fugitive slave to be taken from Massachusetts.' The chairman of a public meeting [Hon. Charles Francis Adams, on October 14th] declared here that 'the law will be resisted, and if the fugitive resists, and if he slay the slave-hunter, or even the Marshal, and if he therefor be brought before a Jury of Massachusetts men, that Jury will not convict him.' And as if there should be nothing wanting to exhibit the madness which has possessed men's minds, *murder and perjury* have been enacted into virtues, and in this city preached from the sacred desk. I must not be suspected of exaggerating in the least degree. I read therefore the following passage from a sermon preached and published in this city: —

"'Let me suppose a case which may happen here and before long. A woman flies from South Carolina to Massachusetts to escape from bondage. Mr. Greatheart aids her in her escape, harbors and conceals her, and is brought to trial for it. The punishment is a fine of one thousand dollars and imprisonment for six months. I am drawn to serve as a juror and pass upon this offence. I may refuse to serve and be punished for that, leaving men with no scruples to take my place, or I may take the juror's oath to give a verdict according to the law and the testimony. The law is plain, let us suppose, and the testimony conclusive. Greatheart himself confesses that he did the deed alleged, saving one ready to perish. The judge charges that if the jurors are satisfied of that fact then they must return that he is guilty. This is a nice matter. Here are two questions. The one put to me in my official capacity as juror, is this: "Did Greatheart aid the woman?" The other, put to me in my natural character as man, is this: "Will you help punish Greatheart with fine and imprisonment for helping a woman obtain her unalienable rights?" If I have extinguished my manhood by my juror's oath, then I shall do my official business and find Greatheart guilty, and I shall seem to be a true man; but if I value my manhood I shall answer after my natural duty to love man and not hate him, to do him justice, not injustice, to allow him the natural rights he has not alienated, and shall say, "Not guilty." Then men will call me forsworn and a liar, but I think human nature will justify the verdict.'"

"I should like to ask," he continued, "the reverend gentleman in what capacity he expects to be punished for his *perjury?*" Gentlemen of the Jury, I rose and said, "Do you want an answer to your question, sir?" He had charged me with preaching murder and perjury; had asked, How I expected to be punished for my own "PERJURY?" When I offered to answer his question he refused me the opportunity to reply! Thus, Gentlemen, he charged me with recommending men to commit perjury! Did he think I advised men to take an oath and break it? On the other side of the page which he read there stood printed: —

"Suppose a man has sworn to keep the Constitution of the United States, and the Constitution is found to be wrong in certain particulars; then his oath is not morally binding, for before his oath, by his very existence, he is morally bound to keep the law of God as fast as he learns it. No oath can absolve him from his natural allegiance to God. Yet I see not how a man can knowingly, and with a good Conscience, swear to keep what he deems it wrong to keep, and will not keep, and does not intend to keep."

Gentlemen, when that speech came to be printed — there was no charge of "perjury" at all, but a quite different sentence![1]

9. In February, 1851, George T. Curtis issued the warrant for the seizure of Shadrach, who was "hauled" in to the court house before that Commissioner; but "the Lord delivered him out of their hands," and he also escaped out of the United States of America.

10. After the escape or rescue of Shadrach, George T. Curtis telegraphed the news to Mr. Webster, at Washington, declaring "it is levying war;" thus constructing high treason out of the rescue of a prisoner by unarmed men, from the hands of a sub-deputy officer of the United States.

11. George T. Curtis also officiated as Commissioner in the kidnapping of Thomas Sims, in April, 1851; and under the pretence of "extradition," sent him to be scourged in the jail of Savannah, and then to suffer eternal bondage. It was rumored at the time that Charles P. Curtis and Benjamin R. Curtis, his law-partner and son-in-law, were the secret legal advisers and chamber-counsel of the Southern slave-hunters in this case. I know not how true the rumor was, nor whether it was based on new observation of facts, or was merely an inference from their general conduct and character.

12. When Mr. Sims was brought before Judge Woodbury, on *habeas corpus*, Benjamin R. Curtis appeared as counsel for the Marshal, and also assisted Judge Woodbury in strengthening his opinion against Sims, by a written note transmitted by an officer of the Court to the Judge, while he was engaged in delivering his opinion.

13. Gentlemen of the Jury, I have shown you how, in Britain, the Government, seeking to oppress the people and to crush down freedom of speech, put into judicial offices such men as were ready to go all lengths in support of profitable wickedness. You do not forget the men whom the Stuarts made judges: surely you remember Twysden, and Kelyng, and Finch, and Saunders, and Scroggs. You will not forget Edmund Thurlow and John Scott. Well, Gentlemen, in 1851, Judge Woodbury died, and on the recommendation of Mr. Webster, Mr. Benjamin R. Curtis was raised to the dignity he now holds. Of course, Gentlemen, the country will judge of the cause and motive of the selection. No lawyer in New England had laid down such southern "Principles" for foundation of law; he outwent Mr. Sprague. None had rendered such service to the Slave Power. In 1836, he had sought to restore slavery to Massachusetts, and to accomplish that had denied the existence of any Higher Law, — the

[1] See the speech in Boston Courier of November 27th, with the editorial comment, and in Daily Advertiser of 28th, *Thanksgiving Day*. See also the Atlas of November 27th. The Sermon is in 2 Parker's Speeches, 241.

written statute was the only standard of judicial morals. In 1850, he had most zealously defended the fugitive slave bill, — coming to the rescue of despotism when it seemed doubtful which way the money of Boston would turn, and showing most exemplary diligence in his attempts to kidnap William and Ellen Craft. Gentlemen, if such services were left unpaid, surely "the Union would be in danger!" But I must go on with my sad chronicle.

14. As Circuit Judge of the United States, Benjamin R. Curtis, as well in the construction of juries, as in the construction of the law, exerted all his abilities against the parties indicted for the rescue of Shadrach, though Mr. Hale says his conduct was far better than Judge Sprague's. He did this especially in the case of Elizur Wright, who appeared withont counsel, and thus afforded a better opportunity to procure a conviction. But it was in vain — all escaped out of his hands.

15. In 1851, George T. Curtis brought an action for libel against Benjamin B. Mussey, bookseller, who had just published a volume of speeches by the Hon. Horace Mann, one of which was against the business of kidnapping in Boston, wherein George T. Curtis found, as he alleged, matter libellous of himself. That suit remains yet undisposed of; but in it he will doubtless recover the full value of his reputation, on which kidnapping has affixed no stain.

16. In May, 1854, Edward G. Loring issued a warrant for the seizure of Mr. Burns; decided the case before he heard it, having advised the counsel not to oppose his rendition, for he would probably be sent back; held him ironed in his "court," and finally delivered him over to eternal bondage. But in that case, it is said, Mr. Loring, who has no Curtis blood in his veins, did not wish to steal a man; and proposed to throw up his commission rather than do such a deed; but he consulted his step-brother, Charles P. Curtis, who persuaded him it would be dishonorable to decline the office of kidnapping imposed upon him as a United States Commissioner by the fugitive slave bill. Benjamin R. Curtis, it is said, I know not how truly — himself can answer, aided Mr. Loring in forming the "opinion" by which he attempted to justify the "extradition" of Mr. Burns; that is to say, the giving him up as a slave without any trial of his right to liberty, merely on a presumptive case established by his claimant.

17. After Commissioner Loring had seized Mr. Burns, Mr. George T. Curtis, by a communication published in the newspapers, informed the public that he still continued the business of man-hunting at the old stand, where all orders for kidnapping would be promptly attended to. For, he says, there was a statement "that I had declined, or was unwilling or afraid to act. I did not choose that

any one whatever should have an excuse for believing that Judge Loring was willing to sit in a case that I had declined." "I thought proper to place myself as it were by his side." "But I never took a fee [for kidnapping], and I never shall take one."[1] Did he remember the fate of the Hebrew Judas, who "betrayed the Innocent Blood," and then cast down the thirty pieces?

Hitherto the kidnapping commissioners, though both members of the same family, had pursued their game separately, each on his own account. After this it appears these two are to hunt in couples: Commissioner Loring and Commissioner Curtis "as it were by his side:" —

> "Swift in pursuit, but matched in mouth like bells,
> *Each under each.*"

Gentlemen of the Jury, it is a very painful thing for me to deliver this very sad chronicle of such wicked deeds. But do not judge these men wholly by those acts. I am by no means stingy of commendation, and would rather praise than blame. The two elder Messrs. Curtis have many estimable and honorable qualities, — in private relations it is said — and I believe it — they are uncommonly tender and delicate and refined in the elegant courtesies of common life. I know that they have often been open-handed and generous in many a charity. In the ordinary intercourse of society, where no great moral principle is concerned, they appear as decorous and worthy men. Hon. Benj. R. Curtis, — he will allow me to mention his good qualities before his face, — though apparently destitute of any high moral instincts, is yet a man of superior powers of understanding, and uncommon industry; as a lawyer he was above many of the petty tricks so common in his profession. Strange as it may seem, I have twice seen Mr. George T. Curtis's name among others who contributed to purchase a slave; Mr. Loring's good qualities I have often mentioned, and always with delight.

But this family has had its hand in all the kidnapping which has recently brought such misery to the colored people and their friends; such ineffaceable disgrace upon Boston, and such peril to the natural Rights of man. These men have laid down and advocated the principles of despotism; they have recommended, enforced, and practised kidnapping in Boston, and under circumstances most terribly atrocious. Without their efforts we should have had no man-stealing here. They cunningly, but perhaps unconsciously, represented the low Selfishness of the Money Power at the North, and the Slave Power at the South, and persuaded the controlling men of Boston to

[1] See Boston Journal of May 29, and Boston Courier of June 7, 1854.

steal Mr. Sims and Mr. Burns. In 1836 they sought to enslave a poor little orphan girl, and restore bondage to Massachusetts; in 1851 they succeeded in enthralling a man. Now, Gentlemen, they are seeking to sew up the mouth of New England; there is a sad consistency in their public behavior.

Gentlemen, they are not ashamed of this conduct; when "A Citizen of Boston," last January, related in the New York Tribune some of the facts I have just set forth, "One of the name" published his card in that paper and thanked the "Citizen" for collecting abundant evidence that the "Curtis Family" "have worked hard to keep the *law* superior to fanaticism, disloyalty, and the *mob*," and declared that "they feel encouraged to continue in the same course and *their children after them*."[1] Mr. Thomas B. Curtis considers some of the acts I have just mentioned "among the most meritorious acts" of his life.[2] Mr. Loring, in his "Remonstrance," justifies Kidnapping!

They may, indeed, speak well of the bridge which carries them safe over. Three of the family are fugitive slave bill commissioners; one of them intellectually the ablest, perhaps morally the blindest, who so charged me with "Perjury," is the Honorable Judge who is to try me for a "Misdemeanor." Of course he is perfectly impartial, and has no animosity which seeks revenge, — the history of courts forbids the supposition!

Such, Gentlemen, are the antecedents of the Hon. Judge Curtis, such his surroundings. You will presently see what effect they have had in procuring this indictment. It is a sad tale that I have presented. He told it, not I; he did the deeds, and they have now found words.

Gentlemen of the Jury, I shall next speak of Judge Curtis's charge to the grand-jury, delivered in Boston, June 7, 1854 — only five days after his kinsman had sent Mr. Burns into Slavery. Here is that part of the charge which relates to our case.

"There is another criminal law of the United States to which I must call your attention, and give you in charge. It was enacted on the 13th of April, 1790, and is in the following words: —

"'If any person shall knowingly or wilfully obstruct, resist, or oppose any officer of the United States, in serving, or attempting to serve, or execute any mesne process, or warrant, or any rule or order of any of the courts of the United States, or any other legal writ or process whatever, or shall assault, beat, or wound any officer, or other person duly authorized, in serving or executing any writ, rule, order, process, or warrant, aforesaid, such person shall, on conviction, be imprisoned not exceeding twelve months, and fined not exceeding three hundred dollars.'

[1] New York Tribune, January 15, 1855.

[2] Daily Advertiser, February 7, 1855.

"You will observe, Gentlemen, that this law makes no provision for a case where an officer, or other person duly authorized, is killed by those unlawfully resisting him. That is a case of murder, and is left to be tried and punished under the laws of the State, within whose jurisdiction the offence is committed. Over that offence against the laws of the State of Massachusetts we have here no jurisdiction. It is to be presumed that the duly constituted authorities of the State will, in any such case, do their duty; and if the crime of murder has been committed, will prosecute and punish all who are guilty.

"Our duty is limited to administering the laws of the United States; and by one of those laws which I have read to you, to obstruct, resist, or oppose, or beat, or wound any officer of the United States, or other person duly authorized, in serving or executing any legal process whatsoever, is an offence against the laws of the United States, and is one of the subjects concerning which you are bound to inquire.

"It is not material that the same act is an offence both against the laws of the United States and of a particular State. Under our system of government the United States and the several States are distinct sovereignties, each having its own system of criminal law, which it administers in its own tribunals; and the criminal laws of a State can in no way affect those of the United States. The offence, therefore, of obstructing legal process of the United States is to be inquired of and treated by you as a misdemeanor, under the Act of Congress which I have quoted, without any regard to the criminal laws of the State, or the nature of the crime under these laws.

"This Act of Congress is carefully worded, and its meaning is plain. Nevertheless, there are some terms in it, and some rules of law connected with it, which should be explained for your guidance. And first, as to the process, the execution of which is not to be obstructed.

"The language of the Act is very broad. It embraces every legal process whatsoever, whether issued by a court in session, or by a judge, or magistrate, or commissioner acting in the due administration of any law of the United States. You will probably experience no difficulty in understanding and applying this part of the law.

"As to what constitutes an obstruction — it was many years ago decided, by Justice Washington, that to support an indictment under this law, it was not necessary to prove the accused used or even threatened active violence. Any obstruction to the free action of the officer, or his lawful assistants, wilfully placed in his or their way, for the purpose of thus obstructing him or them, is sufficient. And it is clear that if a multitude of persons should assemble, even in a public highway, with the design to stand together, and thus prevent the officer from passing freely along the way, in the execution of his precept, and the officer should thus be hindered or obstructed, this would of itself, and without any active violence, be such an obstruction as is contemplated by this law. If to this be added use of any active violence, then the officer is not only obstructed, but he is resisted and opposed, and of course the offence is complete, for either of them is sufficient to constitute it.

"If you should be satisfied that an offence against this law has been perpetrated, you will then inquire by whom; and this renders it necessary for me to instruct you concerning the kind and amount of participation which brings individuals within the compass of this law.

"And first, all who are present and actually obstruct, resist, or oppose, are of course guilty. So are all who are present leagued in the common design, and so situated as to be able, in case of need, to afford assistance to those actually engaged, though they do not actually obstruct, resist, or oppose. If they are present for the purpose of affording assistance in obstructing, resisting, or opposing the officers, and are so situated as to be able in any event which may occur, actually to aid in the common design, though no overt act is done by them, they are still guilty under this law. The offence defined by this act is a misdemeanor; and it is rule of law that whatever participation, in case of felony, would render a person guilty, either as a principal in the second degree, or as an accessory before the fact, does, in a case of misdemeanor, render him guilty as a principal; in misdemeanors all are principals. And, therefore, in pursuance of the same rule, not only those who are present, but those who, though absent when the offence was committed, did procure, counsel, command, or abet others to commit the offence, are indictable as principal.

"Such is the law, and it would seem that no just mind could doubt its propriety. If persons having influence over others use that influence to induce the commission of crime, while they themselves remain at a safe distance, that must be deemed a very imperfect system of law which allows them to escape with impunity. Such is not our law. It treats such advice as criminal, and subjects the giver of it to punishment according to the nature of the offence to which his pernicious counsel has led. If it be a case of felony, he is by the common law an accessory before the fact, and by the laws of the United States and of this State, is punishable to the same extent as the principal felon. If it be a case of misdemeanor, the adviser is himself a principal offender, and is to be indicted and punished as if he himself had done the criminal act. It may be important for you to know what, in point of law, amounts to such an advising or counselling another as will be sufficient to constitute this legal element in the offence. It is laid down by high authority, that though a mere tacit acquiescence, or words, which amount to a bare permission, will not be sufficient, yet such a procurement may be, either by direct means, as by hire, counsel, or command, or indirect, by evincing an express liking, approbation, or assent to another's criminal design. From the nature of the case, the law can prescribe only general rules on this subject. My instruction to you is, that language addressed to persons who immediately afterwards commit an offence, actually intended by the speaker to incite those addressed to commit it, and adapted thus to incite them, is such a counselling or advising to the crime as the law contemplates, and the person so inciting others is liable to be indicted as a principal.

"In the case of the *Commonwealth* v. *Bowen* (13 Mass. R. 359), which was an indictment for counselling another to commit suicide, tried in 1816, Chief Justice Parker instructing the jury, and speaking for the Supreme Court of Massachusetts, said:—

"'The government is not bound to prove that Jewett would not have hung himself, had Bowen's counsel never reached his ear. The very act of advising to the commission of a crime is of itself unlawful. The presumption of law is that advice has the influence and effect intended by the adviser, unless it is shown to have been otherwise; as that the counsel was received with scoff, or was manifestly rejected and ridiculed at the time it was given. It was said in the argument that Jewett's abandoned and depraved character furnishes ground to believe that he would have committed the act without such advice from Bowen. Without doubt he was a hardened and depraved wretch; but it is in man's nature to revolt at self-destruction. When a person is predetermined upon the commission of this crime, the seasonable admonitions of a discreet and respected friend would probably tend to overthrow his determination. On the other hand, the counsel of an unprincipled wretch, stating the heroism and courage the self-murderer displays, might induce, encourage, and fix the intention, and ultimately procure the perpetration of the dreadful deed; and if other men would be influenced by such advice, the presumption is that Jewett was so influenced. He might have been influenced by many powerful motives to destroy himself. Still the inducements might have been insufficient to procure the actual commission of the act, and one word of additional advice might have turned the scale.'

"When applied — as this ruling seems to have been here applied — to a case in which the advice was nearly connected, in point of time, with the criminal act, it is, in my opinion, correct. If the advice was intended by the giver to stir or incite to a crime — if it was of such a nature as to be adapted to have this effect, and the persons incited immediately afterwards committed that crime — it is a just presumption that they were influenced by the advice or incitement to commit it. The circumstances, or direct proof, may or may not be sufficient to control this presumption; and whether they are so, can duly be determined in each case, upon all its evidence.

"One other rule of law on this subject is necessary to be borne in mind — the substantive offence to which the advice or incitement applied must have been committed; and it is for that alone the adviser or procurer is legally accountable. Thus if one should counsel another to rescue one prisoner, and he should rescue another, unless by mistake; or if the incitement was to rescue a prisoner, and he commit a larceny, the inciter is not responsible. But it need not appear *that the precise time, or place, or means advised*, were used. Thus if one incite A. to murder B., but advise him to wait until B. shall be at a certain place at noon, and A. murders B. at a different place in the morning, the adviser is guilty. So if the incitement be to poison, and the murderer shoots, or stabs. So if the counsel be to beat another, and he is beaten to death, the adviser is a murderer; for having incited another to commit an unlawful act, he is responsible for all that ensues upon its execution.

"These illustrations are drawn from cases of felonies, because they are the most common in the books and the most striking in themselves; but the principles on which they depend are equally applicable to cases of misdemeanor. In all such cases the real question is, whether the accused did procure, counsel, command, or abet the substantive offence committed. If he did, it is of no importance that his advice or directions were departed from in respect to the time, or place, or precise mode or means of committing it.

"Gentlemen: The events which have recently occurred in this city, have rendered it my duty to call your attention to these rules of law, and to direct you to inquire whether in point of fact the offence of obstructing process of the United States has been committed; if it has, you will present for trial all such persons as have so participated therein as to be guilty of that offence. And you will allow me to say to you that if you or I were to begin to make discriminations between one law and another, and say this we will enforce and that we will not enforce, we should not only violate our oaths, but so far as in us lies, we should destroy the liberties of our country, which rest for their basis upon the great principle that our country is governed by laws, constitutionally enacted, and not by men.

"In one part of our country the extradition of fugitives from labor is odious; in another, if we may judge from some transactions, the law concerning the extradition of fugitives from justice has been deemed not binding; in another still, the tariff laws of the United States were considered oppressive, and not fit to be enforced.

"Who can fail to see that the government would cease to be a government if it were to yield obedience to those local opinions? While it stands, all its laws must be faithfully executed, or it becomes the mere tool of the strongest faction of the place and the hour. If forcible resistance to one law be permitted practically to repeal it, the power of the mob would inevitably become one of the constituted authorities of the State, to be used against any law or any man obnoxious to the interests and passions of the worst or most excited part of the community; and the peaceful and the weak would be at the mercy of the violent.

"It is the imperative duty of all of us concerned in the administration of the laws to see to it that they are firmly, impartially, and certainly applied to every offence, whether a particular law be by us individually approved or disapproved. And it becomes all to remember, that forcible and concerted resistance to any law is civil war, which can make no progress but through bloodshed, and can have no termination but the destruction of the government of our country, or the ruin of those engaged in such resistance. It is not my province to comment on events which have recently happened. They are matters of fact which, so far as they are connected with the criminal laws of the United States, are for your consideration. I feel no doubt that, as good citizens and lovers of our country, and as conscientious men, you will well and truly observe and keep the oath you have taken, diligently to inquire and true presentment make of all crimes and offences against the laws of the United States given you in charge."[1]

Now gentlemen look at some particulars of this charge.

1. "If a multitude of persons shall assemble *even in a public highway*, with the design to *stand together, and thus prevent the officer from passing freely along that way*, in the execution of his precept, and the officer should thus be *hindered and obstructed*, this would, of itself, and without any active violence, be such an obstruction as is contemplated by this law." Of course, all persons thus assembled in the public highway were guilty of that offence, and liable to be punished with imprisonment for twelve months and a fine of three hundred dollars: "*All who are present*, and obstruct, resist, or oppose, *are of course guilty*." Their "design" is to be inferred from "the fact" that the officer was obstructed.

That is not all, this offence in technical language the Judge calls a "misdemeanor," and in "misdemeanors," he says, "all are principals." So, accordingly, not only are are all guilty who *actually obstruct* but likewise all who are "leagued in the common design, and *so situated as to be able* in case of need *to afford assistance to those actually engaged*, though they do not actually obstruct, resist, or oppose." These are obstructors by construction No. 1; they must have been several thousands in number.

But even that is not all; the judicial logic of deduction goes further still, and he adds, "Not only those who are present, but *those who* though *absent* when the offence was committed, *did procure, counsel, command, or abet* others to commit the offence are indictable as principals." These are obstructors by construction No. 2.

2. Next he determines what it is which "amounts to *such advising or counselling* another as will be sufficient to constitute this legal element in the offence." First he constructs the physical act which is the misdemeanor, namely, standing in the high road and thereby hindering a kidnapper from "passing freely along that way; or being so situated as to be able to afford assistance to others thus standing; or advising another thus to stand, or be situated:" next he constructs the *advice*, the metaphysical act, which is equally a "misdemeanor." This is the square root of construction No. 2. Look at this absurd quantity.

[1] Law Reporter, August, 1854.

"*Such a procurement may be*, either by direct means, as by hire, counsel, or command, or indirect, *by evincing an express liking, approbation, or assent.*" Thus the mere casual expression, "I wish Burns would escape, or I wish somebody would let him out," is a "Misdemeanor;" it is "evincing an express liking." Nodding to any other man's similar wish is a misdemeanor. It is "approbation." Even smiling at the nod is a crime — it is "assent." Such is the threefold shadow of this constructive shade. But even that is not all. A man is held responsible for what he evinced no *express* or implied *liking* for: "*it need not appear that the precise time, or place, or means advised, were used.*" Accordingly, he that "evinces an express liking," "*is responsible for all that ensues upon its execution.*" He evinces his assent to the End and is legally responsible for any Means which any hearer thereof shall, at any time, or in any place, make use of to attain that end!

Gentlemen of the Jury, this charge is a *quo warranto* against all Freedom of Speech. But suppose it were good law, and suppose the Grand-Jury obedient to it, see how it would apply.

All who evinced an express liking, approbation, or assent to the rescue of Mr. Burns are guilty of a misdemeanor; if they "evinced an express liking" that he should be rescued by a miracle wrought by Almighty God, — and some did express "approbation" of that "means," — they are indictable, guilty of a "misdemeanor;" "it need not appear that the precise time, or place, or means advised, were used!" If any colored woman during the wicked week — which was ten days long — prayed that God would deliver Anthony, as it is said his angel delivered Peter, or said "Amen" to such a prayer, she was "guilty of a misdemeanor;" to be indicted as a "principal."

So every man in Boston who, on that bad Friday, stood in the streets of Boston between Court Square and T Wharf, was "guilty of a misdemeanor," liable to a fine of three hundred dollars, and to jailing for twelve months. All who at Faneuil Hall stirred up the minds of the people in opposition to the fugitive slave bill; all who shouted, who clapped their hands at the words or the countenance of their favorites, or who expressed "approbation" by a whisper of "assent," are "guilty of a misdemeanor." The very women who stood for four days at the street corners, and hissed the infamous Slave-hunters and their coadjutors; they, too, ought to be punished by fine of three hundred dollars and imprisonment for a year! Well, there were fifteen thousand persons "assembled" "in the highway" of the city of Boston that day opposed to kidnapping; half the newspapers in the country towns of Massachusetts "evinced an express liking" for freedom, and opposed the kidnapping; they are all "guilty of a misdemeanor;" they are "Principals." Nay, the ministers all over the State, who preached that kidnapping was a sin; those who read brave words out of the Old Testament or the New; those who prayed that the victim might escape; they, likewise, were "guilty of a misdemeanor," liable to be fined three hundred dollars and jailed for twelve months.[1]

But where did Judge Curtis find his right to levy Ship-money, Tonnage, and Poundage on the tongues of men; where did he find his "law?" Surely not in the statute. When the bill was pending in 1790, suppose his construction of the statute had been declared to Congress — who would have voted for a law so monstrous? The statute lay in the Law-book for nearly seventy years, and nobody ever applied it to a case like this.

Gentlemen, I have shown you already how British judges in the time of the Jameses and Charleses perverted the law to the basest of purposes. I mentioned, amongst others, the work of Twysden and Kelyng and Jones. This is a case like those. Just now I spoke of the action of Chief Justice Parker who said it was not for the jury to judge whether a law *were harsh or not;* I showed how he charged the jury in the case of Bowen, and how the jury returned a verdict of "not guilty," thus setting his inhuman charge at nought.[2] But Judge Curtis, for his law, relies upon Judge Parker's charge. It is not a Statute made by the legislature that Judge Curtis relies on for his law; it is not a Custom of the Common law; it is not an Opinion of the Court solemnly pronounced after mature deliberation; it is only the charge of a single judge to a jury in a special case, and one which the jury disregarded even then!

But where did Judge Parker, an estimable man, find his law? Mr. Perez Morton, the Attorney-General, found it in Kelyng's Reports. In the case of Bowen only one authority is referred to for that odious principle on which the judge sought to hang him; that authority is taken from "9 Charles I.;" from the year 1634 — the worst age of the Stuart tyranny! But even that authority was not a Statute law, not a Custom of the People, not the Opinion of a Court solemnly pronounced. It was the charge of a single judge — a charge to a jury, made by an inferior judge, of an inferior court, in a barbarous age, under a despotic king! Hearken to this, — from the volume of Kelyng's Reports.[3] "*Memorandum,* That my Brother Twysden shewed me a Report which he had of the Charge given by Justice Jones to the grand-jury at the King's Bench Barr, in Michaelmas Term, 9 Carl. I." Gentlemen of the Jury, that charge no more settled the law even in 1634, than Judge Sprague's charge telling the *grand-jury to "obey both"* the law of God and the law of man which is ex-

[1] 2 Parker's Additional, 280. [2] See above, p. 112. [3] Page 52. See above, p. 112.

actly opposite thereto, settled the law of the United States and the morality of the People. But yet that is all the law the government had to hang Bowen with. The jury made nothing of it.[1]

But Kelyng's Reports are of no value as authority. Here is what Lord Campbell, now Chief Justice of the King's Bench, says of them and their author. I read it to you long ago. "I ought to mention that among his other vanities he had the ambition to be an author; and he compiled a folio volume of decisions in criminal laws, *which are of no value whatever except to make us laugh at some of the silly egotisms with which they abound.*"[2] Twysden, who showed him the Report of the charge, is of little value, and of no authority. I mentioned his character before.

Justice Jones, who made the charge, would hardly be an authority in the English courts in a nice question of construction. He allowed the king to levy ship-money, as I have shown before,[3] and dared not perform the duties of his office and so protect the Liberty of the Subject when the king smote thereat. He was brought before the House of Commons to answer for his conduct, in 1628. "His memory," says Echard, "suffers upon the account of his open judgment for the ship-money, the unhappy consequence of which he did not live to see."[4]

Judge Kelyng, the great authority in this case, was notorious for violating alike Justice and the law. Out of a riot committed by some apprentices he constructed the crime of High Treason, and sentenced thirteen men to death. He fined and imprisoned jurors because they refused to return the wicked, illegal verdict he demanded. With language too obscene to utter in this century, he mocked at the Great Charter of English Liberty. But at last the scandal was too great even for the reign of Charles II., and in 1667 the "Grand Committee of Justice" in the House of Commons, after examining witnesses and hearing him on his own behalf, reported: —

1. "That the proceedings of the Lord Chief Justice in the cases referred to us are innovations in the trial of men for their lives and liberties, and that he hath used an arbitrary and illegal power which is of dangerous consequence to the lives and liberties of the people of England."

2. "That in place of Judicature, the Lord Chief Justice hath undervalued, vilified, and condemned MAGNA CHARTA, the great preserver of our lives, freedom, and property."

3. "That the Lord Chief Justice be brought to trial, in order to condign punishment, in such manner as the House shall judge most fit and requisite."[5]

[1] Jones's "opinion" relates to a case of *murder* by the advice of an absent person, not at all to *suicide by the advice of another*, so it could not apply to the case of Bowen.

[2] 2 Campbell's Justices, 406.

[3] Above, p. 23.

[4] Parl. Hist. 290; 3 St. Tr. 844, 1181, 162; 2 Echard, 186.

[5] See above, p. 23, 39, 113, 125; 1 Campbell, *Ibid.* 406; 6 St. Tr. 76, 229, 171, 532, 769, 879, 992; Pepy's Diary, 17 Oct., 1667; Commons Journal, 16th Oct., 1667.

Some of the lawyers whom he had browbeaten, generously interceded for him. He made an abject submission "with great humility and reverence," and the House desisted from prosecution. "He was abundantly tame for the rest of his days," says Lord Campbell, "fell into utter contempt," "and *died to the great relief of all who had any regard for the due administration of justice.*"

Gentlemen, I am no lawyer, and may easily be mistaken in this matter, but as I studied Judge Curtis's charge and cast about for the sources of its doctrines and phraseology, I thought I traced them all back to Kelyng's opinions in that famous case, where he made treason out of a common riot among apprentices; and to Judge Chase's "opinions" and "rulings" in the trial of Mr. Fries,—opinions and rulings which shocked the public at the time, and brought legislative judgment on his head. Let any one compare the documents, I think he will find the whole of Curtis in those two impeached Judges, in Kelyng and in Chase.[1]

Here then is the law,—derived from the memorandum of the charge to a grand-jury made in 1634, by a judge so corrupt that he did not hesitate to violate Magna Charta itself; not published till more than seventy years after the charge was given; cited as law by a single authority, and that authority impeached for unrighteously and corruptly violating the laws he was set and sworn to defend, impeached even in that age—of Charles II.;—that is the law! Once before an attempt was made to apply it in Massachusetts, and inflict capital punishment on a man for advising a condemned murderer to anticipate the hangman and die by his own hand in private—and the jury refused. But to such shifts is this Honorable Court reduced! Gentlemen of the Jury, the fugitive slave bill cannot be executed in Massachusetts, not in America, without reviving the worst despotism of the worst of the Stuarts; not without bringing Twysden and Jones and Kelyng on the Bench; no, not without Saunders and Finch, and Jeffreys and Scroggs!

Gentlemen, such was Judge Curtis's charge. I have been told it was what might have been expected from the general character and previous conduct of the man; but I confess it did surprise me: it was foolish as it was wicked and tyrannical. But it all came to nought.

For, alas! there was a grand-jury, and the Salmonean thunder of the fugitive slave bill judge fell harmless—quenched, conquered, disgraced, and brutal,—to the ground. Poor fugitive slave bill Court! It can only gnash its teeth against freedom of speech in Fanueil Hall; only bark and yelp against the unalienable rights of man, and

[1] 1 Wharton, 636; Kelyng, 1–24, 70–77; 6 St. Tr. 879.

howl against the Higher Law of God! it cannot bite! Poor, imbecile, malignant Court! What a pity that the fugitive slave bill judge was not himself the grand-jury, to order the indictment! what a shame that the attorney was not a petty jury to convict! Then New England, like Old, might have had her "bloody assizes," and Boston streets might have streamed with the heart's gore of noble men and women; and human heads might have decked the pinnacles all round the town; and Judge Curtis and Attorney Hallett might have had their place with Judge Jeffreys and John Boilman of old. What a pity that we have a grand-jury and a traverse jury to stand between the malignant arm of the Slave-hunter and the heart of you and me![1]

The grand-jury found no bill and were discharged. In a Fourth of July Sermon "Of the Dangers which Threaten the Rights of Man in America," I said:—

"Perhaps the Court will try again, and find a more pliant Grand-Jury, easier to intimidate. Let me suggest to the Court that the next time it should pack its Jury from the Marshal's 'Guard.' Then there will be Unity of Idea; of action too,— the Court a figure of equilibrium."

The audacious Grand-Jury was discharged. A new one was summoned; this time it was constructed out of the right material. Before that, Gentlemen, we had had the Judge or his kinsmen writing for the fugitive slave bill in the newspapers; getting up public meetings in behalf of man-stealing in Boston; writing letters in support of the same; procuring opinions in favor of the constitutionality of the fugitive slave bill; nay, kidnapping men and sending them into eternal bondage, and in the newspapers defending the act; but we had none of them in the Jury box. On the new Grand-Jury appeared Mr. William W. Greenough, the brother-in-law of Hon. Judge Curtis — each married a daughter of Mr. Charles P. Curtis. Mr. Greenough "was very active in his endeavors to procure an indictment" against me; and a bill was found.

How came the Brother-in-law of the Judge on the Grand-Jury summoned to punish men who spoke against kidnapping? Gentlemen of the Jury, I do not know. Of course it was done honestly; nobody suspects the Mayor of Boston of double-dealing, of intrigue, or of any indirection! Of course there was no improper influence used by the Marshal, or Mr. Curtis, or Mr. Hallett, who had all so much at stake; of course Mr. Greenough "did not wish to be on the Jury;" of course Judge Curtis "was very sorry he was there," and of course "all the family was sorry!" Of course "he went and

[1] 2 Parker's Additional, p. 281.

asked Judge Sprague to excuse him, and the Judge would 'nt let him off!" Well, Gentlemen, I suppose it was a "miracle;" such a miracle as delivered the old or the new Shadrach; a "singular coincidence;" a "very remarkable fact." You will agree with me, Gentlemen, that it was a *very remarkable* FACT. In all the judicial tyranny I have related, we have not found a case before in which the judge had his brother on the Grand-Jury. Even Kelyng affords no precedent for that.

Last summer I met Mr. Greenough in a Bookstore and saluted him as usual; he made no return to my salutation, but doubled up his face and went out of the shop! That was the impartial Grand-Juror, who took the oath to "present no man for envy, hatred, or malice."

"After the impanelling of the new Grand-Jury," — I am reading from a newspaper,[1] "Judge Curtis charged them in reference to their duties at considerable length. In regard to the Burns case he read the law of 1790 respecting opposition to the United States Marshals and their deputies while in discharge of their duty, enforcing the laws of the United States, and referred for further information as to the law upon the point to his charge delivered at a previous term of the Court, and now in the possession *of the District Attorney.*" Thus he delegated the duty of expounding the law to a man who is not a judicial officer of the United States.

Gentlemen of the Jury, look at the facts. I am indicted by a Grand-Jury summoned for that purpose after one Grand-Jury — which had been drawn before the kidnapping of Mr. Burns — had refused to find a bill; a member of the family which has been so distinguished for kidnapping ever since 1832, the Brother-in-law of the Judge, is made one of that Grand-Jury; he is so hostile and malignant as to refuse my friendly salutation when offered as usual; and on the jury is "most active of all in his efforts to procure an indictment," so that "but for his efforts," as one of the Grand-Jury informed me, "no bill would have been found that time;" and "it was obvious that an outside influence affected him." Out of court Mr. Hallett, it is said, jocosely offers to bet ten dollars that he "will get Mr. Parker indicted." I am to be tried before two judges deeply committed to the Slave Power, now fiercely invading our once free soil; they owe their appointment to their hostility against Freedom. Twenty years ago, in the Old Cradle of Liberty, Mr. Sprague could find for Washington no epithet so endearing as "THAT SLAVEHOLDER;" he defended Slavery with all his legal learning, all his personal might. Yes, when other weapons failed him he extemporized a new gospel, and into the mouth of Jesus of Nazareth, — who said,

[1] Evening Traveller, Oct. 16.

"Thou shalt love thy Neighbor as thyself," and pointed out the man who had "fallen among thieves" as neighbor to the Samaritan — he put this most unchristian precept, "SLAVES, OBEY YOUR MASTERS!" Nay, only four years ago, in this very Court, he charged the jury that if they thought there was a contradiction between the Law of God and the Statutes of men they must "obey both."

Gentlemen, the other judge, Mr. Curtis, began his career by asking the Supreme Court of Massachusetts to restore Slavery to Lexington and Bunker Hill; he demanded that our own Supreme Court should grant all that wickedness which Toombs and Hangman Foote, and Atchison and Stringfellow, and Grier and Kane have since sought to perpetuate! He denied the existence of any Law of God to control the Court, there is nothing but the Statutes of men; and declared "Slavery is not immoral;" Massachusetts may interfere actively to establish it abroad as well as at home. In Faneuil Hall, in a meeting which he and his kinsmen had gathered and controlled, a meeting to determine upon kidnapping the citizens of Boston, he charged me with perjury, asked a question, and did not dare listen to my reply! Gentlemen, it is a very proper Court to try me. A fugitive slave bill Court — with a fugitive slave bill Attorney, a fugitive slave bill Grand-Jury, two fugitive slave bill Judges — which scoffs at the natural law of the Infinite God, is a very suitable tribunal to try a Minister of the Christian religion for defending his own parishioners from being kidnapped, defending them with a word in Faneuil Hall!

"No tyranny so secure, — none so intolerable, — none so dangerous, — none so remediless, as that of Executive Courts." "This is a truth all nations bear witness to — all history confirms." These were the words of Josiah Quincy, Jr., in 1772. — Gentlemen, in 1855 you see how true they are! "So sensible are all tyrants of the importance of such courts — that to advance and establish their system of oppression, *they never rest until they have completely corrupted or bought the judges of the land.* I could easily show that the most deep laid and daring attacks upon the rights of a people might, in some measure, be defeated, or evaded by upright judicatories; bad laws with good judges make little progress."[1]

But Gentlemen, — when the fugitive slave bill is "*law*," when the judges are selected for their love of Slavery and their hatred of freedom — men who invent Scripture to justify bondage, or who as Lawyers beseech the courts to establish Slavery in Massachusetts; who declare it is not immoral, that it may be the duty of Massachusetts to interfere actively and establish slavery abroad, nay, that there is no morality but only legality, the statute the only standard of right and

[1] Quincy's Quincy, 68.

wrong — what are you to expect? What you see in Philadelphia, New York; aye, in Boston at this hour. I will add with Mr. Quincy, "Is it possible this should not rouse us and drive us not to desperation but to our duty! The blind may see; the callous must feel; the spirited will act."[1]

It would be just as easy for the Judge to make out divers other crimes from my words, as to construct a misdemeanor therefrom. To charge me with "treason," he has only to vary a few words and phrases; to cite Chase, and not Judge Parker, and to refer to other passages of Kelyng's Reports. James II.'s judges declared it was treason in the seven Bishops to offer their petition to the King. Mr. Webster said, it is only the "clemency of the Government which indicted the Syracuse rescuers for misdemeanors and not for a capital crime!" How easy for a fugitive slave bill judge to hang men for a word against his brother kidnapper — if there were no jury; if, like the New York sheriff in 1735, he could order "his own negro" to do it! Here is a remarkable case of constructive crime, worthy of this Honorable Court. It is the famous case of *Dux* v. *Conrade et Boracio.* Honorable Judge Dogberry thus delivered his charge to the Grand Inquest, "Masters, I charge you accuse these men," — one police-man testified that Conrade said "that Don John, the prince's Brother, was a *villain.*" Judge Dogberry ruled, "This is flat perjury to call a prince's Brother, *villain.*" The next member of the Marshal's guard deposed that Boracio had said, "That he had received a thousand ducats of Don John for accusing the Lady Hero wrongfully." Chief Justice Dogberry decided, "Flat Burglary as ever was committed." Sentence accordingly.[1]

Gentlemen, the indictment is so roomy and vague, that before I came into court, I did not know what special acts of mine would be brought up against me — for to follow out the Judge's charge, all my life is a series of constructive misdemeanors. Nay, I think my mother — the violet has bloomed over that venerable and well-beloved head for more than thirty summers now — I think my mother might be indicted for constructive treason, only for bearing me, her youngest son. Certainly, it was "obstructing an officer," and in "misdemeanors all are principals." I have committed a great many misdemeanors; all my teachings evince an express liking for Piety, for Justice, for Liberty; all my life is obstructing, opposing, and resisting the fugitive slave bill Court, its Commissioners, its Judges, its Marshals and its Marshal's guard. Gentlemen of the jury, you are to judge me. Look at some of my actions and some of my words.

[1] Gazette, Feb. 10, 1772.

[2] 2 Singer's Shakspeare, 192.

In 1850, on the 25th of March, a fortnight after Mr. Webster made his speech against Humanity, there was a meeting of the citizens of Boston, at Faneuil Hall; Gentlemen, I helped procure the meeting. First, I tried to induce the leading Whigs to assemble the people. No, that could not be done; "the Bill would not pass, there was no danger!" Then I tried the leading Free Soilers; "No, it was not quite time, and we are not strong enough." At last the old abolitionists came together. Mr. Phillips made a magnificent speech. Here are some things which I also said.

"There were three fugitives at my house the other night. Ellen Craft was one of them. You all know Ellen Craft is a slave; she, with her husband, fled from Georgia to Philadelphia, and is here before us now. She is not so dark as Mr. Webster himself, if any of you think freedom is to be dealt out in proportion to the whiteness of the skin. If Mason's bill passes, I might have some miserable postmaster from Texas or the District of Columbia, some purchased agent of Messrs. Bruin & Hill, the great slave-dealers of the Capital, have him here in Boston, take Ellen Craft before the caitiff, and on his decision hurry her off to bondage as cheerless, as hopeless, and as irremediable as the grave!

"Let me interest you in a scene which might happen. Suppose a poor fugitive, wrongfully held as a slave — let it be Ellen Craft — has escaped from Savannah in some northern ship. No one knows of her presence on board; she has lain with the cargo in the hold of the vessel. Harder things have happened. Men have journeyed hundreds of miles bent double in a box half the size of a coffin, journeying towards freedom. Suppose the ship comes up to Long Wharf, at the foot of State Street. Bulk is broken to remove the cargo; the woman escapes, emaciated with hunger, feeble from long confinement in a ship's hold, sick with the tossing of the heedless sea, and still further etiolated and blanched with the mingling emotions of hope and fear. She escapes to land. But her pursuer, more remorseless than the sea, has been here beforehand; laid his case before the official he has brought with him, or purchased here, and claims his slave. She runs for her life, fear adding wings. Imagine the scene — the flight, the hot pursuit through State Street, Merchants' Row — your magistrates in hot pursuit. To make the irony of nature still more complete, let us suppose this shall take place on some of the memorable days in the history of America — on the 19th of April, when our fathers first laid down their lives 'in the sacred cause of God and their country;' on the 17th of June, the 22d of December, or on any of the sacramental days in the long sad history of our struggle for our own freedom! Suppose the weary fugitive takes refuge in Faneuil Hall, and here, in the old Cradle of Liberty, in the midst of its associations, under the eye of Samuel Adams, the bloodhounds seize their prey! Imagine Mr. Webster and Mr. Winthrop looking on, cheering the slave-hunter, intercepting the fugitive fleeing for her life. Would not that be a pretty spectacle?

"Propose to support that bill to the fullest extent, with all its provisions! Ridiculous talk! Does Mr. Webster suppose that such a law could be executed in Boston? that the people of Massachusetts will ever return a single fugitive slave, under such an act as that? Then he knows his constituents very little, and proves that he needs "Instruction."

"Perpetuate Slavery, we cannot do it. Nothing will save it. It is girt about by a ring of fire which daily grows narrower, and sends terrible sparkles into the very centre of the shameful thing. 'Joint resolutions' cannot save it; annexations cannot save it — not if we reannex all the West Indies; delinquent representatives cannot —

save it; uninstructed senators, refusing instructions, cannot save it, no, not with all their logic, all their eloquence, which smites as an earthquake smites the sea. No, slavery cannot be saved; by no compromise, no non-intervention, no Mason's Bill in the Senate. It cannot be saved in this age of the world until you nullify every ordinance of nature, until you repeal the will of God, and dissolve the union He has made between righteousness and the welfare of a people. Then, when you displace God from the throne of the world, and instead of His eternal justice, reënact the will of the Devil, then you may keep Slavery; keep it for ever, keep it in peace. Not till then.

"The question is, not if slavery is to cease, and soon to cease, but shall it end as it ended in Massachusetts, in New Hampshire, in Pennsylvania, in New York; or shall it end as in St. Domingo? Follow the counsel of Mr. Webster — it will end in fire and blood. God forgive us for our cowardice, if we let it come to this, that three millions or thirty millions of degraded human beings, degraded by us, must wade through slaughter to their unalienable rights."[1]

Gentlemen, that speech was a "seditious libel" by construction! On the 29th of May, I spoke at the New England Anti-Slavery Convention, and said: —

"Let us not be deceived about the real question at issue. It is not merely whether we shall return fugitive slaves without trial by jury. We will not return them with trial by jury! neither 'with alacrity,' nor with the 'solemnity of judicial proceedings!' It is not merely whether slavery shall be extended or not. By and by there will be a political party with a wider basis than the free soil party, who will declare that the nation itself must put an end to slavery in the nation; and if the Constitution of the United States will not allow it, there is another Constitution that will. Then the title, Defender and expounder of the Constitution of the United States, will give way to this, — 'Defender and expounder of the Constitution of the Universe,' and we shall reaffirm the ordinance of nature, and reënact the will of God. You may not live to see it, Mr. President, nor I live to see it; but it is written on the iron leaf that it must come; come, too, before long. Then the speech of Mr. Webster, and the defence thereof by Mr. Stuart, the letter of the retainers and the letters of the retained, will be a curiosity; the conduct of the whigs and democrats an amazement, and the peculiar institution a proverb amongst all the nations of the earth. In the turmoil of party politics, and of personal controversy, let us not forget continually to move the previous question, whether Freedom or Slavery is to prevail in America. There is no attribute of God which is not on our side; because, in this matter, we are on the side of God."[2]

After the death of General Taylor on the 14th of July, I lifted up my voice in a funeral sermon thus: —

"If he could speak to us from his present position, methinks he would say: Countrymen and friends! You see how little it availed you to agitate the land and put a little man in a great place. It is not the hurrah of parties that will 'save the Union,' it is not 'great men.' It is only Justice. Remember that Atheism is not the first principle of a Republic; remember there is a law of God, the higher law of the universe, the Everlasting Right: I thought so once, and now I know it. Remember that you are

[1] 2 Occasional Speeches, 164, 165, and 172. [2] Ibid, 207, 208.

accountable to God for all things; that you owe justice to all men, the black not less than the white; that God will demand it of you, proud, wicked nation, careful only of your gold, forgetful of God's high law! Before long each of you shall also come up before the Eternal. Then and there it will not avail you to have compromised truth, justice, love, but to have kept them. Righteousness only is the salvation of a State; that only of a man."[1]

All that was before the bill passed, but how easy it would be for Judge Jeffreys or Judge Curtis, Judge Sprague or Judge Scroggs, to construct it into a "misdemeanor," "resisting an officer!"

After the fugitive slave bill passed, on the 22d of September, 1850, not forty-eight hours after the Judge's friends had fired their jubilant cannon at the prospect of kidnapping the men who wait upon their tables, I preached a "Sermon of the Function and Place of Conscience in relation to the Laws of Man, a sermon for the times." I said this:—

"If a man falls into the water and is in danger of drowning, it is the natural duty of the bystanders to aid in pulling him out, even at the risk of wetting their garments. We should think a man a coward who could swim, and would not save a drowning girl for fear of spoiling his coat. He would be indictable at common law. If a troop of wolves or tigers were about to seize a man, and devour him, and you and I could help him, it would be our duty to do so, even to peril our own limbs and life for that purpose. If a man undertakes to murder or steal a man, it is the duty of the bystanders to help their brother, who is in peril, against wrong from the two-legged man, as much as against the four-legged beast. But suppose the invader who seizes the man is an officer of the United States, has a commission in his pocket, a warrant for his deed in his hand, and seizes as a slave a man who has done nothing to alienate his natural rights — does that give him any more natural right to enslave a man than he had before? Can any piece of parchment make right wrong, and wrong right?

"The fugitive has been a slave before: does the wrong you committed yesterday, give you a natural right to commit wrong afresh and continually? Because you enslaved this man's father, have you a natural right to enslave his child? The same right you would have to murder a man because you butchered his father first. The right to murder is as much transmissible by inheritance as the right to enslave! It is plain to me that it is the natural duty of citizens to rescue every fugitive slave from the hands of the marshal who essays to return him to bondage; to do it peaceably if they can, forcibly if they must, but by all means to do it. Will you stand by and see your countrymen, your fellow-citizens of Boston, sent off to slavery by some commissioner? Shall I see my own parishioners taken from under my eyes and carried back to bondage, by a man whose constitutional business it is to work wickedness by statute? Shall I never lift an arm to protect him? When I consent to that, you may call me a hireling shepherd, an infidel, a wolf in sheep's clothing, even a defender of slave-catching if you will; and I will confess I was a poor dumb dog, barking always at the moon, but silent as the moon when the murderer comes near.

"I am not a man who loves violence. I respect the sacredness of human life. But this I say, solemnly, that I will do all in my power to rescue any fugitive slave from the hands of any officer who attempts to return him to bondage. I will resist him as gently as I know how, but with such strength as I can command; I will ring the bells,

[1] 2 Occasional Sermons, 239, 240.

and alarm the town; I will serve as head, as foot, or as hand to any body of serious and earnest men, who will go with me, with no weapons but their hands, in this work. I will do it as readily as I would lift a man out of the water, or pluck him from the teeth of a wolf, or snatch him from the hands of a murderer. What is a fine of a thousand dollars, and jailing for six months, to the liberty of a man? My money perish with me, if it stand between me and the eternal law of God. I trust there are manly men enough in this house to secure the freedom of every fugitive slave in Boston, without breaking a limb or rending a garment.

"One thing more I think is very plain, that the fugitive has the same natural right to defend himself against the slave-catcher, or his constitutional tool, that he has against a murderer or a wolf. The man who attacks me to reduce me to slavery, in that moment of attack alienates his right to life, and if I were the fugitive, and could escape in no other way, I would kill him with as little compunction as I would drive a mosquito from my face. It is high time this was said. What grasshoppers we are before the statute of men! what Goliaths against the law of God! What capitalist heeds your statute of usury when he can get illegal interest? How many banks are content with *six per cent.* when money is scarce? Did you never hear of a merchant evading the duties of the custom-house? When a man's liberty is concerned, we must keep the law, must we? betray the wanderer, and expose the outcast?"[1]

Gentlemen, you know what Mr. Commissioner Hallett said of such language, said at the Union Meeting in Faneuil Hall.[2] He was only fugitive slave bill commissioner then; in consequence of his denial of the Higher Law of God he is now fugitive slave bill Attorney. You know what Mr. Curtis said of the Sermon; now, in consequence he is Judge Curtis — the fugitive slave bill Judge.

On the 14th of October there was another meeting at Faneuil Hall — the Freesoilers came that time. The old flame of Liberty burnt anew in Charles Francis Adams, who presided. Perhaps some of you remember the prayer of the venerable Dr. Lowell which lifted up our souls to the "Father of all men!" I proposed the appointment of a "Committee of Vigilance and Safety to take such measures as they shall deem just and expedient to protect the colored people of this city in the enjoyment of their lives and liberties." I was appointed one of the Committee, and subsequently Chairman of the Executive Committee of the Vigilance Committee; a very responsible office, Gentlemen. At that meeting I told of a fugitive from Boston, who that day had telegraphed to his wife here, asking if it was safe for him to come back from Canada. I asked the meeting, "Will you let him come back; how many will defend him to the worst?" "Here a hand vote was taken," said the newspapers, "a forest of hands was held up." Surely that was "evincing an express liking" for an obstruction of the kidnappers. But did it violate the law of 1790?

All this you might easily have known before. Here is something you did not know. That Meeting, its Resolutions, its Speeches, its

[1] 2 Occasional Sermons, 256, 257, 258.

[2] See above, p. 149.

Action, were brought up in the cabinet of the United States and discussed. *Mr. Webster*, then Secretary of State, *wished to have Mr. Adams, president of the meeting, presented to the grand-jury and indicted for treason!* But the majority thought otherwise.

Gentlemen, when the kidnappers came to Boston I did some things of which this court has not taken notice, and so I will not speak of them now, but only tell your grandchildren of, if I live long enough. Others did more and better than I could do, however. In due time they will have their reward. One thing let me say now. When the two brothers Curtis, with their kinsfolk and coadjutors, were seeking to kidnap the Crafts, I took Ellen to my own house, and kept her there so long as the (Southern) kidnappers remained in the city. For the first time I armed myself, and put my house in a state of defence. For two weeks I wrote my sermons with a sword in the open drawer under my inkstand, and a pistol in the flap of the desk, loaded, ready, with a cap on the nipple. Commissioner Curtis said "a process was in the hands of the marshal . . ." in the execution of which, he *might be called upon to break open dwelling-houses, and perhaps to take life*, by quelling resistance actual or "*threatened*." I was ready for him. I knew my rights.

I went also and looked after William Craft. I inspected his weapons; "his powder had a good kernel, and he kept it dry; his pistols were of excellent proof; the barrels true, and clean, the trigger went easy, the caps would not hang fire at the snap. I tested his poignard; the blade had a good temper, stiff enough and yet springy withal; the point was sharp."[1] After the immediate danger was over and Knight and Hughes had avoided the city, where they had received such welcome from the friends of this Court, such was the tone of the political newspapers and the commercial pulpit that William and Ellen must needs flee from America. Long made one by the wedlock of mutual and plighted faith, their marriage in Georgia was yet "null and void" by the laws of that "Christian State." I married them according to the law of Massachusetts. As a symbol of the husband's peculiar responsibility under such circumstances, I gave William a Sword — it lay on the table in the house of another fugitive, where the wedding took place — and told him of his manly duty therewith, if need were, to defend the life and liberty of Ellen. I gave them both a Bible, which I had bought for the purpose, to be a symbol of their spiritual culture and a help for their soul, as the sword was for their bodily life. "With this sword I thee wed," suited the circumstances of that bridal.

Mr. and Mrs. Craft were parishioners of mine, and besides I have been appointed "minister at large in behalf of all fugitive slaves in

[1] 1 Parker's Additional Speeches, 55.

Boston." I have helped join men and women in wedlock according to the customs of various sects and nations. There is one wedlock, a sacrament, but many forms. Never before did I marry two lovers with the Sword and the Bible — the form of matrimony for fugitive slaves: out of that fact perhaps Mr. Attorney can frame an indictment that will hold water. "If it only resists law and obstructs its officers," quoth he, "it is treason, and he who risks it must risk hanging for it!"

At the great Union meeting, November 26, when Mr. Curtis said "I should like to ask the Reverend Gentleman in what capacity he expects to be punished for his *perjury*," I said, "Do you want an answer to your question, Sir?" No doubt that was obstructing a (prospective) "officer," then preparing for process. How easily could Scroggs make a "misdemeanor," or "a seditious libel," out of that question! Allybone would call it "treason," "levying war."

Thirty-six hours after the Union meeting, on Thanksgiving day, 28th November, 1850, in a "Sermon of the State of the Nation," I said: —

"I have sometimes been amazed at the talk of men who call on us to keep the fugitive slave law, one of the most odious laws in a world of odious laws — a law not fit to be made or kept. I have been amazed that they should dare to tell us the law of God, writ on the heavens and our hearts, never demanded we should disobey the laws of men! Well, suppose it were so. Then it was old Daniel's duty at Darius' command to give up his prayer; but he prayed three times a day, with his windows up. Then it was John's and Peter's duty to forbear to preach of Christianity; but they said, 'Whether it be right in the sight of God to hearken unto you more than unto God, judge ye.' Then it was the duty of Amram and Jochebed to take up their new-born Moses and cast him into the Nile, for the law of king Pharoah, commanding it, was 'constitutional,' and 'political agitation' was discountenanced as much in Goshen as in Boston. But Daniel did not obey; John and Peter did not fail to preach Christianity; and Amram and Jochebed refused 'passive obedience' to the king's decree! I think it will take a strong man all this winter to reverse the judgment which the world has passed on these three cases. But it is 'innocent' to try.

"However, there is another ancient case, mentioned in the Bible, in which the laws commanded one thing and conscience just the opposite. Here is the record of the law: — 'Now both the chief priests and the Pharisees had given a commandment, that if any one knew where he [Jesus] were, he should show it, that they might take him.' Of course, it became the official and legal business of each disciple who knew where Christ was, to make it known to the authorities. No doubt James and John could leave all and follow him, with others of the people who knew not the law of Moses, and were accursed; nay, the women, Martha and Mary, could minister unto him of their substance, could wash his feet with their tears, and wipe them with the hairs of their head. They did it gladly, of their own freewill, and took pleasure therein, I make no doubt. There was no merit in that — 'Any man can perform an agreeable duty.' But there was found one disciple who could 'perform a disagreeable duty.' He went, perhaps 'with alacrity,' and betrayed his Saviour to the marshal of the district of Jerusalem, who was called a centurion. Had he no affection for Jesus? No doubt; but he could conquer his prejudices, while Mary and John could not.

"Judas Iscariot has rather a bad name in the Christian world: he is called 'The son of perdition,' in the New Testament, and his conduct is reckoned a 'transgression;' nay, it is said the devil 'entered into him,' to cause this hideous sin. But all this it seems was a mistake; certainly, if we are to believe our 'republican' lawyers and statesmen, Iscariot only fulfilled his 'constitutional obligations.' It was only 'on that point,' of betraying his Saviour, that the constitutional law required him to have any thing to do with Jesus. He took his 'thirty pieces of silver'—about fifteen dollars; a Yankee is to do it for ten, having fewer prejudices to conquer—it was his legal fee, for value received. True, the Christians thought it was 'The wages of iniquity,' and even the Pharisees—who commonly made the commandment of God of none effect by their traditions—dared not defile the temple with this 'price of blood;' but it was honest money. Yes, it was as honest a fee as any American commissioner or deputy will ever get for a similar service. How mistaken we are! Judas Iscariot is not a traitor! he was a great patriot; he conquered his 'prejudices,' performed 'a disagreeable duty,' as an office of 'high morals and high principle;' he kept the 'law' and the 'Constitution,' and did all he could to 'save the Union;' nay, he was a saint, 'not a whit behind the very chiefest apostles.' 'The law of God never commands us to disobey the law of man.' *Sancte Iscariote ora pro nobis.*

"Talk of keeping the fugitive slave law! Come, come, we know better. Men in New England know better than this. We know that we ought not to keep a wicked law, and that it must not be kept when the law of God forbids!

"One of the most awful spectacles I ever saw, was this: A vast multitude attempting, at an orator's suggestion [Hon. Mr. Hallett], to howl down the 'Higher law,' and when he said, Will you have this to rule over you? they answered, 'Never!' and treated the 'Higher law' to a laugh and a howl! It was done in Fanueil Hall; under the eyes of the three Adamses, Hancock, and Washington; and the howl rung round the venerable arches of that hall! I could not but ask, 'Why do the heathen rage, and the people imagine a vain thing? the rulers of the earth set themselves, and kings take counsel against the Lord and say, Let us break his bands asunder, and cast off his yoke from us.' Then I could not but remember that it was written, 'He that sitteth in the heavens shall laugh; the Lord shall have them in derision.' 'He taketh up the isles as a very little thing, and the inhabitants of the earth are as grasshoppers before Him.' Howl down the law of God at a magistrate's command! Do this in Boston! Let us remember this—but with charity."

"I do not believe there is more than one of the New England men who publicly helped the law into being, but would violate its provisions; conceal a fugitive; share his loaf with a runaway; furnish him golden wings to fly with. Nay, I think it would be difficult to find a magistrate in New England, willing to take the public odium of doing the official duty. I believe it is not possible to find a regular jury, who will punish a man for harboring a slave, for helping his escape, or fine a marshal or commissioner for being a little slow to catch a slave. Men will talk loud in public meetings, but they have some conscience after all, at home. And though they howl down the 'Higher law' in a crowd, yet conscience will make cowards of them all, when they come to lay hands on a Christian man, more innocent than they, and send him into slavery for ever! One of the commissioners of Boston talked loud and long, last Tuesday, in favor of keeping the law. When he read his litany against the law of God, and asked if men would keep the 'Higher law,' and got 'Never' as the welcome, and amen for response—it seemed as if the law might be kept, at least by that commissioner, and such as gave the responses to his creed. But slave-hunting Mr. Hughes, who came here for two of our fellow-worshippers, in his Georgia newspaper, tells a different story. Here it is from the 'Georgia Telegraph,' of last Friday. 'I called at eleven o'clock at night, at his [the commissioner's] residence, and stated to him my business, and asked him for a warrant, saying that if I could get a warrant, I could have the negroes [William and Ellen Craft] arrested. He said the law did not authorize a warrant to be issued: that it was my duty to go and arrest the negro without a warrant, and bring him before him!' This is more than I expected. 'Is Saul among the prophets?' The men who tell us that the law must be kept, God willing, or against His will — there are Puritan fathers behind them also; Bibles in their houses; a Christ crucified, whom they think of; and a God even in their world, who slumbers not, neither is weary, and is as little a respecter of parchments as of persons! They know there is a people, as well as politicians, a posterity not yet assembled, and they would not like to have certain words writ on their tomb-stone. 'Traitor to the rights of mankind,' is no pleasant epitaph. They, too, remember there is a day after to-day; aye, a forever; and 'Inasmuch as ye have not done it unto one of the least of these my brethren, ye have not done it unto me,' is a sentence they would not like to hear at the day of judgment."[1]

Gentlemen, you see by the faces of this Honorable Court, and you know by what these honorable functionaries and their coadjutors have done out of its limit, how much I was mistaken in the notion that no Boston Commissioner would ever kidnap a man! Perhaps you will pardon me for the mistake. I will soon explain it by a quotation.

After the rescue of Shadrach, in my Sunday prayer I publicly gave God the thanks of the congregation for the noble deed. Perhaps that was a crime. I think Judge Saunders could make it appear that I was an "accessory after the fact," and then Judge Curtis could call the offence not a felony but a "misdemeanor," and "in misdemeanors all are principals." Nay, it might be "levying war" "with force and arms."

After the Hon. Judge Sprague had made himself glorious by charging the jury "to obey both" the will of God and the laws of men, which forbid that will; and after Commissioner Curtis had kidnapped Mr. Sims, while he still had him in his unlawful jail, on Fast-day, April 10, 1851, I preached a sermon "of the Chief Sins of the People," and said,—

"He [Judge Sprague] supposes a case: that the people ask him, 'Which shall we obey, the law of man or the will of God?' He says, 'I answer, obey both. The incompatibility which the question assumes does not exist.'

"So, then, here is a great general rule, that between the 'law of man' and the 'will of God' there is no incompatibility, and we must 'obey both.' Now let us see how this rule will work.

"If I am rightly informed, King Ahab made a law that all the Hebrews should serve Baal, and it was the will of God that they should serve the Lord. According to this rule of the judge, they must 'obey both.' But if they served Baal, they could not serve the Lord. In such a case, 'what is to be done?' We are told that Elijah gathered the prophets together: 'and he came unto all the people, and said, How long halt ye? If the Lord be God, follow him; but if Baal, then follow him.' Our modern

[1] 2 Parker's Occasional Sermons, pp. 298–300, 301, 302, 304, 305.

prophet says, 'Obey both. The incompatibility which the question assumes does not exist.' Such is the difference between Judge Elijah and Judge Peleg.

"Let us see how this rule will work in other cases; how you can make a compromise between two opposite doctrines. The king of Egypt commanded the Hebrew nurses, 'When you do the office of a midwife to the Hebrew women, if it be a son ye shall kill him.' I suppose it is plain to the Judge of the Circuit Court that this kind of murder, killing the new-born infants, is against 'the will of God;' but it is a matter of record that it was according to 'the law of man.' Suppose the Hebrew nurses had come to ask Judge Sprague for his advice. He must have said, 'Obey both!' His rule is a universal one.

"Another decree was once made, as it is said in the Old Testament, that no man should ask any petition of any God for thirty days, save of the king, on penalty of being cast into the den of lions. Suppose Daniel — I mean the old Daniel, the prophet — should have asked him, What is to be done? Should he pray to Darius or pray to God? 'Obey both!' would be the answer. But he cannot, for he is forbid to pray to God. We know what Daniel did do.

"The elders and scribes of Jerusalem commanded the Christians not to speak or to teach at all in the name of Jesus; but Peter and John asked those functionaries, 'Whether it be right in the sight of God to hearken unto you more than unto God, judge ye.' Our judge must have said, There is no 'incompatibility;' 'obey both!' What 'a comfortable Scripture' this would have been to poor John Bunyan! What a great ethical doctrine to St. Paul! He did not know such Christianity as that. Before his time a certain man had said, 'No man can serve two masters.' But there was one person who made the attempt, and he also is eminent in history. Here was 'the will of God,' to do to others as you would have others do to you: 'Love thy neighbor as thyself.' Here is the record of 'the law of man:' 'Now both the chief priests and the Pharisees had given a commandment, that, if any man knew where he [Jesus] were, he should show it that they might take him.' Judas, it seems, determined to 'obey both,' — 'the law of man' and 'the will of God.' So he sat with Jesus at the Last Supper, dipped his hand in the same dish, and took a morsel from the hand of Christ, given him in token of love. All this he did to obey 'the will of God.' Then he went and informed the Commissioner or Marshal where Jesus was. This he did to obey 'the law of man.' Then he came back, and found Christ, — the agony all over, the bloody sweat wiped off from his brow presently to bleed again, — the Angel of Strength there with him to comfort him. He was arousing his sleeping disciples for the last time, and was telling them, 'Pray, lest ye enter into temptation.' Judas came and gave him a kiss. To the eleven it seemed the friendly kiss, obeying 'the will of God.' To the Marshal it also seemed a friendly kiss, — obeying 'the law of man.' So, in the same act, he obeys 'the law of God' and 'the will of man,' and there is no 'incompatibility!'

"Of old it was said, 'Thou canst not serve God and mammon.' He that said it, has been thought to know something of morals, — something of religion.

"Till the fugitive slave law was passed, we did not know what a great saint Iscariot was. I think there ought to be a chapel for him, and a day set apart in the calendar. Let him have his chapel in the navy yard at Washington. He has got a priest there already. And for a day in the calendar — set apart for all time the seventh of March!"

"Last Thanksgiving day, I said it would be difficult to find a magistrate in Boston to take the odium of sending a fugitive back to slavery. I believed, after all, men had some conscience, although they talked about its being a duty to deliver up a man to bondage. Pardon me, my country, that I rated you too high! Pardon me, town of Boston, that I thought your citizens all men! Pardon me, lawyers, that I thought you had been all born of mothers! Pardon me, ruffians, who kill for hire! I thought you had some animal mercy left, even in your bosom! Pardon me, United States' commissioners, marshals, and the like, I thought you all had some shame! Pardon me, my hearers, for such mistakes. One commissioner was found to furnish the warrant [Mr. George T. Curtis]! Pardon me, I did not know he was a commissioner; if I had, I never would have said it!

"Spirits of tyrants, I look down to you! Shade of Cain, you great first murderer, forgive me that I forgot your power, and did not remember that you were parent of so long a line! And you, my brethren, if hereafter I tell you that there is any limit of meanness or wickedness which a Yankee will not jump over, distrust me, and remind me of this day, and I will take it back!

"Let us look at the public conduct of any commissioner who will send an innocent man from Boston into slavery. I would speak of all men charitably; for I know how easy it is to err, yea, to sin. I can look charitably on thieves, prowling about in darkness; on rum-sellers, whom poverty compels to crime; on harlots, who do the deed of shame that holy woman's soul abhors and revolts at; I can pity the pirate, who scours the seas doing his fiendish crimes — he is tempted, made desperate by a gradual training in wickedness. The man, born at the South, owning slaves, who goes to Africa and sells adulterated rum in exchange for men to retail at Cuba, — I cannot understand the consciousness of such a man; yet I can admit that by birth and by breeding he has become so imbruted he knows no better. Nay, even that he may perhaps justify his conduct to himself. I say I think his sin is not so dreadful as that of a commissioner in Boston who sends a man into slavery. A man commits a murder, inflamed by jealousy, goaded by desire of great gain, excited by fear, stung by malice, or poisoned by revenge, and it is a horrid thing. But to send a man into slavery is worse than to murder him. I should rather be slain than enslaved. To do this, inflamed by no jealousy, goaded by no desire of great gain, — only ten dollars! — excited by no fear, stung by no special malice, poisoned by no revenge, — I cannot comprehend that in any man, not even in a hyena. Beasts that raven for blood do not kill for killing's sake, but to feed their flesh. Forgive me, O ye wolves and hyenas! that I bring you into such company. I can only understand it in a devil!

"When a man bred in Massachusetts, whose Constitution declares that 'All men are born free and equal;' within sight of Faneuil Hall, with all its sacred memories; within two hours of Plymouth Rock; within a single hour of Concord and Lexington; in sight of Bunker Hill, — when he will do such a deed, it seems to me that there is no life of crime long enough to prepare a man for such a pitch of depravity; I should think he must have been begotten in sin, and conceived in iniquity, and been born 'with a dog's head on his shoulders;' that the concentration of the villany of whole generations of scoundrels would hardly be enough to fit a man for a deed like this!"

"Last Thursday night, — when odious beasts of prey, that dare not face the light of heaven, prowl through the woods, — those ruffians of the law seized on their brother man. They lie to the bystanders, and seize him on a false pretence. There is their victim — they hold him fast. His faithless knife breaks in his hand; his coat is rent to pieces. He is the slave of Boston. Can you understand his feelings? Let us pass by that. His 'trial!' Shall I speak of that? He has been five days on trial for more than life, and has not seen a judge! A jury? No, — only a commissioner! O justice! O republican America! Is this the liberty of Massachusetts?

"Where shall I find a parallel with men who will do such a deed, — do it in Boston? I will open the tombs, and bring up most hideous tyrants from the dead. Come, brood of monsters, let me bring you up from the deep damnation of the graves wherein your hated memories continue for all time their never-ending rot. Come, birds of evil omen! come, ravens, vultures, carrion-crows, and see the spectacle! come, see the meeting of congenial souls! I will disturb, disquiet, and bring up the greatest monsters of the human race! Tremble not, women; tremble not, children; tremble not, men! They are all dead! They cannot harm you now! Fear the living, not the dead!

"Come hither, Herod the wicked! Thou that didst seek after that young child's life, and destroyedst the Innocents! Let me look on thy face! No; go! Thou wert a heathen! Go, lie with the Innocents thou hast massacred. Thou art too good for this company!

"Come, Nero! Thou awful Roman Emperor! Come up! No; thou wast drunk with power! schooled in Roman depravity. Thou hadst, besides, the example of thy fancied gods! Go, wait another day. I will seek a worser man.

"Come hither, St. Dominic! come, Torquemada! — Fathers of the Inquisition! Merciless monsters, seek your equal here! No; pass by! You are no companions for such men as these! You were the servants of atheistic popes, of cruel kings. Go to, and get you gone. Another time I may have work for you, — not now; lie there and persevere to rot. You are not yet quite wicked and corrupt enough for this comparison. Go, get ye gone, lest the sun turn back at sight of ye!

"Come up, thou heap of wickedness, George Jeffreys! — thy hands deep purple with the blood of thy murdered fellow men! Ah, I know thee! awful and accursed shade! Two hundred years after thy death, men hate thee still, not without cause! Let me look upon thee! I know thy history. Pause and be still, while I tell it to these men.

"Brothers, George Jeffreys 'began in the sedition line.' 'There was no act, however bad, that he would not resort to to get on.' 'He was of a bold aspect, and cared not for the countenance of any man.' 'He became the avowed, unblushing slave of the court, and the bitter persecutor and unappeasable enemy of the principles he had before supported.' 'He was universally insolent and overbearing.' 'As a judge, he did not consider the decencies of his post, nor did he so much as affect to be impartial, as became a judge.' His face and voice were always unamiable. 'All tenderness for the feelings of others, all self-respect were obliterated from his mind.' He had 'a delight in misery, merely as misery,' and 'that temper which tyrants require in their worst instruments.' 'He made haste to sell his forehead of brass and his tongue of venom to the court.' He had 'more impudence than ten carted street-walkers;' and was appropriately set to a work 'which could be trusted to no man who reverenced law, or who was sensible of shame.' He was a 'Commissioner' in 1685. You know of the 'Bloody assizes' which he held, and how he sent to execution three hundred and twenty persons in a single circuit. 'The whole country was strewed with the heads and limbs of his victims.' Yet a man wrote that 'A little more hemp might have been usefully employed.' He was the worst of the English judges. 'There was no measure, however illegal, to the execution of which he did not devotedly and recklessly abandon himself.' 'During the Stuart reigns, England was cursed by a succession of ruffians in ermine, who, for the sake of court favor, wrested the principles of law, the precepts of religion, and the duties of humanity; but they were all greatly outstripped by Jeffreys.' Such is his history.

"Come, shade of a judicial butcher! Two hundred years thy name has been pilloried in face of the world, and thy memory gibbeted before mankind. Let us see how thou wilt compare with those who kidnap men in Boston! Go seek companionship with them! Go claim thy kindred, if such they be! Go tell them that the memory of the wicked shall rot, — that there is a God; an Eternity; ay! and a Judgment too! where the slave may appeal against him that made him a slave, to Him that made him a man.

"What! Dost thou shudder? Thou turn back! These not thy kindred! Why dost thou turn pale, as when the crowd clutched at thy life in London Street? It is true, George Jeffreys, and these are not thy kin. Forgive me that I should send thee on such an errand, or bid thee seek companionship with such — with Boston hunters of the slave! Thou wert not base enough! It was a great bribe that tempted thee! Again I say, pardon me for sending thee to keep company with such men! Thou only struckst at men accused of crime; not at men accused only of their birth! Thou wouldst not send a man into bondage for two pounds! I will not rank thee with men who, in Boston, for ten dollars, would enslave a negro now! Rest still, Herod! Be quiet, Nero! Sleep, St. Dominic, and sleep, O Torquemada! in your fiery jail! Sleep, Jeffreys, underneath 'the altar of the church' which seeks with Christian charity to hide your hated bones."

"Well, my brethren, these are only the beginning of sorrows. There will be other victims yet; this will not settle the question. What shall we do? I think I am a calm man and a cool man, and I have a word or two to say as to what we shall do. Never obey the law. Keep the law of God. Next I say, resist not evil with evil; resist not now with violence. Why do I say this? Will you tell me that I am a coward? Perhaps I am; at least I am not afraid to be called one. Why do I say, then, do not now resist with violence? Because it is not time just yet; it would not succeed. If I had the eloquence that I sometimes dream of, which goes into a crowd of men, and gathers them in its mighty arm, and sways them as the pendent boughs of yonder elm shall be shaken by the summer breeze next June, I would not give that counsel. I would call on men, and lift up my voice like a trumpet through the whole land, until I had gathered millions out of the North and the South, and they should crush slavery for ever, as the ox crushes the spider underneath his feet. But such eloquence is given to no man. It was not given to the ancient Greek who 'shook the arsenal and fulmined over Greece.' He that so often held the nobles and the mob of Rome within his hand, had it not. He that spoke as never man spake, and who has since gathered two hundred millions to his name, had it not. No man has it. The ablest must wait for time! It is idle to resist here and now. It is not the hour. If in 1765 they had attempted to carry out the Revolution by force, they would have failed. Had it failed, we had not been here to-day. There would have been no little monument at Lexington 'sacred to liberty and the rights of mankind,' honoring the men who 'fell in the cause of God and their country.' No little monument at Concord; nor that tall pile of eloquent stone at Bunker Hill, to proclaim that 'Resistance to tyrants is obedience to God.' Success is due to the discretion, heroism, calmness, and forbearance of our fathers: let us wait our time. It will come — perhaps will need no sacrifice of blood."[1]

Gentlemen, I think Judge Finch could construct a misdemeanor out of these words; you will find in them nothing but the plain speech of a minister of the Christian religion.

On the 6th of July, 1851, I preached "Of the three chief Safeguards of Society," and said: —

"Nowhere in the world is there a people so orderly, so much attached to law, as the people of these Northern States. But one law is an exception. The people of the North hate the fugitive slave law, as they have never hated any law since the stamp act. I know there are men in the Northern States who like it, — who would have invented slavery, had it not existed long before. But the mass of the Northern people hate this law, because it is hostile to the purpose of all just human law, hostile to the

[1] 2 Parker's Occasional Sermons, p. 334–337, 343–348, 351, 352.

purpose of society, hostile to the purpose of individual life; because it is hostile to the law of God, — bids the wrong, forbids the right. We disobey that, for the same reason that we keep other laws: because we reverence the law of God. Why should we keep that odious law which makes us hated wherever justice is loved? Because we must sometimes do a disagreeable deed to accomplish an agreeable purpose? The purpose of that law is to enable three hundred thousand slaveholders to retake on our soil the men they once stole on other soil! Most of the city churches of the North seem to think that is a good thing. Very well; is it worth while for fifteen million freemen to transgress the plainest of natural laws, the most obvious instincts of the human heart, and the plainest duties of Christianity, for that purpose? The price to pay is the religious integrity of fifteen million men; the thing to buy is a privilege for three hundred thousand slaveholders to use the North as a hunting field whereon to kidnap men at our cost. Judge you of that bargain."

"I adjure you to reverence a government that is right, statutes that are right, officers that are right; but to disobey every thing that is wrong. I intreat you by your love for your country, by the memory of your fathers, by your reverence for Jesus Christ, yea, by the deep and holy love of God which Jesus taught, and you now feel."[1]

You will say all this is but indispensable duty; but the judge who hanged a man for treason because he promised to make his son "heir to the Crown" — meaning the "Crown Tavern" that he lived in — would doubtless find treason in my words also.

On the 12th of April, 1852, I delivered an address to commemorate the first anniversary of the Kidnapping of Thomas Sims, and said: —

"But when the rulers have inverted their function, and enacted wickedness into a law which treads down the unalienable rights of man to such a degree as this, then I know no ruler but God, no law but natural Justice. I tear the hateful statute of kidnappers to shivers; I trample it underneath my feet. I do it in the name of all law; in the name of Justice and of Man; in the name of the dear God."

"You remember the decision of the Circuit judge, — himself soon to be summoned by death before the Judge who is no respecter of persons, — not allowing the destined victim his last hope, 'the great writ of right.' The decision left him entirely at the mercy of the other kidnappers. The Court-room was crowded with 'respectable people,' 'gentlemen of property and standing:' they received the decision with 'applause and the clapping of hands.' Seize a lamb out of a flock, a wolf from a pack of wolves, the lambs bleat with sympathy, the wolves howl with fellowship and fear; but when a competitor for the Presidency sends back to eternal bondage a poor, friendless negro, asking only his limbs, wealthy gentlemen of Boston applaud the outrage.

'O judgment! thou art fled to brutish beasts,
And men have lost their reason!'"

"When the Fugitive Slave Bill passed, the six New England States lay fast asleep: Massachusetts slept soundly, her head pillowed on her unsold bales of cotton and of woollen goods, dreaming of 'orders from the South.' Justice came to waken her, and whisper of the peril of nine thousand citizens; and she started in her sleep, and, being frighted, swore a prayer or two, then slept again. But Boston woke, — sleeping, in her shop, with ears open, and her eye on the market, her hand on her purse, dreaming

[1] 2 Parker's Occasional Sermons, p. 392–394.

of goods for sale, — Boston woke broadly up, and fired a hundred guns for joy. O Boston, Boston! if thou couldst have known, in that thine hour, the things which belong unto thy peace! But no: they were hidden from her eyes. She had prayed to her god, to Money; he granted her the request, but sent leanness into her soul."

"Yet one charge has been made against the Government, which seems to me a little harsh and unjust. It has been said the administration preferred low and contemptible men as their tools; judges who blink at law, advocates of infamy, and men cast off from society for perjury, for nameless crimes, and sins not mentionable in English speech; creatures 'not so good as the dogs that licked Lazarus's sores; but, like flies, still buzzing upon any thing that is raw.' There is a semblance of justice in the charge: witness Philadelphia, Buffalo, Boston; witness New York. It is true, for kidnappers the Government did take men that looked 'like a bull-dog just come to man's estate;' men whose face declared them, 'if not the devil, at least his twin-brother.' There are kennels of the courts wherein there settles down all that the law breeds most foul, loathsome, and hideous and abhorrent to the eye of day; there this contaminating puddle gathers its noisome ooze, slowly, stealthily, continually, agglomerating its fetid mass by spontaneous cohesion, and sinking by the irresistible gravity of rottenness into that abhorred deep, the lowest, ghastliest pit in all the subterranean vaults of human sin. It is true the Government has skimmed the top and dredged the bottom of these kennels of the courts, taking for its purpose the scum and sediment thereof, the Squeers, the Fagins, and the Quilps of the law, the monsters of the court. Blame not the Government; it took the best it could get. It was necessity, not will, which made the selection. Such is the stuff that kidnappers must be made of. If you wish to kill a man, it is not bread you buy: it is poison. Some of the instruments of Government were such as one does not often look upon. But, of old time, an inquisitor was always 'a horrid-looking fellow, as beseemed his trade.' It is only justice that a kidnapper should bear 'his great commission in his look.'"

"I pity the kidnappers, the poor tools of men almost as base. I would not hurt a hair of their heads; but I would take the thunder of the moral world, and dash its bolted lightning on this crime of stealing men, till the name of kidnapping should be like Sodom and Gomorrah. It is piracy to steal a man in Guinea; what is it to do this in Boston?

"I pity the merchants who, for their trade, were glad to steal their countrymen; I wish them only good. Debate in yonder hall has shown how little of humanity there is in the trade of Boston. She looks on all the horrors which intemperance has wrought, and daily deals in every street; she scrutinizes the jails, — they are filled by rum; she looks into the alms-houses, crowded full by rum; she walks her streets, and sees the perishing classes fall, mowed down by rum; she enters the parlors of wealthy men, looks into the bridal chamber, and meets death: the ghosts of the slain are there, — men slain by rum. She knows it all, yet says, 'There is an interest at stake!' — the interest of rum; let man give way! Boston does this to-day. Last year she stole a man; her merchants stole a man! The sacrifice of man to money, when shall it have an end? I pity those merchants who honor money more than man. Their gold is cankered, and their soul is brass, — is rusted brass. They must come up before the posterity which they affect to scorn. What voice can plead for them before their own children? The eye that mocketh at the justice of its son, and scorneth to obey the mercy of its daughter, the ravens of posterity shall pick it out, and the young eagles eat it up!

"But there is yet another tribunal: 'After the death the judgment!' When he maketh inquisition for the blood of the innocent, what shall the stealers of men reply? Boston merchants, where is your brother, Thomas Sims? Let Cain reply to Christ."[1]

[1] 1 Parker's Additional Speeches, p. 50, 70, 88, 89, 92, 93, 100, 101.

The Sunday after Mr. Webster's death, Oct. 31, 1852, I spoke of that powerful man; listen to this:—

"Mr. Webster stamped his foot, and broke through into the great hollow of practical atheism, which undergulfs the State and Church. Then what a caving in was there! The firm-set base of northern cities quaked and yawned with gaping rents. 'Penn's sandy foundation' shook again, and black men fled from the city of brotherly love, as doves, with plaintive cry, flee from a farmer's barn when summer lightning stabs the roof. There was a twist in Faneuil Hall, and the doors could not open wide enough for Liberty to regain her ancient Cradle; only soldiers, greedy to steal a man, themselves stole out and in. Ecclesiastic quicksand ran down the hole amain. Metropolitan churches toppled, and pitched, and canted, and cracked, their bowing walls all out of plumb. Colleges, broken from the chain which held them in the stream of time, rushed towards the abysmal rent. Harvard led the way, '*Christo et Ecclesiæ*' in her hand. Down plunged Andover, 'Conscience and the Constitution' clutched in its ancient, failing arm. New Haven began to cave in. Doctors of Divinity, orthodox, heterodox, with only a doxy of doubt, 'no settled opinion,' had great alacrity in sinking, and went down quick, as live as ever, into the pit of Korah, Dathan, and Abiram, the bottomless pit of lower law,—one with his mother, cloaked by a surplice, hid beneath his sinister arm, and an acknowledged brother grasped by his remaining limb. Fossils of theology, dead as Ezekiel's bones, took to their feet again, and stood up for most arrant wrong. 'There is no higher law of God,' quoth they, as they went down; 'no golden rule, only the statutes of men.' A man with mythologic ear might fancy that he heard a snickering laugh run round the world below, snorting, whinnying, and neighing, as it echoed from the infernal spot pressed by the fallen monsters of ill-fame, who, thousands of years ago, on the same errand, had plunged down the self-same way. What tidings the echo bore, Dante nor Milton could not tell. Let us leave that to darkness, and to silence, and to death.

"But spite of all this, in every city, in every town, in every college, and in each capsizing church, there were found Faithful Men, who feared not the monster, heeded not the stamping;—nay, some doctors of divinity were found living. In all their houses there was light, and the destroying angel shook them not. The word of the Lord came in open vision to their eye; they had their lamps trimmed and burning, their loins girt; they stood road-ready. Liberty and Religion turned in thither, and the slave found bread and wings. 'When my father and my mother forsake me, then the Lord will hold me up!'

"After the 7th of March, Mr. Webster became the ally of the worst of men, the forefront of kidnapping. The orator of Plymouth Rock was the advocate of slavery; the hero of Bunker Hill put chains round Boston Court House; the applauder of Adams and Jefferson was a tool of the slaveholder, and a keeper of slavery's dogs, the associate of the kidnapper, and the mocker of men who loved the right. Two years he lived with that rabble rout for company, his name the boast of every vilest thing.

'Oh, how unlike the place from whence he fell!'"

"Do men mourn for him? See how they mourn! The streets are hung with black. The newspapers are sad colored. The shops are put in mourning. The Mayor and Aldermen wear crape. Wherever his death is made known, the public business stops, and flags drop half-mast down. The courts adjourn. The courts of Massachusetts—at Boston, at Dedham, at Lowell, all adjourn; the courts of New Hampshire, of Maine, of New York; even at Baltimore and Washington, the courts adjourn; for the great lawyer is dead, and Justice must wait another day. Only the

United States Court, in Boston, trying a man for helping Shadrach out of the furnace of the kidnappers, — the court which executes the Fugitive Slave Bill, — that does not adjourn; that keeps on; its worm dies not, and the fire of its persecution is not quenched, when death puts out the lamp of life! Injustice is hungry for its prey, and must not be balked. It was very proper! Symbolical court of the Fugitive Slave Bill — it does not respect life, why should it death? and, scorning liberty, why should it heed decorum?"[1]

On the 12th of February, 1854, I preached "Some Thoughts on the new Assault upon Freedom in America."

"Who put Slavery in the Constitution; made it Federal? who put it in the new States? who got new soil to plant it in? who carried it across the Mississippi — into Louisiana, Florida, Texas, Utah, New Mexico? who established it in the Capital of the United States? who adopted Slavery and volunteered to catch a runaway, in 1793, and repeated the act in 1850, — in defiance of all law, all precedent, all right? Why, it was the North. 'Spain armed herself with bloodhounds,' said Mr. Pitt, 'to extirpate the wretched natives of America.' In 1850, the Christian Democracy set worse bloodhounds afoot to pursue Ellen Craft; offered them five dollars for the run, if they did not take her; ten if they did! The price of blood was Northern money; the bloodhounds — they were Kidnappers born at the North, bred there, kennelled in her church, fed on her sacraments, blessed by her priests! In 1778, Mr. Pitt had a yet harsher name for the beasts wherewith despotic Spain hunted the red man in the woods — he called them '*Hell Hounds.*' But they only hunted 'savages, heathens, men born in barbarous lands.' What would he say of the pack which in 1851 hunted American Christians, in the 'Athens of America,' and stole a man on the grave of Hancock and Adams — all Boston looking on, and its priests blessing the deed!'

"See what encourages the South to make new encroachments. She has been eminently successful in her former demands, especially with the last. The authors of the fugitive slave bill did not think that enormity could be got through Congress: it was too atrocious in itself, too insulting to the North. But Northern men sprang forward to defend it — powerful politicians supported it to the fullest extent. The worse it was, the better they liked it. Northern merchants were in favor of it — it 'would conciliate the South.' Northern ministers in all the churches of commerce baptized it, defended it out of the Old Testament, or the New Testament. The Senator of Boston gave it his mighty aid, — he went through the land a huckster of Slavery, peddling Atheism: the Representative of Boston gave it his vote. Their constituents sustained both! All the great cities of the North executed the bill. The leading Journals of Boston advised the merchants to withhold all commercial intercourse from Towns which opposed Kidnapping. There was a 'Union Meeting' at Faneuil Hall. You remember the men on the platform: the speeches are not forgotten. The doctrine that there is a Law of God above the passions of the multitude and the ambition of their leaders, was treated with scorn and hooting: a loud guffaw of vulgar ribaldry went up against the Justice of the Infinite God! All the great cities did the same. Atheism was inaugurated as the first principle of Republican government; in politics, religion makes men mad! Mr. Clay declared that 'no Northern gentleman will ever help return a fugitive Slave!' What took place at Philadelphia? New York? Cincinnati? — nay, at Boston? The Northern churches of commerce thought Slavery was a blessing, Kidnapping a 'grace.' The Democrats and Whigs vie with each other in devotion to the fugitive slave bill. The 'Compromises' are the golden rule. The

1 1 Parker's Additional Speeches, 235-37, 246-47.

North conquered her prejudices. The South sees this, and makes another demand. Why not? I am glad of it. She serves us right."

"In 1775, what if it had been told the men all red with battle at Lexington and Bunker Hill, — 'your sons will gird the Court House with chains to kidnap a man; Boston will vote for a Bill which puts the liberty of any man in the hands of a Commissioner, to be paid twice as much for making a Slave as for declaring a freeman; and Boston will call out its soldiers to hunt a man through its streets!' What if on the 19th of April, 1775, when Samuel Adams said, 'Oh! what a glorious morning is this!' as he heard the tidings of war in the little village where he passed the night, — what if it had been told him, — 'On the 19th of April, seventy-six years from this day, will your City of Boston land a poor youth at Savannah, having violated her own laws, and stained her Magistrates' hands, in order to put an innocent man in a Slave-master's jail?' What if it had been told him that Ellen Craft must fly out of Democratic Boston, to Monarchic, Theocratic, Aristocratic England, to find shelter for her limbs, her connubial innocence, and the virtue of her woman's heart? I think Samuel would have cursed the day in which it was said a man-child was born, and America was free! What if it had been told Mayhew and Belknap, that in the pulpits of Boston, to defend kidnapping should be counted to a man as righteousness? They could not have believed it. They did not know what baseness could suck the Northern breast, and still be base."[1]

You will think all this is good morality; but Mr. Curtis in 1836, maintained that kidnapping in Massachusetts, would "promote harmony and good-will where it is extremely desirable to promote it, encourage frequent intercourse, and soften prejudice by increasing acquaintance, and tend to peace and good-will." Nay, that it may be "perfectly consistent with our policy . . . *to interfere actively to enable the citizens of those States* [the slave States] *to enjoy those institutions at home.*" "Slavery is not immoral;" "By the law of this Commonwealth slavery is not immoral."[2]

After Commissioner Loring had kidnapped Anthony Burns, I attended the meeting at Faneuil Hall, and spoke. Gentlemen, I did not finish the speech I had begun, for news came that an attack was made on the Court House, and the meeting was thrown into confusion. I did not speak in a corner, but in the old Cradle of Liberty. Here is the report of the speech which was made by a phonographer, and published in the newspapers of the time — I have no other notes of it. You shall see if there be a misdemeanor in it. Here is the speech: —

"FELLOW-SUBJECTS OF VIRGINIA — [Loud cries of 'No,' 'no,' and 'you must take that back!'] FELLOW-CITIZENS OF BOSTON, then — ['Yes,' 'yes,'] — I come to condole with you at this second disgrace which is heaped on the city made illustrious by *some* of those faces that were once so familiar to our eyes. [Alluding to the portraits which *once hung* conspicuously in Faneuil Hall, but which had been

[1] 1 Parker's Additional Speeches, p. 351, 352, 357–359, 368, 369.

[2] Med Case, p. 9, 11.

removed to obscure and out-of-the-way locations.] Fellow-citizens — A deed which Virginia commands has been done in the city of John Hancock and the 'brace of Adamses.' It was done by a Boston hand. It was a Boston man who issued the warrant; it was a a Boston Marshal who put it in execution; they are Boston men who are seeking to kidnap a citizen of Massachusetts, and send him into slavery for ever and ever. It is our fault that it is so. Eight years ago, a merchant of Boston 'kidnapped a man on the high road between Faneuil Hall and Old Quincy,' at 12 o'clock, — at the noon of day, — and the next day, mechanics of this city exhibited the half-eagles they had received for their share of the spoils in enslaving a brother man. You called a meeting in this hall. It was as crowded as it is now. I stood side by side with my friend and former neighbor, your honorable and noble Chairman to-night [George R. Russell, of West Roxbury], [Loud Cheers,] while this man who had fought for liberty in Greece, and been imprisoned for that sacred cause in the dungeons of Poland, [Dr. Samuel G. Howe,] stood here and introduced to the audience that 'old man eloquent,' John Quincy Adams. [Loud Cheers.]

"It was the last time he ever stood in Faneuil Hall. He came to defend the unalienable rights of a friendless negro slave, kidnapped in Boston. There is even no picture of John Quincy Adams to-night.

"A Suffolk Grand-Jury would find no indictment against the Boston merchant for kidnapping that man. ['Shame,' 'shame.'] If Boston had spoken then, we should not have been here to-night. We should have had no fugitive slave bill. When that bill passed, we fired a hundred guns.

"Don't you remember the Union meeting held in this very hall? A man stood on this platform, — he is a Judge of the Supreme Court now, — and he said — When a certain 'Reverend gentleman' is indicted for perjury, I should like to ask him how he will answer the charge? And when that 'Reverend gentleman' rose, and asked, 'Do you want an answer to your question?' Faneuil Hall cried out, — 'No,' 'no,' — 'Throw him over!' Had Faneuil Hall spoken then on the side of Truth and Freedom, we should not now be the subjects of Virginia.

"Yes, we are the vassals of Virginia. She reaches her arm over the graves of our mothers, and kidnaps men in the city of the Puritans; over the graves of Samuel Adams aud John Hancock. [Cries of 'Shame!'] 'Shame!' so I say; but who is to blame? 'There is no north,' said Mr. Webster. There is none. The South goes clear up to the Canada line. No, gentlemen, there is no Boston to-day. There *was* a Boston once. Now, there is a North suburb to the city of Alexandria,— that is what Boston is. [Laughter.] And you and I, fellow-subjects of the State of Virginia— [Cries of 'no,' 'no.' 'Take that back again.'] — I will take it back when you show me the fact is not so. — Men and brothers, (brothers, at any rate,) I am not a young man; I have heard hurrahs and cheers for liberty many times; I have not seen a great many deeds done for liberty. I ask you, are we to have deeds as well as words? ['Yes,' 'yes,' and loud cheers.]

"Now, brethren, you are brothers at any rate, whether citizens of Massachusetts or subjects of Virginia — I am a minister — and, fellow-citizens of Boston, there are two great laws in this country; one of them is the LAW OF SLAVERY; that law is declared to be a 'finality.' Once the Constitution was formed 'to establish justice, promote tranquillity, and secure the blessings of liberty to ourselves and our posterity.' *Now*, the Constitution is not to secure liberty; it is to extend slavery into Nebraska. And when slavery is established there, in order to show what it is, there comes a sheriff from Alexandria, to kidnap a man in the city of Boston, and he gets a Judge of Probate, in the county of Suffolk, to issue a writ, and another Boston man to execute that writ! [Cries of 'shame,' 'shame.']

"Slavery tramples on the Constitution; it treads down State Rights. Where are the Rights of Massachusetts? A fugitive slave bill Commissioner has got them all in his pocket. Where is the trial by jury? Watson Freeman has it under his Marshal's staff. Where is the great writ of personal replevin, which our fathers wrested, several hundred years ago, from the tyrants who once lorded it over Great Britain? Judge Sprague trod it under his feet! Where is the sacred right of *habeas corpus?* Deputy Marshal Riley can crush it in his hands, and Boston does not say any thing against it. Where are the laws of Massachusetts forbidding State edifices to be used as prisons for the incarceration of fugitives? They, too, are trampled underfoot. 'Slavery is a finality.'

"These men come from Virginia, to kidnap a man here. Once, this was Boston; now, it is a Northern suburb of Alexandria. At first, when they carried a fugitive slave from Boston, they thought it was a difficult thing to do it. They had to get a Mayor to help them; they had to put chains round the Court House; they had to call out the 'Sims Brigade'; it took nine days to do it. Now, they are so confident that we are subjects of Virginia, that they do not even put chains round the Court House; the police have nothing to do with it. I was told to-day that one of the officers of the city said to twenty-eight police-men, 'If any man in the employment of the city meddles in this business, he will be discharged from service, without a hearing.' [Great applause.] Well, gentlemen, how do you think they received that declaration? They shouted, and hurrahed, and gave three cheers. [Renewed applause.] My friend here would not have had the honor of presiding over you to-night, if application had been made a little sooner to the Mayor. Another gentleman told me that, when that man (the Mayor) was asked to preside at this meeting, he said that he regretted that all his time to-night was previously engaged. If he had known it earlier, he said, he might have been able to make arrangements to preside. When the man was arrested, he told the Marshal he regretted it, and that his sympathies were wholly with the slave. [Loud applause.] Fellow-citizens, remember that word. Hold your Mayor to it, and let it be seen that he has got a background and a foreground, which will authorize him to repeat that word in public, and act it out in Faneuil Hall. I say, so confident are the slave agents now, that they can carry off their slave in the daytime, that they do not put chains round the Court House; they have got no soldiers billeted in Faneuil Hall, as in 1851. They think they can carry this man off tomorrow morning in a cab. [Voices — 'They can't do it.' 'Let's see them try.']

"I say, there are two great laws in this country. One is the slave law. That is the law of the President of the United States; it is the law of the Commissioner; it is the law of every Marshal, and of every meanest ruffian whom the Marshal hires to execute his behests.

"There is another law, which my friend, Mr. Phillips, has described in language such as I cannot equal, and therefore shall not try; I only state it in its plainest terms. It is the Law of the People when they are sure they are right and determined to go ahead. [Cheers and much confusion.]

"Now, gentlemen, there was a Boston once, and you and I had fathers — brave fathers; and mothers who stirred up those fathers to manly deeds. Well, gentlemen, once it came to pass that the British Parliament enacted a 'law' — *they* called it law — issuing stamps here. What did your fathers do on that occasion? They said, in the language of Algernon Sydney, quoted in your resolutions, 'that which is not just is not law, and that which is not law ought not to be obeyed.' — [Cheers.] They did not obey the stamp act. They did not call it law, and the man that did call it a law, here, eighty years ago, would have had a very warm coat of tar and feathers on him. They called it an 'act,' and they took the Commissioner who was here to execute it, took him solemnly, manfully, — *they did n't hurt a hair of his head;* they were non-resistants, of a very potent sort, [Cheers,] — and made him take a solemn oath that he would not issue a single stamp. He was brother-in-law of the Governor of the State, the servant of a royal master, 'exceedingly respectable,' of great wealth, and once very popular; but they took him, and made him swear not to execute his commission; and he kept his oath, and the stamp act went to its own place, and you know what that was. [Cheers.] That was an instance of the people going behind a wicked law to enact Absolute Justice into their statute, and making it Common Law. You know what they did with the tea.

"Well, gentlemen, in the South there is a public opinion, it is a very wicked public opinion, which is stronger than law. When a colored seaman goes to Charleston from Boston, he is clapped instantly into jail, and kept there until the vessel is ready to sail, and the Boston merchant or master must pay the bill, and the Boston black man must feel the smart. That is a wicked example, set by the State of South Carolina. When Mr. Hoar, one of our most honored and respected fellow-citizens, was sent to Charleston to test the legality of this iniquitous law, the citizens of Charleston ordered him off the premises, and he was glad to escape to save himself from further outrage. There was no violence, no guns fired. That was an instance of the strength of public opinion — of a most unjust and iniquitous public opinion.

"Well, gentlemen, I say there is one law — slave law; it is everywhere. There is another law, which also is a finality; and that law, it is in your hands and your arms, and you can put it in execution, just when you see fit.

"Gentlemen, I am a clergyman and a man of peace; I love peace. But there is a means, and there is an end; Liberty is the end, and sometimes peace is not the means towards it. [Applause.] Now, I want to ask you what you are going to do. [A voice — 'shoot, shoot.'] There are ways of managing this matter without shooting anybody. Be sure that these men who have kidnapped a man in Boston, are cowards, every mother's son of them; and if we stand up there resolutely, and declare that this man shall not go out of the city of Boston, *without shooting a gun* — [cries of 'that's it,' and great applause,] — then he won't go back. Now, I am going to propose that when you adjourn, it be to meet at *Court Square, to-morrow morning at nine o'clock*. As many as are in favor of that motion will raise their hands. [A large number of hands were raised, but many voices cried out, 'Let's go to-night,' 'let's pay a visit to the slave-catchers at the Revere House,' etc. 'Put that question.'] Do you propose to go to the Revere House to-night, then show your hands. (Some hands were held up.) It is not a vote. We shall meet at *Court Square, at nine o'clock to-morrow morning*."

On the following Sunday, May 28, in place of the usual Scripture passages, I extemporized the following "Lesson for the Day," which on Monday appeared in the newspapers: —

"Since last we came together, there has been a man stolen in the city of our fathers. It is not the first; it may not be the last. He is now in the great slave-pen in the city of Boston. He is there against the law of the Commonwealth, which, if I am rightly informed, in such cases prohibits the use of State edifices as United States jails."

"A man has been killed by violence. Some say he was killed by his own coadjutors: I can easily believe it; there is evidence enough that they were greatly frightened. They were not United States soldiers, but volunteers from the streets of Boston, who, for their pay, went into the Court House to assist in kidnapping a brother man. They were so cowardly that they could not use the simple cutlasses they had in their hands, but smote right and left, like ignorant and frightened ruffians as they are. They may have slain their brother or not — I cannot tell."

"Why is Boston in this confusion to-day? The fugitive slave bill Commissioner has just now been sowing the wind, that we may reap the whirlwind. The old fugitive slave bill Commissioner stands back; he has gone to look after his 'personal popularity.' But when Commissioner Curtis does not dare appear in this matter, another man comes forward, and for the first time seeks to kidnap his man also in the city of Boston."

"But he has sown the wind, and we are reaping the whirlwind. All this confusion is his work. He knew he was stealing a Man born with the same unalienable right to 'life, liberty, and the pursuit of happiness,' as himself. He knew the slave-holders had no more right to Anthony Burns than to his own daughter. He knew the consequences of stealing a man. He knew that there are men in Boston who have not yet conquered their prejudices — men who respect the Higher Law of God. He knew there would be a meeting at Faneuil Hall, gatherings in the streets. He knew there would be violence."

"Edward Greeley Loring, Judge of Probate for the County of Suffolk, in the State of Massachusetts, fugitive slave bill Commissioner of the United States, before these citizens of Boston, on Ascension Sunday, assembled to worship God, I charge you with the death of that man who was killed on last Friday night. He was your fellow-servant in kidnapping. He dies at your hand. You fired the shot which makes his wife a widow, his child an orphan. I charge you with the peril of twelve men, arrested for murder, and on trial for their lives. I charge you with filling the Court House with one hundred and eighty-four hired ruffians of the United States, and alarming not only this city for her liberties that are in peril, but stirring up the whole Commonwealth of Massachusetts with indignation, which no man knows how to stop—which no man can stop. You have done it all!"[1]

June 4th, I preached "of the New Crime against Humanity," and said:—

"Wednesday, the 24th of May, the city was all calm and still. The poor black man was at work with one of his own nation, earning an honest livelihood. A Judge of Probate, Boston born and Boston bred, a man in easy circumstances, a Professor in Harvard College, was sitting in his office, and with a single spurt of his pen he dashes off the liberty of a man—a citizen of Massachusetts. He kidnaps a man endowed by his Creator with the unalienable right to life, liberty, and the pursuit of happiness. He leaves the writ with the Marshal, and goes home to his family, caresses his children, and enjoys his cigar. The frivolous smoke curls round his frivolous head, and at length he lays him down to sleep, and, I suppose, such dreams as haunt such heads. But when he wakes next morn, all the winds of indignation, wrath, and honest scorn, are let loose. Before night, they are blowing all over this commonwealth—ay, before another night they have gone to the Mississippi, and wherever the lightning messenger can tell the tale. So have I read in an old mediæval legend that one summer afternoon, there came up a 'shape, all hot from Tartarus,' from hell below, but garmented and garbed to represent a civil-suited man, masked with humanity. He walked quiet and decorous through Milan's stately streets, and scattered from his hand an invisible dust. It touched the walls; it lay on the streets; it ascended to the cross on the minster's utmost top. It went down to the beggar's den. Peacefully he walked through the streets, vanished and went home. But the next morning, the pestilence was in Milan, and ere a week had sped half her population were in their graves; and half the other half, crying that hell was clutching at their hearts, fled from the reeking City of the Plague!"

"I have studied the records of crime—it is a part of my ministry. I do not find that any College Professor has ever been hanged for murder in all the Anglo-Saxon family of men, till Harvard College had that solitary shame. Is not that enough? Now she is the first to have a Professor that kidnaps men. 'The Athens of America' furnished both!

"I can understand how a man commits a crime of passion, or covetousness, or rage, nay, of revenge, or of ambition. But for a man in Boston, with no passion, no covetousness, no rage, with no ambition nor revenge, to steal a poor negro, to send him into bondage,—

[1] 2 Parker's Additional, 74, 75, 81, 83.

I cannot comprehend the fact. I can understand the consciousness of a lion, not a kidnapper's heart."

"But there is another court. The Empsons and the Dudleys have been summoned there before: Jeffreys and Scroggs, the Kanes, and the Curtises, and the Lorings, must one day travel the same unwelcome road. Imagine the scene after man's mythological way. 'Edward, where is thy brother, Anthony?' 'I know not; am I my brother's keeper, Lord?' 'Edward, where is thy brother, Anthony?' 'Oh, Lord, he was friendless, and so I smote him; he was poor, and I starved him of more than life. He owned nothing but his African body. I took that away from him, and gave it to another man!'

"Then listen to the voice of the Crucified — 'Did I not tell thee, when on earth, "Thou shalt love the Lord thy God with all thy understanding and thy heart?"' 'But I thought thy kingdom was not of this world.'

"'Did I not tell thee that thou shouldst love thy neighbor as thyself? Where is Anthony, thy brother? I was a stranger, and you sought my life; naked, and you rent away my skin; in prison, and you delivered me to the tormentors — fate far worse than death. Inasmuch as you did it to Anthony Burns, you did it unto me.'"[1]

Gentlemen, I suppose the honorable Judge had the last three addresses in his mind while concocting his charge to the Grand-Jury which refused to find a bill. I infer this partly from what took place in the room of the next Grand-Jury which found this indictment, and partly also from another source which you will look at for a moment.

I preach on Sundays in the Music Hall, which is owned by a Corporation who rent it to the 28th Congregational Society for their religious meetings. Mr. Charles P. Curtis, father-in-law of the Hon. Judge Curtis, and step-brother of Commissioner Loring, and a more distant relation but intimate friend of George T. Curtis, was then president of that Corporation, and one of its directors. At a meeting of the corporation, held presently after the kidnapping of Mr. Burns, Mr. Charles P. Curtis and his family endeavored to procure a vote of the Corporation to instruct the directors "to terminate the lease of the 28th Congregational Society as soon as it can be legally done, and not to renew it." Mr. Charles P. Curtis managed this matter clandestinely, but not with his usual adroitness, for at the meeting he disclosed the cause of his act, — that *Mr. Parker had called his brother a murderer*, probably referring to the passage just read from the "Lesson for the Day." But he took nothing by that motion.[2]

[1] Parker's Additional, 167, 168, 169, 170, 171, 172.

[2] See the communications of Messrs. Chas. P. Curtis and Thomas B. Curtis, in the Boston Daily Advertiser of June, 1854; and the other articles setting forth the facts of the case.

What influence this private and familistic disposition had in framing the Judge's charge, I leave it for you and the People of America to determine. You also can conjecture whether it had any effect on Mr. Greenough, the other son-in-law of Mr. Charles P. Curtis, who refused to return my salutation, and who, "by a miracle," was put on the new Grand-Jury after the old one was discharged, and then was so "very anxious to procure an indictment" against me. I leave all that with you. You can easily appreciate the efforts made to silence not only my Sunday preaching, but also the magnificent eloquence of Wendell Phillips; yes, to choke all generous speech, in order that kidnappers might pursue their vocation with none to molest or make them afraid.

But, Gentlemen, I fear you do not yet quite understand the arrogance of our Southern masters, and the fear and hatred they bear towards all who dare speak a word in behalf of the Rights of outraged Humanity. The gag-law of Congress which silenced the House of Representatives till John Quincy Adams, that noble son of a noble sire, burst through the Southern chain; the violation of the United States mails to detect "incendiary publications;" the torturing of men and women for an opinion against Slavery — all these are notorious; but they and all that I have yet stated of the action of the Federal Courts in the fugitive slave bill cases, with the "opinions" of Northern Judges already mentioned, do not fill up the cup of bitterness and poison which is to be poured down our throats. Let me, therefore, here give you one supplementary piece of evidence to prove how intensely the South hates the Northern Freedom of Speech. I purposely select this case from a period when Southern arrogance and Northern servility were far less infamous than now.

About twenty years ago Mr. R. G. Williams of New York published this sentence in a newspaper called the Emancipator, — "God commands and all nature cries out, that man should not be held as property. The system of making men property has plunged 2,250,000 of our fellow countrymen into the deepest physical and moral degradation, and they are every moment sinking deeper."

For this he was indicted by a Grand-Jury of the State of Alabama, and the Governor of that State made a demand on the Executive of New York insisting that Mr. Williams should be delivered up to take his trial in Alabama — a State where he had never been! But the New York Governor, after consulting with his law-advisers, did not come to the conclusion that it was consistent with the public policy of New York to "interfere actively" and promote Slavery in Alabama. *So he refused to deliver up Mr. Williams!* [1]

[1] Med Case, p. 25.

Gentlemen of the Jury, before you can convict me of the crime charged, you must ask three several sets of questions, and be satisfied of all these things which I will now set forth.

I. THE QUESTION OF FACT. Did I do the deed charged, and obstruct Marshal Freeman while in the peace of the United States, and discharging his official duty? This is a quite complicated question. Here are the several parts of it: —

1. Was there any illegal obstruction or opposition at all made to the Marshal? This is not clear. True, an attack was made on the doors and windows of the Court House, but that is not necessarily an attack on the Marshal or his premises. He has a right in certain rooms of the Court House, and this he has in virtue of a lease. He has also a right to use the passage-ways of the house, in common with other persons and the People in general. His rights as Tenant are subject to the terms of his lease and to the law which determines the relation of Tenant and Landlord. Marshal Freeman as tenant has no more rights than Freeman Marshal, or John Doe, or Rachel Roe would have under the same circumstances. Of course he had a legal right to defend himself if attacked, and to close his own doors, bar and fortify the premises he rented against the illegal violence of others. But neither his lease nor the laws of the land authorized him to close the other doors, or to obstruct the passages, no more than to obstruct the Square or the Street. No lease, no law gave him that right.

Now there have been three secret examinations of witnesses relative to this assault, before three Grand-Juries. No evidence has been offered which shows *that any attack was made on the premises of the Marshal.* The Supreme Court of Massachusetts was in session at the moment the attack was made on the Court House; the venerable Chief Justice was on the Bench; the jury had retired to consider the capital case then pending, and were expected to return with their verdict. The People had a right in the court-room, a right in the passage-ways and doors which lead thither. That court had not ordered the room to be cleared or the doors to be shut. Marshal Freeman closed the outer doors of the Court House, and thus debarred men of their right to enter a Massachusetts Court of Justice solemnly deciding a capital case. You are to consider whether an attack on the outer doors of the Court House, is an illegal attack on the Marshal who had shut those doors without any legal authority. If you decide this point as the government wishes, then you will proceed to the next question.

2. Did I actually obstruct him? If not, then the inquiry stops here. You answer " not guilty." But if I did, then it is worth while to consider how I obstructed him. (1.) Was it by a physical act, by material force; or, (2.) by a metaphysical act, immaterial or spiritual

force — a word, thought, a feeling, a wish, approbation, assent, consent, "evincing an express liking."

3. Was Marshal Freeman, at the time of the obstruction, in the peace of the United States, or was he himself violating the law thereof? For if he were violating the law and thereby injuring some other man, and I obstructed him in that injury, then I am free from all legal guilt, and did a citizen's duty in obstructing his illegal conduct. Now it appears that he was kidnapping and stealing Anthony Burns for the purpose of making him the slave of one Suttle of Virginia, who wished to sell him and acquire money thereby; and that Mr. Freeman did this at the instigation of Commissioner Loring who was entitled to receive ten dollars if he enslaved Mr. Burns, and five only for setting him free. It appears also that Marshal Freeman was to receive large, official money for this kidnapping, and such honor as this Administration, and the Hunker newspapers, and lower law divines can bestow.

Now you are to consider whether a man so doing was in the peace of the United States. He professes to have acted under the fugitive slave bill which authorizes him to seize, kidnap, steal, imprison, and carry off any person whatsoever, on the oath of any slaveholder who has fortified himself with a piece of paper of a certain form and tenor from any court of slaveholders in the slave States. Is that bill Constitutional? The Constitution of the United States is the People's Power of Attorney by which they authorize certain servants, called Legislative, Judicial, and Executive officers, to do certain matters and things in a certain way, but prohibit them from doing in the name of the People, any thing except those things specified, or those in any but the way pointed out. Does the fugitive slave bill attempt those things and only those, in the way provided for in that Power of Attorney; or other things, or in a different way?

To determine this compound question you will look (1.) at the ultimate Purpose of the Constitution, the End which the People wanted to attain; and (2.) at the provisional Means, the method by which they proposed to reach it. Here of course the Purpose is more important than the Means. The Preamble to this Power of Attorney clearly sets forth this Purpose aimed at: here it is, "to form a more perfect Union, establish Justice, insure domestic Tranquillity, provide for the Common Defence, promote the General Welfare, and secure the Blessings of Liberty." Is the fugitive slave bill a Measure tending to that End?

To answer that question you are to consult your own mind and conscience. You are not to take the opinion of the Court. For (1.) it would probably be their purchased *official* opinion which the government pays for, and so is of no value whatever; or (2.) if it be their *personal* opinion, from what Mr. Sprague and Mr. Curtis have said and done before, you know that their personal opinion in the matter would be of no value whatsoever. To me it is very plain that kidnapping a man in Boston and making him a slave, is not the way to form a more perfect Union, establish Justice, insure domestic Tranquillity, provide for the Common Defence, promote the General Welfare, or secure the Blessings of Liberty. But you are to judge for yourselves. If you think the fugitive slave bill not a Means towards that End, which this national Power of Attorney proposes, then you will think it is unconstitutional, that Mr. Freeman was not in the peace of the United States, but acting against it; and then it was the Right of every citizen to obstruct his illegal wickedness and might be the Duty of some.

But not only does the fugitive slave bill contravene and oppose the Purpose of the Constitution, it also transcends the Means which that Power of Attorney declares the People's agents shall make use of, and whereto it absolutely restricts them. The Constitution prescribes that "the Judicial power shall be vested in one Supreme Court, and in such inferior courts as the Congress may ordain and establish." "The Judges . . . shall hold their offices during good behavior, and shall . . . receive a compensation which shall not be diminished during their continuance in office." Now the Commissioner who kidnaps a man and declares him a slave, exercises *judicial power.* Commissioner Loring himself confesses it, in his Remonstrance against being removed from the office of Judge of Probate. You are to consider whether a Commissioner appointed by the Judge of the Court as a ministerial officer to take "bail and affidavits," and paid twice as much for stealing a victim as for setting free a man, is either such a "supreme" or such an "inferior court" as the Constitution vests the "judicial powers" in. If not, then the fugitive slave bill is unconstitutional because it does not use the Means which the People's Power of Attorney points out. Of course the inquiry stops at this point, and you return "not guilty."

4. It is claimed that the fugitive slave bill is sustained by this clause in the Constitution, "No person held to service or labor in one State, under the laws thereof, escaping into another, shall, in consequence of any law or regulation therein, be discharged from such service or labor, but shall be delivered up on claim of the party to whom such service or labor may be due."[1] But if you try the fugitive slave bill by this rule, you must settle two questions. (1.) Who is meant by persons "held to service or labor?" and (2.) by whom shall they "be delivered up on claim?" Let us begin with the first.

[1] Art. iv. § 2, ¶ 2.

(1.) Who are the persons "held to service or labor?" The preamble to this People's Power of Attorney, sets forth the matters and things which the People's agents are empowered to achieve. "They are to form a more perfect Union, establish Justice, insure domestic Tranquillity, provide for the common Defence, promote the General Welfare and secure the Blessings of Liberty." Now the fugitive-from-labor clause must be interpreted in part by the light of the Purpose of the Constitution. So it would appear that this Power of Attorney, requires the delivery of only such as are *justly* "held to service or labor;" and only to those men to whom this "service" is *justly* "due." Surely, it would be a monstrous act to deliver up to his master a person *unjustly* "held to service or labor," or one justly held to those to whom his service was not *justly* due: it would be as bad to deliver up the *wrong fugitive*, as to deliver the right fugitive to the *wrong claimant:* it would be also monstrous to suppose that the People of the United States, with the Declaration of Independence in their memory, should empower their attorneys to deliver up a man *unjustly* held to service or labor, and that too by the very instrument which directs them to "establish Justice" and "secure the Blessings of Liberty." Whatsoever interpretation was at the time put on the Constitution, whatsoever the People thereby intended, two things are plain — namely, (1.) that the language implies only such as are *justly* held to service, or labor, and (2.) that the People had no moral right to deliver up any except such as were *justly* held, and had *unjustly* escaped.

If the opposite interpretation be accepted, and that clause be taken without restrictions, then see what will follow. South Carolina has already made a law by which she imprisons all *colored* citizens of the free States who are found on her soil. Let us suppose she makes a new law for reducing to perpetual slavery all the white citizens of Massachusetts whom she finds on her soil; that a Boston vessel with 500 Boston men and women — sailing for California, — is wrecked on her inhospitable coast, and those persons are all seized and reduced to slavery; but some ten or twenty of the most resolute escape from the "service or labor" to which they are held, and return to their business in Boston. But their "owners" come in pursuit; the kidnapping Commissioners, Curtis and Loring, with the help of the rest of the family of men-stealers, arrest them under the fugitive slave bill. On the mock trial, it is shown by the kidnapper that they were legally "held to service or labor," and according to the constitution "shall be delivered up;" that this enslavement is perfectly "legal" in South Carolina; and the constitution says that no "law or regulation" of Massachusetts shall set them free. They must go with Sims and Burns. Gentlemen, you see where you are going, if you allow the Constitution of parchment to override the Constitution of Justice.

(2.) By whom shall they "be delivered up?" Either by the Federal Government, or else by the Government of the State into which they have escaped. Now the Federal Government has no constitutional power, except what the Constitution gives it. Gentlemen, there is not a line in that Power of Attorney by which the People authorize the Federal Government to make a man a slave in Massachusetts or anywhere else. I know the Government has done it, as the British Government levied ship-money, and put men to the rack, but it is against the Constitution of the land.

Gentlemen, you will settle these constitutional questions according to your conscience, not mine. But if the fugitive slave bill demands the rendition of men from whom service is not *justly* due — due by the Law of God, or if the Government unconstitutionally aims to do what the Constitution gave it no right to do — then the Marshal was not "in the peace of the United States." Your inquiry stops at this point.

5. But, if satisfied on all which relates to this question of his being in the peace of the United States, you are next to inquire if Mr. Freeman, at the time of the obstruction was "Marshal of the United States," and "in the due and lawful discharge of his duties as such officer." There is no doubt that he was Marshal; but there may be a doubt that he was in the "lawful discharge of his duties as such officer." Omitting what I first said, (I. 1.) see what you must determine in order to make this clear.

(1.) Was Commissioner Loring, who issued the warrant to kidnap Mr. Burns, legally qualified to do that act. Gentlemen, there is no record of his appointment and qualification by the form of an oath. No evidence has been adduced to this point. Mr. Loring says he was duly appointed and qualified. There is no written line, no other word of mouth to prove it.

(2.) Admitting that Mr. Loring had the legal authority to command Mr. Freeman to steal Mr. Burns, it appears that stealing was done feloniously. The Marshal's guard seized him on the charge of Burglary — a false charge. You are to consider whether Mr. Freeman had legally taken possession of his victim.

(3.) If satisfied thus far, you are to inquire if he held him legally. It seems he was imprisoned in a public building of Massachusetts, which was by him used as a jail for the purpose of keeping a man claimed as a fugitive slave, contrary to the express words of a regular and constitutional statute of Massachusetts.

If you find that Mr. Freeman was not in the lawful discharge of his duties as Marshal, then the inquiry stops here, and you return a verdict of "not guilty."

But if you are convinced that an obstruction was made against a Marshal in the peace of the United States, and in the legal discharge of a legal, constitutional duty, then you settle the question of Fact against me, and proceed to the next point.

II. *The Question of Law.*

1. Is there a law of the United States punishing this deed of mine? The answer will depend partly on the kind of opposition or obstruction which I made. If you find (1.) that I obstructed him, while in the legal discharge of his legal duties, with physical force, violence, then there is a law, clear and unmistakable, forbidding and punishing that offence. But if you find (2.) that I obstructed him with only metaphysical force, — "words," "thoughts," "feelings," "wishes," "consent," "assent," "evincing an express liking," "or approbation," then it may be doubtful to you whether the law of 1790, or any other law of the United States forbids that.

2. But if you find there is such a law, punishing such metaphysical resistance — and the court by the charge to the Grand-Jury seems plainly of that opinion, which is fortified by the authority of Chief Justice Kelyng and Judge Chase, two impeached judges — then you will consider whether that law is constitutional. And here you will look at two things, (1.) The Purpose of the Constitution already set forth; and (2.) at the Means provided for by that Power of Attorney. For if the agents of the People — legislative, judiciary, or executive — have exceeded their delegated authority, then their act is invalid and binding on no man. If I, in writing, authorize my special agent to sell my Ink-stand for a dollar, I am bound by his act in obedience thereto. But if on that warrant he sells my Writing-Desk for that sum, I am not bound by his unauthorized act. Now I think there will be grave doubts, whether any law, which with fine and imprisonment punishes such words, thoughts, feelings, consent, assent, "express liking," approbation, is warranted by the People's Power of Attorney to their agents. The opinion of the Court on such a matter, Gentlemen, I think is worth as much as Bacon's opinion in favor of the rack; or Jones's opinion that Charles I. had the right to imprison members of Parliament for words spoken in the Commons' Debate; or the opinion of the ten judges that Ship-money was lawful; or of the two chief justices that the Seven Bishops' Petition to James II. was high treason; or Thurlow's opinion that a jury is the natural enemy of the King. Gentlemen, I think it is worth nothing at all. But if you think otherwise, you have still to ask: —

3. Is this law just? That is does it coincide with the Law of God, the Constitution of the Universe? There your own conscience must decide. Mr. Curtis has told you there is no Morality but Legality, no standard of Right and Wrong but the Statute, your only

light comes from this printed page, "Statutes of the United States," and through these sheepskin covers. Gentlemen, if your conscience is also bound in sheepskin you will think as these Honorable Judges, and recognize only Judge Curtis's "Standard of Morality," — no Higher Law. But even if you thus dispose of the Question of Law, there will yet remain the last part of your function.

III. *The Question of the Application of the Law to the Fact.* To determine this Question you are to ask: —

1. Does the law itself, the act of 1790, apply to such acts, that is, to such words, thoughts, wishes, feelings, consent, assent, approbation, express liking, and punish them with fine and imprisonment? If not, the consideration ends: but if it does, you will next ask: —

2. Is it according to the Constitution of the United States — its Purpose, its Means — thus to punish such acts? If not satisfied thereof, you stop there; but if you accept Judge Curtis's opinion then you will next inquire: —

3. Is it expedient in this particular case to apply this law, under the circumstances, to this man, and punish him with fine and imprisonment? If you say "yes" you will then proceed to the last part of the whole investigation, and will ask: —

4. Is it just and right; that is according to the Natural Law of God, the Constitution of the Universe? Here you will consider several things.

(1.) What was the Marshal legally, constitutionally, and justly doing at the time he was obstructed? He was stealing, kidnapping, and detaining an innocent man, Anthony Burns, with the intention of depriving him of what the Declaration of Independence calls his natural and unalienable Right to liberty and the pursuit of happiness. Mr. Burns had done no wrong or injury to any one — but simply came to Massachusetts, to possess and enjoy these natural rights. Marshal Freeman had seized him on the false charge of burglary, had chained him in a dungeon contrary to Massachusetts law, — there were irons on his hands.

It is said he was a slave: now a slave is a person whom some one has stolen from himself, and by force keeps from his natural rights. Mr. Burns sought to rescue himself from the thieves who held him; Marshal Freeman took the thieves' part.

(2.) Was there any effectual mode of securing to Mr. Burns his natural and unalienable Right except the mode of forcible rescue? Gentlemen of the Jury, it is very clear there was none at all. The laws of Massachusetts were of no avail. Your own Supreme Court, which in 1832, at the instigation of Mr. Charles P. Curtis, sent a little boy not fourteen years old into Cuban Slavery to gratify a slave-hunting West Indian, in 1851, had voluntarily put its neck under the

Southern chain. Your Chief Justice, who acquired such honorable distinction in 1836 by setting free the little girl Med from the hands of the Curtises, in 1851 spit in the face of Massachusetts, and spurned her laws with his judicial foot. It was plain that Commissioner Loring did not design to allow his victim a fair trial — for he had already prejudged the case; he advised Mr. Phillips to make no defence, put no 'obstruction' in the way of the man's going back, as he probably will," and, before hearing the defence sought to settle the matter by a sale of Mr. Burns.

Gentlemen, the result showed there was no chance of what the United States law reckons justice being done in the case — for Commissioner Loring not only decided the fate of Mr. Burns against law, and against evidence, but communicated his decision to the slave-hunters nearly twenty-four hours before he announced it in open court! No, Gentlemen, when a man claimed as a fugitive is brought before either of these two members of this family of kidnappers — who run now in couples, hunting men and seeking whom they may devour — there is no hope for him: it is only a mock-trial, worse than the Star-chamber inquisition of the Stuart kings. Place no "obstructions in the way of the man's going back," said the mildest of the two, "as he probably will." Over that door, historic and actual, as over that other, but fabulous, gate of Hell should be written: —

> "Through me they go to the city of sorrow;
> Through me they go to endless agony;
> Through me they go among the nations lost:
> Leave every hope, all ye that enter here!"

The only hope of freedom for Mr. Burns lay in the limbs of the People! Anarchy afforded him the only chance of Justice.

(3.) Did they who it is alleged made the attack on the Marshal, or they who it is said instigated them to the attack, do it from any wicked, unjust, or selfish motive? Nobody pretends it — Gentlemen, we had much to lose — ease, honor — for with many persons in Boston it is a disgrace to favor the unalienable Rights of man, as at Rome to read the Bible, or at Damascus to be a Christian — ease, honor, money, liberty — if this Court have its way, — nay, life itself; for one of the family which preserves the Union by kidnapping men, counts it a capital crime to rescue a victim from their hands, and Mr. Hallett, when only a democratic expectant of office, declared "if it only resists law and obstructs its officers . . . it is treason . . . and he who risks it must risk hanging for it." No, Gentlemen, I had much to lose by my words. I had nothing to gain. Nothing I mean but the satisfaction of doing my duty to Myself, my Brother, and my God.

And tried by Judge Sprague's precept, "Obey both," that is nothing; or by Judge Curtis's "Standard of Morality" it is a crime; and according to his brother it is "Treason;" and according to, I know not how many ministers of commerce, it is "infidelity" — "treasonable, damnable doctrine."

No, Gentlemen, no selfish motive could move me to such conduct. The voice of Duty was terribly clear: "Inasmuch as ye have done it unto the least of these my brethren, ye have done it unto me."

Put all these things together, Gentlemen. Remember there is a duty of the strong to help the weak: that all men have a common interest in the common duty to keep the Eternal Law of Justice; remember we are all of us to appear one day before the Court which is of purer eyes than to love iniquity. Ask what says Conscience — what says God. Then decide as you must decide.

The eyes of the nation are upon you. The Judges of this Honorable Court hold their office in Petty Serjeantry on condition of wresting the Laws and Constitution to the support of the fugitive slave bill, and of preventing, as far as possible, all noble thought which opposes the establishment of Despotism, now so rapidly encroaching upon our once Free Soil: they hold by this Petty Serjeantry — a menial service not mentioned in any book even of "Jocular Tenures."

If you could find me guilty — it is not possible, only conceivable with a contradiction, — you would delight the Slave Power — Atchison, Cushing, Stringfellow, and their Northern and Southern crew — for to them I seem identified with New England Freedom of Speech. "Aha," they will neigh and snicker out, "Judge Curtis has got the North under his feet! Mr. Webster knew what he was about when putting him in place!"

English is the only tongue in which Freedom can speak her political or religious word. Shall that tongue be silenced; tied in Faneuil Hall; torn out by a Slave-hunter? The Stamp Act only taxed commercial and legal documents; the fugitive slave bill makes our words misdemeanors. The Revenue Act did but lay a tax on tea, three-pence only on a pound: the Slave-hunters' act taxes our thoughts as a crime. The Boston Port Bill but closed our harbor, we could get in at Salem; but the Judge's Charge shuts up the mouth of all New England, not a word against man-hunting but is a "crime," — the New Testament is full of "misdemeanors." Andros only took away the Charter of Massachusetts; Judge Curtis's "law" is a *quo warranto* against Humanity itself. "Perfidious General Gage" took away the arms of Boston; Judge Curtis *charges* upon our Soul; he would wring all religion out of you, — no "Standard of Morality" above the fugitive slave bill; you must not, even to God in your prayers, evince "an express liking" for the deliverance of an innocent man whom his family seek to transform to a beast of burthen and then sacrifice to the American Moloch.

Decide according to your own Conscience, Gentlemen, not after mine.

Gentlemen of the Jury, I must bring this defence to a close. Already it is too long for your patience, though far too short for the mighty interest at stake, for it is the Freedom of a Nation which you are to decide upon. I have shown you the aim and purposes of the Slave Power — to make this vast Continent one huge Despotism, a House of Bondage for African Americans, a House of Bondage also for Saxon Americans. I have pointed out the course of Despotism in Monarchic England; you have seen how there the Tyrants directly made wicked laws, or when that resource failed, how they reached indirectly after their End, and appointed officers to pervert the law, to ruin the people. You remember how the King appointed base men as Attorneys and Judges, and how wickedly they used their position and their power, scorning alike the law of God and the welfare of Man. "The Judges in their itinerant Circuits," says an old historian,[1] "the more to enslave the people to obedience, being to speak of the king, would give him sacred titles as if their advancement to high places must necessarily be laid upon the foundation of the People's debasement." You have not forgotten Saunders, Kelyng, and Jeffreys and Scroggs; Sibthorpe and Mainwaring you will remember for ever, — denouncing "eternal damnation" on such as refused the illegal tax of Charles I. or evinced an express disapprobation of his tyranny.

Gentlemen, you recollect how the rights of the jury were broken down, — how jurors were threatened with trial for perjury, insulted, fined, and imprisoned, because they would be faithful to the Law and their Conscience. You remember how the tyrannical king clutched at the People's purse and their person too, and smote at all freedom of speech, while the purchased Judges were always ready, the tools of Despotism. But you know what it all came to — Justice could not enter upon the law through the doors of Westminster Hall; so she tried it at Naseby and Worcester and with her "Invincible Ironsides" took possession by means of pike and gun. Charles I. laid his guilty head on the block; James II. only escaped the same fate by timely flight. If Courts will not decree Justice, then Civil War will, for it must be done, and a battle becomes a "Crowning Mercy."

Gentlemen, I have shown you what the Slave Power of America

[1] In 2 Kennett, 753.

aims at, — a Despotism which is worse for this age than the Stuarts' tyranny for that time. You see its successive steps of encroachment. Behold what it has done within ten years. It has made Slavery perpetual in Florida; has annexed Texas, a Slave State as big as the kingdom of France; has fought the Mexican War, with Northern money, and spread bondage over Utah, New Mexico, and California; it has given Texas ten millions of Northern dollars to help Slavery withal; it has passed the fugitive slave bill and kidnapped men in the West, in the Middle States, and even in our own New England; it has given ten millions of dollars for a little strip of worthless land, the Mesilla valley, whereon to make a Slave Railroad and carry bondage from the Atlantic to the Pacific; it has repealed the Prohibition of Slavery, and spread the mildew of the South all over Kansas and Nebraska. Ask your capitalists, who have bought Missouri lands and railroads, how their stock looks just now; not only your Liberty but even their Money is in peril. You know the boast of Mr. Toombs. Gentlemen, you know what the United States Courts have done — with poisoned weapons they have struck deadly blows at Freedom. You know Sharkey and Grier and Kane. You recollect the conduct of Kidnappers' Courts at Milwaukie, Sandusky, Cincinnati, Philadelphia — in the Hall of Independence. But why need I wander so far? Alas! you know too well what has been done in Boston, our own Boston, the grave of Puritan piety. You remember the Union Meeting, Ellen Craft, Sims, chains around the Court House, the Judges crawling under, soldiers in the street, drunk, smiting at the citizens; you do not forget Anthony Burns, the Marshal's guard, the loaded cannon in place of Justice, soldiers again in the streets smiting at and wounding the citizens. You recollect all this — the 19th of April, 1851, Boston delivering an innocent man at Savannah to be a slave for ever, and that day scourged in his jail while the hirelings who enthralled him were feasted at their Inn; — Anniversary week last year — a Boston Judge of Probate, the appointed guardian of orphans, kidnapping a poor and friendless man! You cannot forget these things, no, never!

You know who did all this: a single family — the Honorable Judge Curtis, with his kinsfolk and friends, himself most subtly active with all his force throughout this work. When Mr. Webster prostituted himself to the Slave Power this family went out and pimped for him in the streets; they paraded in the newspapers, at the Revere House, and in public letters; they beckoned and made signs at Faneuil Hall. That crime of Sodom brought Daniel Webster to his grave at Marshfield, a mighty warning not to despise the Law of the Infinite God; but that sin of Gomorrah, it put the Hon. Benj. R. Curtis on this Bench; gave him his judicial power to construct his "law," construct his "jury," to indict and try me. Try me! No, Gentlemen, it is you, your wives and your children, who are up for swift condemnation this day. Will you wait, will you add sin to sin, till God shall rain fire and brimstone on your heads, and a Dead Sea shall cover the place once so green and blossoming with American Liberty? Decide your own fate. When the Judges are false let the Juries be faithful, and we have "a crowning mercy" without cannon, and the cause of Justice is secure. For "when wicked men seem nearest to their hopes, the godly man is furthest from his fears."

You know my "offence," Gentlemen. I have confessed more than the government could prove. You are the "Country:" the Nation by twelve Delegates is present here to-day. In the name of America, of mankind, you are to judge of the Law, the Fact, and the Application of the Law to the Fact. You are to decide whether you will spread Slavery and the Consequences of Slavery all over the North; whether Boston, New England, all the North, shall kidnap other Ellen Crafts, other Thomas Sims, other Anthony Burns, — whether Sharkey and Grier, and Kane and Curtis, shall be Tyrants over you — forbidding all Freedom of Speech: or whether Right and Justice, the Christian Religion, the natural service of the Infinite God shall bless our wide land with the numberless Beatitudes of Humanity. Should you command me to be fined and go to jail, I should take it very cheerfully, counting it more honor to be inside of a jail in the austere silence of my dungeon, rather than outside of it, with a faithless Jury, guilty of such treason to their Country and their God. But, forgive me! you cannot commit such a crime against Humanity. Pardon the monstrous figure of my speech, — it is only conceivable, not also possible. These Judges could do it — their speeches, their actions, that Charge, this Indictment, proves all that — but you cannot; — not you. You are the Representatives of the People, the Country, not idiotic in Conscience and the Affections.

Gentlemen, I am a minister of Religion. It is my function to teach what is absolutely true and absolutely right. I am the servant of no sect, — how old soever, venerable and widely spread. I claim the same religious Rights with Luther and Calvin, with Budha and Mohammed; yes, with Moses and Jesus, — the unalienable Right to serve the God of Nature in my own way. I preach the Religion which belongs to Human Nature, as I understand it, which the Infinite God imperishably writes thereon, — Natural Piety, love of the infinitely perfect God, Natural Morality, the keeping of every law He has written on the body and in the soul of man, especially by loving and serving his creatures. Many wrong things I doubtless do, for which I must ask the forgiveness of mankind. But do you suppose I can keep the fugitive slave bill, obey these Judges, and kidnap my own Parishioners? It is no part of my "Christianity" to "send the mother that bore me into eternal bondage." Do you think I can suffer Commissioner Curtis and Commissioner Loring to steal my friends, — out of my meeting-house? Gentlemen, when God bids me do right and this Court bids me do wrong, I shall not pretend to "obey both." I am willing enough to suffer all that you will ever lay on me. But I will not do such a wrong, nor allow such wickedness to be done — so help me God! How could I teach Truth, Justice, Piety, if I stole men; if I allowed Saunders, Jeffreys, Scroggs, or Sharkey, Grier, Kane, or in one word, Curtis, to steal them? I love my Country, my kindred of Humanity; I love my God, Father and Mother of the white man and the black; and am I to suffer the Liberty of America to be trod under the hoof of Slaveholders, Slave-drivers; yes, of the judicial slaves of slaveholders' slave-drivers? I was neither born nor bred for that. I drew my first breath in a little town not far off, a poor little town where the farmers and mechanics first unsheathed that Revolutionary sword which, after eight years of hewing, clove asunder the Gordian knot that bound America to the British yoke. One raw morning in spring — it will be eighty years the 19th of this month — Hancock and Adams, the Moses and Aaron of that Great Deliverance, were both at Lexington; they also had "obstructed an officer" with brave words. British soldiers, a thousand strong, came to seize them and carry them over sea for trial, and so nip the bud of Freedom auspiciously opening in that early spring. The town militia came together before daylight "for training." A great, tall man, with a large head and a high, wide brow, their Captain, — one who "had seen service," — marshalled them into line, numbering but seventy, and bad "every man load his piece with powder and ball." "I will order the first man shot that runs away," said he, when some faltered; "Do n't fire unless fired upon, but if they want to have a war, — let it begin here." Gentlemen, you know what followed: those farmers and mechanics "fired the shot heard round the world." A little monument covers the bones of such as before had pledged their fortune and their sacred honor to the Freedom of America, and that day gave it also their lives. I was born in that little town, and bred up amid the memories of that day. When a boy my mother lifted me up, one Sunday, in her religious, patriotic arms, and held me while I read the first monumental line I ever saw: —

"SACRED TO LIBERTY AND THE RIGHTS OF MANKIND."

Since then I have studied the memorial marbles of Greece and Rome in many an ancient town; nay, on Egyptian Obelisks have read what was written before the Eternal roused up Moses to lead

Israel out of Egypt, but no chiselled stone has ever stirred me to such emotions as those rustic names of men who fell

"In the Sacred Cause of God and their Country."

Gentlemen, the Spirit of Liberty, the Love of Justice, was early fanned into a flame in my boyish heart. That monument covers the bones of my own kinsfolk; it was their blood which reddened the long, green grass at Lexington. It is my own name which stands chiselled on that stone; the tall Captain who marshalled his fellow farmers and mechanics into stern array and spoke such brave and dangerous words as opened the War of American Independence,—the last to leave the field,—was my father's father. I learned to read out of his Bible, and with a musket he that day captured from the foe, I learned also another religious lesson, that

"Rebellion to Tyrants is Obedience to God."

I keep them both, "Sacred to Liberty and the Rights of Mankind," to use them both "In the Sacred Cause of God and my Country."

Gentlemen of the Jury, and you my fellow-countrymen of the North, I leave the matter with you. Say "Guilty!" You cannot do it. "Not Guilty." I know you will, for you remember there is another Court, not of fugitive slave bill law, where we shall all be tried by the Justice of the Infinite God. Hearken to the last verdict, "Inasmuch as ye have done it unto one of the least of these my brethren, ye have done it unto me."

END.

ERRATA.

Page 19,	line 16	from top,	instead of	*rest*, read *government*.
" 23	" 10	"	"	" 1618, read 1215.
" 76	" 2	"	"	" *Aoncilia*, read *Ancilia*.
" 78	" 3	" bottom,	"	" *not*, read *or*.
" 84	" 11	"	"	" *promoting*, read *perverting*.
" 89	" 18	"	"	omit *his*, before *vengeance*.

OTHER WORKS BY THE SAME AUTHOR.

A Discourse of Matters Pertaining to Religion. 1 Vol. 12mo. New Edition will appear in December.	$1.25
An Introduction to the Old Testament. From the German of De Wette. 2d edition. 2 Vols. 8vo.	3.75
Critical and Miscellaneous Writings. 1 Vol. 12mo. New Edition will soon appear.	1.25
Occasional Sermons and Speeches. 2 Vols. 12mo.	2.50
Ten Sermons of Religion. 1 Vol. 12mo.	1.00
Sermons of Theism, Atheism, and the Popular Theology. 1 Vol. 12mo.	1.25
Additional Sermons and Speeches. 2 Vols. 12mo.	2.50

PAMPHLETS.

Two Sermons on leaving the Old and entering the New place of Worship. (1852.)	20
Discourse of Daniel Webster. (1853.) Cloth.	50
A Sermon of Old Age. (1854.)	15
The New Crime against Humanity. (1854.)	20
The Laws of God and the Statutes of Man. (1854.)	15
The Dangers which Threaten the Rights of Man in America. (1854.)	20
The Moral Dangers Incident to Prosperity. (1855.)	15
Consequences of an Immoral Principle. (1855.)	15
Function of a Minister. (1855.)	20
Two Sermons in Proceedings of Progressive Friends. (1855.)	15

www.ingramcontent.com/pod-product-compliance
Lightning Source LLC
LaVergne TN
LVHW050521100826
845148LV00002B/403

* 9 7 8 1 4 2 5 5 2 0 7 6 2 *